Studies of Organized Crime

Volume 17

Series Editor

Dina Siegel, Willem Pompe Institute, Utrecht University, Utrecht, The Netherlands

More information about this series at http://www.springer.com/series/6564

Roos de Wildt

Post-War Prostitution

Human Trafficking and Peacekeeping in Kosovo

Springer

Roos de Wildt
Verwey-Jonker Institute
Utrecht, The Netherlands

ISSN 1571-5493
Studies of Organized Crime
ISBN 978-3-030-19473-4 ISBN 978-3-030-19474-1 (eBook)
https://doi.org/10.1007/978-3-030-19474-1

Cover Illustration: Photographs: Willem Poelstra
Graphic design of photographs: Regina Geerts

This Springer imprint is published by the registered company Springer Nature Switzerland AG
The registered company address is: Gewerbestrasse 11, 6330 Cham, Switzerland

Foreword

A walk around Pristina, the capital of Kosovo, is a journey of historical discovery. Half-abandoned buildings in socialist realist style—leftovers from the socialist era—coexist alongside ancient and newly built mosques calling the faithful to prayer, colourful neon advertisements and modern European-style late night bars, clubs, hotels and souvenir shops. Many miles from the capital, the landscape is not that different with its traditional and modern mix of beautiful green scenery interspersed with modern business premises and small, mysterious-looking motels along the main roads.

It was in this sometimes confusing and contradictory mix of past and present that Roos de Wildt, the author of the present book, conducted her field research on post-war prostitution in Kosovo. She did so within the framework of cultural criminology, a discipline that involves the ethnographic research of criminality and deviance. In cultural criminology, we are still reflecting on how this strand of criminology differs from other schools. This author's research provides an excellent example of the special character of the Utrecht School of Cultural Criminology, which entails spending long periods of time among respondents in remote understudied settings that are often considered 'dangerous' because of the ongoing conflicts, wars or other troubles, observing and communicating intensively with the people living there, participating in their activities and, above all, listening to their stories.

The strength of this approach was *not* seeing sex workers – some of whom were victims of human trafficking—as *victims* per se, with the label 'victim' written on their foreheads as their 'master status', as Goffman would have it. Rather, the researcher approached them as fully informed, active individuals. She described and analysed their social world, their biographies, their decision-making moments and emotions, their dreams and their desires. In other words, she gave them a voice. But these voices seem to contradict many existing stereotypes and clichés about prostitution, human trafficking and the 'unacceptable' behaviour of UN peacekeepers.

When I first visited the author in Pristina, I was struck by how warmly and enthusiastically she was greeted, not only by women working in the sex industry but also by law enforcement officers, social workers, medical doctors and even politicians. They all knew her and were eager to share information and news with her. This kind of trust is precious when conducting anthropological research, especially when the object of study is as complex and controversial as the involvement of international peacekeepers in prostitution and alleged sex trafficking in post-war Kosovo.

Historically, Kosovo can be compared to a volcano of ongoing ethnic hostility. In different periods in history, this volcano has either been dormant or in a state of eruption, emitting an avalanche of violence, war and murder. One result of the last outburst of ethnic conflict was economic and political chaos which gave birth to a post-war or rather a 'peacekeeping' economy, including a sex industry. The presence of international peacekeepers, most of whom are men, attracted many women from Kosovo and other East European countries who saw an opportunity to earn money doing sex work in order to improve their economic situation and provide for their families.

The author presents an analysis of the sex industry in Kosovo as a logical social process: prostitution flourishes when there is supply and demand. On the one hand, it is a business in which all participants receive some reward. On the other hand, there are codes of behaviour and ethical issues, as well as the risk of abuse and exploitation. Roos de Wildt challenges the prevailing discourse that sex workers operating within the context of peacekeeping missions are by definition victims of human trafficking. Such stereotypical claims can affect the lives of Kosovar and foreign sex workers who have not experienced victimhood and do not want to be considered as victims.

Moral entrepreneurs around the world still view voluntary sex work as impossible or immoral. Even countries where sex work has been decriminalized, legalized or regulated have not been able to convince the rest of the world that sex work can be a profession deserving of respect and acceptance. There are still too many rescue organizations that can only survive and function if myths of the 'fallen woman' and her 'criminal pimp' are kept alive. These often exaggerated images of exploitation and victimization seem to get more attention from media and politicians than the very real problems of social exclusion, economic inequality and migration. In addition, when there is a stereotype of victims of human trafficking, there is inevitably a stereotype of the offenders; in this case, it is one of the UN peacekeepers exploiting women and violating ethical codes laid down in official regulations. For moral entrepreneurs, the persistence of these 'black or white' stereotypes is essential to their abolitionist message.

This book makes an important theoretical and empirical contribution to the critical social sciences. For those who are curious about the experiences of sex workers in the understudied context of the Balkans, this book can be an eye-opener. It also proves that ethnographic research is possible in 'exotic' areas, such as Kosovo, and demonstrates that the same dilemmas regarding the regulation of sex work and the status of sex workers apply everywhere in the world.

December 2018

Dina Siegel
Utrecht University

Acknowledgements

At Utrecht University, I would like to thank my supervisor, Dina Siegel, whose enthusiasm for criminological fieldwork is contagious. She encouraged me throughout every stage of this project, ranging from motivating me to take seriously my initial ideas about studying post-war prostitution to accompanying me to one of the bars in Kosovo and getting me in the writing mood by inviting me to edit a book together. It has been a great pleasure to work with her. My co-supervisor, Brenda Oude Breuil, has contributed to my development as a researcher in the best possible way. I cannot thank Brenda enough for her keen interest and heartwarming support ever since my very first step into the world of academia. At Hamburg University, my supervisor, Susanne Krasmann, has challenged and enriched my ideas.

I am grateful for the support of the consortium of the Doctorate in Cultural and Global Criminology program, especially Damián Zaitch. My fellow PhD students within this program have been the best partners in crime one could wish for. Special hugs go to Camille Stengel, Veronika Nagy and Rosa Koenraadt.

Most of my time writing these texts has been spent at the Willem Pompe Institute for Criminal Law and Criminology at Utrecht University. What a stellar place to work! Thanks to all the *Pompeanen*, Kristien Hepping and Daan van Uhm in particular.

This book would not have seen the light of the day without the help of many people in Kosovo. While it is impossible to thank all of them—as I sincerely believe that I did not meet a single Kosovar who did not want to discuss my research and ways to help me over (what else) a macchiato—the following is the beginning of my gratitude. I am indebted to the bar owners and bartenders who opened their doors to this surprising guest. Most importantly, I thank the women in these bars. I remain humbled by and grateful for their willingness to share their time and stories with me. This book is dedicated to them.

A special thanks goes to *shoqe kallamoqe* Dafina Muçaj, who accompanied me during most of my visits to bars. It is hard to put into words how much it meant to share the sometimes hilarious, other times ugly, but always intense impressions of life at the bars with her. Rifat Batusha and Ramiz Dukaj from the Kosovo Population

Foundation (KOPF) helped put me in contact with women who engaged in prostitution in Kosovo in the first place. I greatly admire their work and thank them for supporting this.

I thank Valentina Bejtullahu, anti-trafficking officer at the Organization for Security and Co-operation in Europe (OSCE), as well as Artur Marku, former delegate of Terre des Hommes Kosovo, for being supportive of my research from the very start (and even a bit before that). I am indebted to Besim Kelmendi of the State Prosecution Office, the Kosovo Police Directorate for Investigation of Trafficking in Human Beings and the national and international prosecutors, legal advisors and police officers of UNMIK and EULEX who kindly shared their experiences with me, most notably Ramiz Durmishi and Natasha Vicary.

I owe gratitude to Hyrie Veliu for teaching me Albanian. *Faleminderit Jeta, je një mike e mrekullueshme të cilen e admiroj shumë.* Fatime Aliu, Leonora Azemi, Brikenë Bunjaku, Besnik Dreshaj and Rrahim Ternava made sure that studying human trafficking was successfully combined with hiking in the stunning Sharr and Rugova Mountains, dancing in Pristina's nightlife and beach bumming in Albania. I feel blessed by their friendship.

Back home in the Netherlands, I met Willem Poelstra during the early stages of this study. No one has more clearly marked these pages than Willem. Readers will most likely marvel at his photographs long before turning to the texts. I thank Willem for our great cooperation within *Future Stories from the Past*, his photo project on post-war Kosovo, for his beautiful pictures and for his friendship. He is greatly missed. Regina Geerts kindly offered to anonymize the photographs in this book. I am grateful to her for generously providing her talents.

I thank my friends Nikkie Wiegink, Sofie Smeets, Oka Storms, Anne Lucassen, Karin van Bemmel and all the others who lent their ears to my fieldwork tales whenever they threatened to overwhelm me and who never failed to join in celebrations whenever a momentous occasion was reached. Nikkie commented on almost every page of this book irrespective of her stay in rural Mozambique, Sudan, or the back of a car in the midst of a snowstorm. Sofie quickly arranged for us to take a beginner's course in car repair in order to prepare for our various road trips to and from Kosovo in my little car. I could not ask for more dedicated *paranympfen.*

I feel extremely lucky for the unwavering support of my lovely large family: Ellen Bakker, Piet de Wildt, Emmy Kanon, Pieternel Broos, Sjon Brands, Dorith van der Lee, Fleur Zwemmer, Klaas Jan Leuring, Simon de Wildt, Rong Zwemmer and all the others. They made sure that I never doubted that this project could be finished and often took loving care of the boys so that I could actually get to it. Finally, my deepest thanks go to Tijn Brands and our sons, Manuel and Casper, for being altogether marvellous.

Contents

List of Abbreviations

EULEX	European Union Rule of Law Mission in Kosovo
KFOR	Kosovo Force (NATO-led international peacekeeping force)
KLA	Kosovo Liberation Army (the Albanian acronym is UÇK)
LDK	Lidhja Demokratike e Kosovës (The Democratic League of Kosovo)
NATO	North Atlantic Treaty Organization
PDK	Partia Demokratike e Kosovës (The Democratic Party of Kosovo)
UÇK	Ushtria Çlirimtare e Kosovës (the English acronym is KLA)
UN	United Nations
UNMIBH	United Nations Mission in Bosnia and Herzegovina
UNMIK	United Nations Mission in Kosovo

List of Figures

Maps

Map 1: Southeast Europe

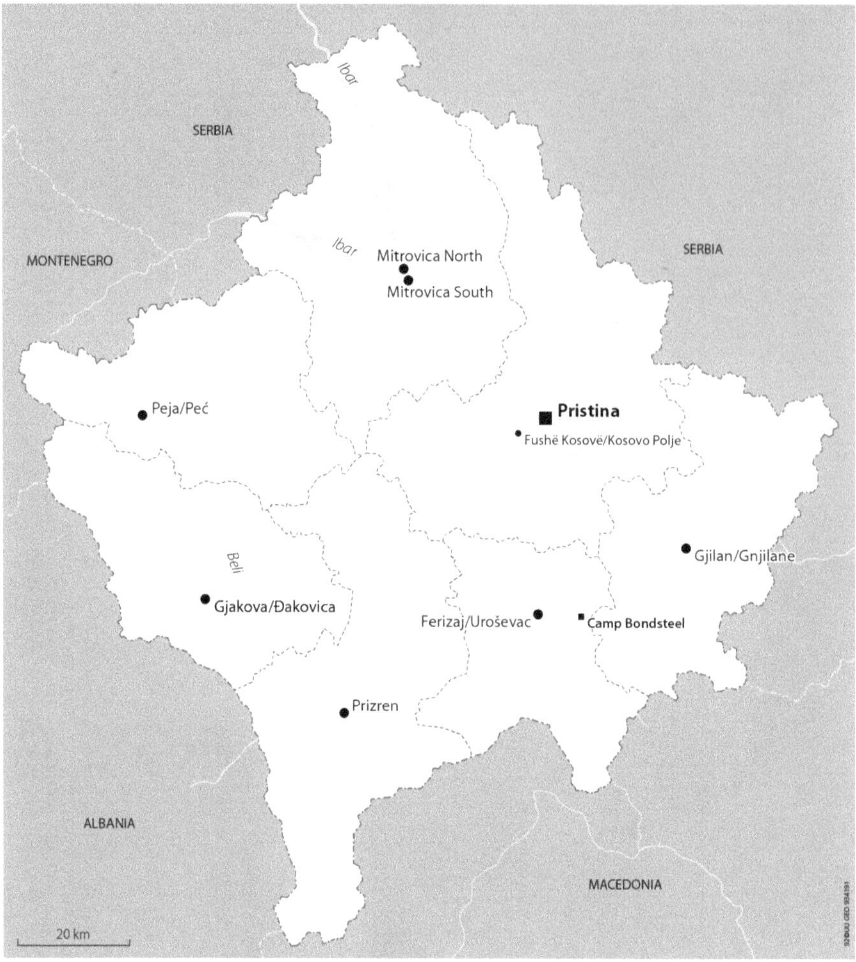

Map 2: Kosovo[1]

[1] Names are a matter of contention in Kosovo. Kosovo's municipalities all have double names, as both Serbian and Albanian are official languages. Throughout this work, I use English names (e.g. Pristina) or the combined Albanian/Serbian names when an English option is not available (e.g. Ferizaj/Uroševac).

Fig. 1.1 Motel

Chapter 1
Introduction

> It was a quiet evening in a brothel close to Camp Bondsteel, the main U.S. military base in Kosovo. Mimoza and Shqipe did not have any clients.[1] They were killing time by dreaming about possibilities abroad, but a Kosovar passport does not allow for much traveling. "Where would you go if you could travel anywhere?" I asked. Shqipe took a moment to think and said, "Afghanistan."
>
> Mimoza nodded in agreement. "A lot of our friends are in Afghanistan."
>
> I was puzzled. "Americans and other soldiers from Bondsteel, Roos; they left Kosovo but work in Afghanistan now. We could make money there."[2]

Mimoza and Shqipe learned from experience that the wake of a war can be economically lucrative. Both women tried to earn money when Kosovo's small-scale prostitution market was transformed into a large-scale sex industry with high demand for commercial sex in the context of the peacekeeping mission right after the war (Amnesty International, 2004; Friman & Reich, 2007; Mertus & Bertone, 2007; Terre des Hommes, 2010).

Sex industries worldwide tend to flourish during United Nations (UN) peacekeeping missions. Academic studies have reported an increase in Dominican and local sex workers during the UN Stabilization Mission in "postquake" Haiti (Jennings, 2008; Martin, 2005),[3] as well as a rapid increase in prostitution during UN peacekeeping missions in Bosnia and Herzegovina, Cambodia, Timor-Leste, West Africa, and the Democratic Republic of the Congo (Higate, 2007; Jennings, 2015; Mendelson, 2005; Murray, 2002; Oldenburg, 2015; Simic, 2012; Whitworth, 2004).[4] The rise in

[1] Mimoza and Shqipe are pseudonyms. I have used pseudonyms for all the women and bar owners mentioned in this book as a precautionary measure to guarantee anonymity. All pseudonyms or codes given to informants, along with basic information about each, are listed in the overview in Annex Two.

[2] Informal conversation with Mimoza and Shqipe, April 16, 2013.

[3] See also Desvarieux (2010) and Lynch (2005).

[4] UN General Assembly (2005). In 2004, the UN invited Prince Zeid Ra'ad Zeid Al-Hussein, Jordan's ambassador to the UN, to analyze sexual exploitation and abuse by UN peacekeeping personnel. The critical report that he published one year later became known as the Zeid Report.

R. de Wildt, *Post-War Prostitution*, Studies of Organized Crime 17,
https://doi.org/10.1007/978-3-030-19474-1_1

prostitution in the context of peacekeeping missions is predominantly explained as a matter of forced prostitution, which follows the demand of (largely male) UN peacekeepers (Higate, 2003; Martin, 2005).

This is also the case for Kosovo. The Kosovar sex industry has substantially increased since the end of the war in 1999, when the UN was tasked with governing the area through the Interim Administration Mission in Kosovo (UNMIK) and the North Atlantic Treaty Organization (NATO) started to lead an international peacekeeping force (KFOR). According to Mertus and Bertone (2007, p. 42), "[…] the arrival of an international community catalysed the growth of the sex industry" in Kosovo, supposedly stimulating the trafficking of women and girls for sexual purposes (Amnesty International, 2004; Friman & Reich, 2007).[5] Amnesty International (2004, p. 7) proclaimed that "within months of KFOR's arrival, brothels were reported around military bases occupied by international peace-keepers. Kosovo soon became a major destination country for women trafficked into forced prostitution." In May 2000, the chief of mission of the International Organization for Migration (IOM), the lead anti-trafficking agency in Kosovo at the time, stated that "KFOR troops and UN staff in Kosovo had fed a mushrooming of nightclubs in which young girls were being forced into prostitution."[6]

The claim that UN peacekeepers engage in and sometimes orchestrate prostitution in war-torn and otherwise vulnerable regions where they are expected to "do good" has provoked concerned reactions in academic and non-academic publications alike. Higate (2003, 2007) described prostitution in the context of peacekeeping missions in terms of "sexual exploitation" and "abuse of vulnerable people." Newspapers printed articles with titles such as "What the UN Doesn't Want You to Know" and "The Dark Side of U.N. Peacekeepers."[7] This turmoil results in international donors' extensive support of information campaigns about trafficking for sexual purposes, as well as reintegration programs for "survivors" of human trafficking in Kosovo and other places where peacekeeping missions are deployed (De Wildt, 2015).

Yet, the claims that, first, international peacekeepers create the demand for prostitution and, second, that this demand tends to be met through the trafficking of women for sexual purposes, are poorly substantiated by empirical data that takes insider perspectives into account. A number of questions therefore remain unanswered: Which characteristics of post-war societies can contribute to the growth of the sex industry? What are the lived experiences of women engaged in post-war prostitution? Who are their clients? How did these women become involved in

---

This report also included an analysis of prostitution, which the UN defines as a manifestation of sexually exploitative behavior. This depiction will be discussed in more detail in Chap. 4.

[5] Human trafficking is defined in the Protocol to Prevent, Suppress and Punish Trafficking in Persons, Especially Women and Children, supplementing the United Nations Convention against Transnational Organized Crime. The definition is given in Annex One. See also UNODC (2004).

[6] Pasquale Lupoli, IOM chief of mission, in "Group launches campaign against forced prostitution in Kosovo." *AFP*, May 24, 2000; cited in Amnesty International (2004).

[7] Diu (2012) and Patrick (2015).

prostitution? Do they actually want to be "saved"? What are the (unintended) consequences of one-dimensionally portraying prostitution in the context of peacekeeping missions as human trafficking for sexual purposes? In order to answer these questions, the narratives of the women actually engaged in prostitution in the context of peacekeeping missions need to be considered. In this ethnographic study, conducted amongst women engaged in post-war prostitution in Kosovo, I aim to do just that.

I spent several periods of time (ranging from one week to 8 months) in Kosovo, intensively researching sex work settings throughout the country, from 2008 to 2015. The central research question of this study was:

> What are the lived experiences of women engaged in prostitution in post-war Kosovo, and how did war and its aftermath (e.g., the presence of a peacekeeping mission) shape these experiences as well as the prostitution business at large?

By examining this question, I aim to widen "the rather restrictive lenses" (Yea, 2005, p. 459) through which women engaged in prostitution in the context of peacekeeping missions are generally viewed.

1.1 Methodology[8]

Between 2011 and 2015, I conducted approximately 12 months of ethnographic research that built on relationships I had established in Kosovo beginning in 2008. This included participant observation among women involved in the sex industry, as well as those facilitating it. Furthermore, I conducted in-depth interviews with trafficking and prostitution "experts," including policymakers, police, shelters, and local and international NGOs, as well as women (previously) involved in the sex industry and facilitators of prostitution. Finally, I analyzed court cases (e.g., Leman & Janssens, 2008) and police and official reports (international, national and local) in this field. I will expound on these methods below.

1.1.1 Participant Observation

In their theoretical and historical background of the method, DeWalt and DeWalt (2002, p. 1) define participant observation as "a method in which a researcher takes part in the daily activities, rituals, interactions, and events of a group of people as

[8] Parts of this section have been published as: De Wildt (2016). This publication also addresses various ethical and safety concerns that aim to protect respondents and researchers. I there argue that guiding principles such as "do no harm," informed consent, anonymity, confidentiality, and clarity about researchers' role and responsibility can advise them on how to deal with certain situations. Nevertheless, following the general guidelines does not guarantee successful research on the sex industry. Imposing these guidelines on researchers, as institutional review boards tend to do, can hinder research progress.

one of the means of learning the explicit and tacit aspects of their life routines and their culture." I conducted participant observation to analyze the daily endeavors and interactions that constitute the daily lives of the Eastern European and local women involved in the Kosovar sex industry and, by listening to anecdotes and tracing the way the sex industry changed over time, come to apprehend the transformation that turned an initial small-scale prostitution market into a large-scale industry.

In the beginning of my fieldwork in Kosovo, I established contacts in premises where prostitution was taking place by joining an outreach organization involved in distributing condoms and information about sexually transmitted infections. Some of the women with whom I established good relationships subsequently took me to other premises, where they introduced me to friends or acquaintances who were also involved in prostitution. Throughout the entire course of my fieldwork, I made a habit of spending several days and evenings a week in bars and motels where these women were working. These visits were spread across different bars and motels in different cities in Kosovo, since dynamics at the various premises varied vastly from posh pole dance clubs, where elegantly dressed Moldovan women danced for wealthy customers, to smoky basements where Kosovar Albanian women drank beer and played darts with older men.

I hung out with women when they were waiting for customers, joined them for lunch, drinks or necessary visits to institutions and health clinics, and in some cases visited them at home and met their families. In premises where commercial sex was being offered, I also discussed "business" with bar owners and observed them being offered new employees; this was primarily possible in places where I had become a regular and had also gained the trust of facilitators of the prostitution business. Additionally, I spent time with a woman in witness protection, whom I had met several years before when she was living and offering commercial sex in a Kosovar motel.

Finally, I observed various criminal hearings in the framework of three different court cases on human trafficking and the facilitation of prostitution. This meant that I was present when charges were read out, during the presentation of evidence (e.g., calling witnesses, listening to telephone taps) and the cross-examination of defense witnesses, as well as when a decision was made on sentencing. All observations were elaborated upon in daily fieldwork notes.

1.1.2 In-depth Interviews

While I had countless informal conversations as a participant observer hanging around premises where prostitution was taking place, I also conducted in-depth interviews with some of the people in this scene, as well as trafficking and prostitution "experts" including policymakers, police, prosecutors, gynecologists working on the promotion of sexual and reproductive health among women involved in prostitution, and people working at shelters and NGOs. In total I conducted 111 interviews and extensive informal conversations with 43 women (formerly) engaged in prostitution, and 16 interviews and extensive informal conversations with four facilitators of prostitution (i.e., bar owners and barmen). Moreover, I held 70 interviews and extensive informal conversations with 45 professionals and interviewed 10 additional people related in various ways to the context of my study, such as former Kosovo Liberation Army (KLA) combatants. Some of these informants I met only once, but I interviewed the majority of them two or more times.[9] Interviews were generally semi-structured, with a topic list guiding the direction of the conversation (see also Beyens & Tournel, 2010, p. 207).

While my knowledge of the Albanian language allowed me to have conversations in Albanian, the interviews were primarily conducted in English or in Albanian with the assistance of my Kosovar Albanian research assistant. I have been working with the same research assistant in Kosovo since 2011; she is a psychologist who is at ease in conversations about women's experiences, since she had worked with a similar group of women prior to our cooperation. In addition to language translation when necessary, my research assistant regularly provided cultural translations. Especially at the beginning of my research, I couldn't judge, for instance, whether it was exceptional when a woman told me she had lost all contact with her children after being separated from her husband. My research assistant could place these stories in the Kosovar context. I found it particularly valuable to be able to discuss the impressions of an interview with her afterward.

1.1.3 Analysis of Brochures and Reports

Although they account for only a small part of the data presented in this book, local publications on human trafficking and prostitution in Kosovo were analyzed to grasp the way in which the Kosovar sex industry is being presented by organizations working with or for the women involved. Highly symbolic and stereotypical images of victims of trafficking are often the basis of posters and brochures warning about the dangers of trafficking (Andrijasevic, 2007, p. 42). Empirical studies (e.g., Agustín, 2007; Brunovskis & Surtees, 2008; De Wildt, 2009; Oude Breuil, 2008, 2009; Siegel, 2005) show that such images rarely correspond to lived experiences. But as insights from cultural criminology demonstrate, "in this world the street scripts the screen and the screen scripts the street; there is no clearly linear sequence, but rather a shifting interplay between the real and the virtual, the factual and the fictional" (Ferrell, Hayward, & Young, 2008, pp. 123–124).

The way in which imaginations "script the scene" in the sex business is studied through the analysis of posters and brochures warning about the dangers of trafficking, as well as the examination of newspaper clippings. These imaginations of sex trafficking not only reflect values of society, but simultaneously influence the

[9] An overview of these four categories of informants is provided in Annex Two.

experience of people involved in the sex industry. Integrating an analysis of the highly symbolic and stereotypical constructions of women and men involved in the sex industry, as displayed in local images of trafficking and prostitution, is therefore essential in understanding the friction between the imaginary and the actual experience of involvement in the sex industry in Kosovo.

Local and international official reports provided additional historical context. Reports of the Kosovar office of the national coordinator against trafficking in human beings (Republic of Kosovo, Ministry of Internal Affairs, Office of National Coordinator against Trafficking in Human Beings, 2009; Republic of Kosovo, Ministry of Internal Affairs, Koordinatori Nacional Kundër Trafikimit Me Qenie Njerëzore, 2010), for instance, specified the numbers of victims of trafficking whom the police had encountered and how the demographic background of these victims changed over the years.

Finally, I analyzed the indictments of four cases on human trafficking or the facilitation of prostitution. I supplemented the information from these indictments using interviews with special prosecutors and police who had been—or were still—working on these cases, as well as observations in court for three of these cases. The study of recent indictments of trafficking cases was particularly valuable for gaining insight into international money transfers, as well as the transcriptions of telephone taps I include throughout this book. Conversations between different bar owners, or between bar owners and the women working for them, had a different—often rougher—tone than the conversations I observed in bars.

1.1.4 Visual Method

The inclusion of photographs aims to contribute to a more nuanced visual representation of women engaged in (post-war) prostitution, and the world they inhabit. Andrijasevic and Mai (2016) show that the plethora of documentaries, artistic works, and fiction films on prostitution (migration) and human trafficking provide a narrow representation of the experiences of women engaged in prostitution. Women are framed either as ideal victims that are nothing more than "wounded and inanimate female bodies" (Andrijasevic, 2007, p. 26) or as "unworthy prostitutes" (Krsmanovic, 2016). In an attempt to challenge these representations, I cooperated with professional documentary photographer Willem Poelstra who portrayed my respondents in their own accounts and on their own terms. The women decided on their visual representation. This approach feeds into a more visually attuned criminology as suggested by Ferrell and Van de Voorde (2010, p. 45).

Poelstra and I showed the final photographs to everyone whose picture was taken. The reactions were positive: on various occasions women expressed a sense of pride as they looked at the pictures, and one of the women immediately showed the images to all of the customers in the bar where she was working. The use of the pictures was discussed and agreed upon with all of the people portrayed. This participatory element meant that, first, confidentiality was not harmed, as those portrayed had agreed on the use of images and, second, we portrayed women engaged in prostitution in such a way that they identified with it.[10] Moreover the photographs provided an instrument to discuss how people viewed themselves and the world they inhabit.

The motels that Poelstra photographed are not necessarily involved in my research. Motels can be found all over Kosovo, and in some instances there are several along a single street. Poelstra took pictures of a random selection of motels he passed by. It has to be said that not all of these motels earn money through the facilitation of prostitution; motels in Kosovo also earn money by renting rooms to couples who cannot meet at home because the family members with whom they are living will not accept it.

The selection of, primarily contextual, images of Kosovo included in this work aim to shed light on the post-conflict Kosovar society in which the sex industry blossomed.[11] They invite the reader to contemplate what it means to live in a post-conflict society with the strong presence of an international peacekeeping community.

By no means do I intend to suggest that the pictures included in this work are "objective" representations. For instance, by choosing the moment a picture was taken (a Kosovar souvenir shop with only a few customers in the rain versus the same shop on a bright and sunny day) and inviting women to pose instead of portraying them when they are dancing and drinking with male customers, Poelstra and I colored the images. Our fingerprints on the photographs are even more explicit in the anonymized portraits of women and men involved in the sex industry.[12] Although everyone portrayed agreed to their photographs being taken in ways so that they could be recognized, the pictures are presented here with participants' faces covered. I cannot foresee the consequences if people were to be identified as being involved in the sex industry, and I do not wish to trigger any negative reactions.

"Mutually independent, and fully collaborative" (Agee & Evans, 1960, pp. xiv–xv), this verbal and photographic account of post-war prostitution in Kosovo aims to provide a complex, layered analysis of sex trafficking and prostitution that emphasizes the work of imaginations, as well as the embattled space within which the phenomenon takes shape and continues to change. Although the written description of my understanding of the Kosovar sex industry remains dominant in this work, the pictures are included as more than textual illustrations. As Ferrell and Van de Voorde (2010, p. 45) outline in their analysis of the use of documentary photography in cultural criminology, both "text and image each complement the

---

[10] As opposed to the images of women portrayed as wounded and helpless victims (Andrijasevic, 2007).

[11] These pictures were made within the framework of a larger, long-term photo project on the aftermath of the Kosovo War by Willem Poelstra, for which I conducted background research and drafted some of the text. This complete work has resulted in exhibitions in the Balkans and the Netherlands, as well as a photobook. More information on this project can be found at http://forhanna.com/future-stories-from-the-past/.

[12] Graphic designer Regina Geerts carefully anonymized all pictures, for which I am very thankful.

other—that is, serve to illustrate and illuminate the other—as fragments of a larger narrative." I hope the images can help readers to envision post-war prostitution in Kosovo as something different—something more mundane—than the highly symbolic and stereotypical images that tend to dominate documentaries, artistic works and fictional films on prostitution (Andrijasevic & Mai, 2016) which likely feed the association we have with it.

1.2 Academic Relevance

This book responds to the call for more "high-quality microlevel empirical studies [...] regarding human trafficking" (Weitzer, 2014, p. 21). Criminologists Zhang (2009) and Weitzer (2007, 2014) highlight the importance of more empirical data, zooming into insiders' perspectives in order to contest dubious claims put forward by individuals and organizations with an ideological agenda that influence policy and practices in the field.[13] This is especially relevant with regard to prostitution during peacekeeping missions: no other empirical studies have been conducted amongst women engaged in prostitution in these contexts, although claims about their situation are plentiful. This research aims to fill that gap.

This study also thus contributes to a critical reflection on victimization within the hegemonic discourse. Such a reflection has been insightfully established by scholars such as Autesserre (2012), who examines why certain categories of victims achieve prominence in the public discourse, unraveling the negative consequences of simple narratives featuring "ideal victims" (Christie, 1986). Anderson and Andrijasevic (2008) have added to this reflection, putting forward that solutions to exploitation and abuse in the sex industry should "move beyond identifying victims and imprisoning traffickers" and instead address the role of immigration and labour regulations in increasing the vulnerability of people. In line with these works, I examine why certain women engaged in prostitution in Kosovo are depicted as victims while others are not, investigating the (unintended) consequences of this categorization, as well as the agency of all these women. Specifically, I zoom in on the (geo-)political and socio-economic context that has situated the agency of women engaged in prostitution in Kosovo. In doing so, I tap into the structure-and-agency debate within the social sciences, which contests whether individuals control their own actions and destinies (i.e., agency; see Weber, 1978; Barth, 1967) or simply obey powerful social forces (i.e., structures; see Durkheim, 1938; Radcliff-Brown, 1940). In tandem, I draw on critical criminology, which provides a focus on the ways in which power hierarchies impact crime and criminalization (Becker, 1963; Taylor, Walton, & Young, 1973).[14]

[13] See also the theoretical chapter (Chap. 2).

[14] Giddens (1984) in his structuration theory, and Bourdieu (1977) in coining habitus, propose a dialectical relationship between structure and agency whereby individuals constantly shape and reshape structures though their actions while these actions are at the same time impacted by these ever dynamic structures.

A cross-fertilization of viewpoints from anthropology, criminology, and conflict studies challenges existing narratives on the growth of sex industries in the context of peacekeeping missions. A cultural criminology perspective is essential, as this approach to the study of crime "places criminality and its control squarely in the context of culture" (Hayward, 2012).[15]

While some studies touch upon the context from which alleged victims of trafficking and prostitution migrants originate (e.g., Friman & Reich, 2007; Surtees, 2008), few ethnographic studies thus far have been conducted within Western Balkan countries. Challenges related to (out-country) prostitution for countries in Central and Eastern Europe require more thorough analysis, as does the influence of the movement of people from "the West" to "the East" during peacekeeping missions on the shaping of sex industries worldwide.[16]

Such ethnographic studies outside Western Europe and North America are not "exotic" studies that highlight their—versus our "Western"—reality. Criminologist Wayne Morrison (2006, pp. 1–2) argues that such a fictitious divide has already led to intellectual incoherence, as "in the West our concern is with living the 'good life' within 'civilised space', blind to the interconnection that render that space in a dependent relation to its external." The specific development and construction of deviance outside the Western realm is very much connected to the West (and vice versa). The growth of the Kosovar sex industry during a UN peacekeeping mission is only one example of this. Therefore, this research project considers how transnational processes (e.g., UN peacekeeping missions, immigration laws) are embedded in locally specific circumstances outside the Western realm while taking international power hierarchies into account.

1.3 Social Relevance

The societal relevance of this study lies in providing insight into the lived experience of women involved in post-war prostitution along the entire continuum from voluntary sex workers to forced victims of human trafficking, as well as all possible forms of prostitution between these two extremes. These women's narratives, together with an analysis of the negative consequences of (often well-intended) initiatives focusing on those engaged in prostitution, can support future policy and programmes. They will also help counter inflated claims and generalized horror

[15] Cultural criminologists often focus on cultural and media studies, but cultural criminologists who take a more anthropological approach to culture combine decent ethnographic work with the study of crime and deviance (see, for instance, Zaitch, 2002; Oude Breuil, 2009).

[16] I use the term "out-country" to refer to the situation wherein women engage in prostitution in a country other than their country of origin. In this book, it is primarily applied to the Ukrainian, Moldovan, Romanian, Bulgarian, Serbian, and Albanian women who engage in prostitution in Kosovo.

stories put forward by activists and organizations as a part of a moral crusade against the sex industry at large (Weitzer, 2007; Zhang, 2009, p. 185) and in the context of peacekeeping missions in particular.

Second, challenging the dominant narrative—that the growth of the post-war sex industry is a direct consequence of internationals' demand for commercial sex—allows for more tailor-made reactions to the prevalence of sex industries during future UN missions by both mission organizations themselves and NGOs. As will be outlined, the UN tends to deal with the rise of a local sex industry as if it is the consequence of the act of some delinquent individuals, "rotten apples," that can be dismissed (Jennings & Nikolić-Ristanović, 2009, p. 21). However, if the growth of the sex industry can be linked to peacekeeping missions and a post-war setting more structurally (rather than temporally and haphazardly), this might open up pathways toward a more durable approach to combating cases of exploitation and protecting the rights of women who opt to engage in commercial sex in these contexts.

1.4 Outline of the Book

Following this introduction, Chap. 2 sets the stage of the research by providing an overview of the contemporary theoretical debate on prostitution and human trafficking for sexual purposes. The two dominant perspectives on prostitution will be discussed not as two opposing views on reality, but rather as two instrumental discourses aimed at achieving different goals. This analysis seeks to contribute to a better understanding of the hegemonic discourse on prostitution.

I will then turn to my empirical data. The first two ethnographic chapters relate to the claim that the growth of the sex industry in the wake of the Kosovo War was a direct consequence of the demand of international peacekeepers. Chapter 3 zooms in to focus on Kosovo. Following a description of the breakup of former Yugoslavia and the unfolding of the war, I will identify some socio-economic features of post-war Kosovo, in which the sex industry blossomed. I will argue that these features have also contributed to the growth of the sex industry.

Chapter 4 discusses the clientele of the nascent sex industry. Did the demand of peacekeepers indeed singlehandedly feed the prostitution business in Kosovo, as the dominant representation of post-war prostitution suggests? This chapter discusses various types of clients as identified by the women who are actually servicing them.

The final two empirical chapters examine the claim that the demand for commercial sex was met through forced prostitution. The foreign women who were initially involved in the Kosovar sex industry will be introduced in Chap. 5. In 1999, shortly after the end of the Kosovo War, women from Moldova, Romania, and Ukraine—and, to a lesser extent, Serbia and Bulgaria—entered Kosovo and engaged in prostitution. Studies on prostitution in the context of peacekeeping missions that feature foreign women tend to portray these women singularly as victims of trafficking. But does this depiction do justice to the life trajectories of foreign women involved in post-war prostitution in Kosovo? I will examine where these women came from, why and how they came to Kosovo, as well as their expectations before departure and their experiences after arrival.

Kosovar women engaged in prostitution in their home country in larger numbers when it became virtually impossible for foreign women to live in Kosovo and work in its sex industry. A large number of the Kosovar women who engaged in prostitution in bars were not identified as victims of trafficking by Kosovar law enforcement. Instead, these women were considered to be "voluntary prostitutes." Their lived experiences are discussed in Chap. 6, where I will specifically address the consequences of being identified as a "voluntary prostitute."

I will bring the various claims of the book together in conclusion in Chap. 7. Women engaged in post-war prostitution are thus the focal point.[17] More specifically, I have focused on women engaged in prostitution in bars and motels, spaces with the most widespread and public display of prostitution in Kosovo that are relatively accessible. I have occasionally included women who engaged in prostitution in other premises (e.g., apartments) in my research. As the bulk of my work centers around women who offer commercial sexual services in bars and motels so, too, do my conclusions.

References

Agee, J., & Evans, W. (1960). *Let us now praise famous men* (2nd ed.). Boston, MA: Houghton Mifflin.

Agustín, L. M. (2007). *Sex at the margins: Migration, labour markets and the rescue industry*. London, UK: Zed Books.

Amnesty International. (2004). So does it mean I have rights? In *Protecting the human rights of women and girls trafficked for forced prostitution in Kosovo*. London, UK: Amnesty International.

Anderson, B., & Andrijasevic, R. (2008). Sex, slaves and citizens: The politics of anti-trafficking. *Soundings, 40*, 135–145.

Andrijasevic, R. (2007). Beautiful dead bodies: Gender, migration and representation in anti-trafficking campaigns. *Feminist Review, 86*(1), 24–44.

Andrijasevic, R., & Mai, N. (2016). Understanding the recurring appeal of victimhood and slavery in neoliberal times. *Anti-Trafficking Review*, (7), 1–10. https://doi.org/10.14197/atr.20121771

Autesserre, S. (2012). Dangerous tales: Dominant narratives on the Congo and their unintended consequences. *African Affairs, 111*(443), 202–222.

Barth, F. (1967). On the study of social change. *American Anthropologist, 69*(6), 661–669.

Becker, H. (1963). *Outsiders: Studies in the sociology of deviance*. New York, NY: The Free Press.

Beyens, K., & Tournel, H. (2010). Mijnwerkers of ontdekkingsreiziger? Het kwalitatieve interview. In T. Decorte & D. Zaitch (Eds.), *Kwalitatieve methoden en technieken in de criminologie* (2nd ed., pp. 99–233). Leuven, Belgium: Acco.

Bourdieu, P. (1977). *Outline of a theory of practice*. Cambridge, UK: Cambridge University Press.

Brunovskis, A., & Surtees, R. (2008). Agency or illness – the conceptualization of trafficking: Victims' choices and behaviors in the assistance system. *Gender, Technology and Development, 12*(1), 53–76.

[17] This is not to deny that men offer commercial sexual services in Kosovo or in the context of other peacekeeping missions. However, male sex workers are beyond the scope of this research.

Christie, N. (1986). The ideal victim. In E. A. Fattah (Ed.), *From crime policy to victim policy* (pp. 17–30). London, UK: Palgrave Macmillan.

De Wildt, R. (2009). Tasten in het duister: Roemeense straatprostituees in Rome. In Y. van der Pijl, D. Raven, L. Brouwer, & B. Oude Breuil (Eds.), *Antropologische vergezichten: Mondialisering, migratie en multiculturaliteit* (pp. 207–224). Amsterdam, The Netherlands: Aksant.

De Wildt, R. (2015). In the wake of war: A cultural criminological perspective on the growth of the sex industry in Kosovo. In F. de Jong, J. A. E. Vervaele, M. M. Boone, C. Kelk, F. A. M. M. Koenraadt, F. G. H. Kristen, D. Rozenblit, & E. Sikkema (Eds.), *Overarching views of crime and deviancy – rethinking the legacy of the Utrecht School* (pp. 507–526). The Hague, The Netherlands: Eleven International Publishing.

De Wildt, R. (2016). Ethnographic research on the sex industry: The ambivalence of ethical guidelines. In D. Siegel & R. de Wildt (Eds.), *Ethical concerns in research on human trafficking* (pp. 51–69). New York, NY: Springer International Publishing.

Desvarieux, J. (2010, August 2). In postquake Haiti, an Influx of Dominican prostitutes. *Time*. Retrieved October 23, 2015, from http://content.time.com/time/world/article/0,8599,2007131,00.html

Dewalt, K. M., & Dewalt, B. R. (2002). *Participant observation. A guide for fieldworkers*. Walnut Creek, CA: Altamira Press.

Diu, N. L. (2012, February 6). What the UN Doesn't want you to know. *The Telegraph*. Retrieved from http://www.telegraph.co.uk/culture/film/9041974/What-the-UN-Doesnt-Want-You-to-Know.html

Durkheim, E. (1938). *The rules of sociological method*. New York, NY: The Free Press.

Ferrell, J., Hayward, K., & Young, J. (2008). *Cultural criminology: An invitation*. London, UK: Sage.

Ferrell, J., & Van de Voorde, C. (2010). The decisive moment: Documentary photography and cultural criminology. In K. J. Hayward & M. Presdee (Eds.), *Framing crime: Cultural criminology and the image* (pp. 36–52). New York, NY: Routledge.

Friman, R., & Reich, S. (2007). *Human trafficking, human security, and the Balkans*. Pittsburgh, PA: Pittsburgh Press.

Giddens, A. (1984). *The constitution of society: Outline of the theory of structuration*. Cambridge, UK: Polity Press.

Hayward, K. (2012). *Cultural criminology. Oxford bibliography*. Retrieved March 17, 2018, from http://www.oxfordbibliographies.com/view/document/obo-9780195396607/obo-9780195396607-0003.xml

Higate, P. (2003). Gender and peacekeeping. Case studies: The DRC and Sierra Leone. *Africa Portal*. Retrieved November 7, 2017, from https://www.africaportal.org/publications/gender-and-peacekeeping-case-studies-the-drc-and-sierra-leone/

Higate, P. (2007). Peacekeepers, masculinities, and sexual exploitation. *Men and Masculinities, 10*(1), 99–119.

Jennings, K., & V. Nikolić-Ristanović (2009). *UN peacekeeping economies and local sex industries: Connections and implications* (Microcon Working Paper no. 17). Retrieved from http://www.peacewomen.org/assets/file/Resources/NGO/PK_SexIndustries_MICROCON_2009.pdf

Jennings, K. M. (2008). *Protecting whom? Approaches to sexual exploitation and abuse in UN peacekeeping operations (report)*. Oslo, Norway: Fafo.

Jennings, K. M. (2015). Life in a 'peace-kept' City: Encounters with the peacekeeping economy. *Journal of Intervention and Statebuilding, 9*(3), 296–315.

Krsmanovic, E. (2016). Captured 'realities' of human trafficking: Analysis of photographs illustrating stories on trafficking into the sex industry in Serbian media. *Anti-Trafficking Review*, (7), 139–160. https://doi.org/10.14197/atr.20121778

Leman, J., & Janssens, S. (2008). The Albanian and post-soviet business of trafficking women for prostitution: Structural developments and financial modus operandi. *European Journal of Criminology, 5*(4), 433–451.

Lynch, C. (2005, March 23). U.N. faces more accusations of sexual misconduct. *The Washington Post*. Retrieved October 23, 2015, from http://www.washingtonpost.com/wp-dyn/articles/A30286-2005Mar12.html

Martin, S. (2005). *Must boys be boys? Ending sexual exploitation & abuse in UN peacekeeping missions*. Washington, DC: Refugees International.

Mendelson, S. E. (2005). *Barracks and brothels: Peacekeepers and human trafficking in the Balkans*. Washington, DC: Csis.

Mertus, J., & Bertone, A. (2007). Combating trafficking: International efforts and their ramifications. In R. Friman & S. Reich (Eds.), *Human trafficking, human security and the Balkans* (pp. 40–60). Pittsburgh, PA: University of Pittsburgh Press.

Morrison, W. (2006). *Criminology, civilization and the new world order*. London, UK: Glasshouse.

Murray, J. (2002). Who will police the peace-builders? The failure to establish accountability for the participation of United Nations Civilian Police in the trafficking of women in post-conflict Bosnia and Herzegovina. *Columbia Human Rights Law Review, 34*(2), 475–528.

Oldenburg, S. (2015). The politics of love and intimacy in Goma, Eastern DR Congo: Perspectives on the market of intervention as contact zone. *Journal of Intervention and Statebuilding, 9*(3), 316–333.

Oude Breuil, B. C. (2008). Precious children in a heartless world? The complexities of child trafficking in Marseille. *Children & Society, 22*(3), 223–234.

Oude Breuil, B. C. (2009). Nachtblind. (On)zichtbaarheid van prostitutiemigratie in Marseille. In C. Brants & S. van der Poel (Eds.), *Diverse kwesties. Liber amicorum Prof. Dr. Frank Bovenkerk* (pp. 125–141). The Hague, The Netherlands: Boom Juridische Uitgevers.

Patrick, S. (2015). *The Dark Side of U.N. Peacekeepers*. Retrieved July 19, 2019, from: https://www.newsweek.com/why-are-un-peacekeepers-still-sexually-abusing-children-361065.

Radcliff-Brown, A. R. (1940). On social structure. *The Journal of the Royal Anthropological Institute of Great Britain and Ireland, 70*(1), 1–12.

Republic of Kosovo, Ministry of Internal Affairs, Koordinatori Nacional Kundër Trafikimit Me Qenie Njerëzore. (2010). *Rapport per Zbatimin e Strategjisë Nacionale dhe Plani i Veprimit Kunder Trafikimit të Qenieve Njerëzore. Vepro me Përgjegjësi. Të gjithë kundër Trafikimit me Qenie Njerëzore. Janar- Dhjetor*. Pristina, Kosovo: Republic of Kosovo, Ministry of Internal Affairs, Koordinatori Nacional Kundër Trafikimit Me Qenie Njerëzore.

Republic of Kosovo, Ministry of Internal Affairs, Office of National Coordinator against Trafficking in Human Beings. (2009). *Progress report: Implementation of strategy and action plan against trafficking in human beings. Zero tolerance against organized crime*. Pristina, Kosovo: Republic of Kosovo, Ministry of Internal Affairs, Office of National Coordinator against Trafficking in Human Beings.

Siegel, D. (2005). Recent trends in women trafficking and voluntary prostitution: Russian-speaking sex-workers in the Netherlands. *Transnational Crime, 4*(1), 4–23.

Simic, O. (2012). *Regulation of sexual conduct in UN peacekeeping operations*. New York, NY: Springer.

Surtees, R. (2008). Traffickers and trafficking in Southern and Eastern Europe: Considering the other side of human trafficking. *European Journal of Criminology, 5*(1), 39–68.

Taylor, I., Walton, P., & Young, J. (1973). *The new criminology: For a social theory of deviance*. London, UK: Routledge.

Terre des Hommes. (2010). *Regional Report on the Implementation of the "UNICEF Guidelines for the Protection of the Rights of Child Victims of Trafficking in South Eastern Europe": Assessment of the Situation in Albania, Kosovo and the Former Yugoslav Republic of Macedonia*. Geneva, Switzerland: Terre des Hommes. Retrieved from http://tdh-childprotection.org/documents/regional-report-on-the-implementation-of-the-unicef-guidelines-for-the-protection-of-the-rights-of-child-victims-of-trafficking-in-south-eastern-europe

UN General Assembly. (2005, March 24). *Letter dated March 24, 2005 from the Secretary General to the President of the General Assembly* (UN Doc A/59/710). Retrieved from https://cdu.unlb.org/Portals/0/Documents/KeyDoc5.pdf

UNODC. (2004). *United Nations convention against transnational organized crime and the protocols thereto*. New York, NY: United Nations. Retrieved from https://www.unodc.org/documents/treaties/UNTOC/Publications/TOC%20Convention/TOCebook-e.pdf

Weber, M. (1978). *Economy and society*. Berkeley, CA: University of California Press.

Weitzer, R. (2007). The social construction of sex trafficking: Ideology and institutionalization of a moral crusade. *Politics and Society, 35*(3), 447–475.

Weitzer, R. (2014). New directions in research on human trafficking. *The Annals of the American Academy of Political and Social Science, 653*(1), 6–24.

Whitworth, S. (2004). *Men, militarism, and UN peacekeeping: A gendered analysis*. Boulder, CO: Lynne Rienner Publishers.

Yea, S. (2005). Labour of love: Filipina entertainers' narratives of romance and relationships with GIs in US Military camp towns in Korea. *Women's Studies International Forum, 28*(6), 456–472.

Zaitch, D. (2002). *Trafficking cocaine: Colombian drug entrepreneurs in the Netherlands*. The Hague, The Netherlands: Kluwer Law International.

Zhang, S. X. (2009). Beyond the 'Natasha' story – a review and critique of current research on sex trafficking. *Global Crime, 10*(3), 178–195.

Fig. 2.1 Woman in a bar

Chapter 2
Theorizing Prostitution

In the context of peacekeeping missions, the view that prostitution equals human trafficking has come to the fore (Higate, 2007; Mendelson, 2005). This discourse is accompanied by stereotypical and highly symbolic visual representations that emphasize the horror of trafficking; images tend to portray distraught young women and children forced into prostitution (Andrijasevic, 2007; Andrijasevic & Mai, 2016).

Claims over human trafficking often accompany worldwide events where large groups of men gather. One can think of sports tournaments, such as the soccer World Cups in South Africa (Gould, 2010) and Germany (Henning, Craggs, Laczko, & Larsson, 2007; Segrave, Milivojevic, & Pickering, 2009), mining settlements—from corporate mining towns in Chile to copper and gold mines in Kenya (Lahiri-Dutt, 2011; Laite, 2009)—and even historical events, such as the diplomatic meetings in the Netherlands that led to the establishment of the Treaty of Utrecht in 1713 (Freschot, 2013; Siegel, 2015). The soccer spectators, miners, and diplomats present for such events allegedly create an increased demand for commercial sex, which is met through the trafficking of women and children. These claims are not necessarily supported by available evidence, but nonetheless, cause turmoil that in turn creates opportunities for campaigns against human trafficking for sexual purposes. The World Cup in South Africa is one such case in point: posters were distributed that depicted a referee holding a red card stating "OUT with trafficking" (Gould, 2010, p. 36).

Similar allegations have emerged in relation to peacekeeping missions from Bosnia and Herzegovina (Mendelson, 2005; Murray, 2002) to Cambodia (Whitworth, 2004) and Sierra Leone (Higate, 2007). The largely male international peacekeepers, diplomats, and relief workers in these war-torn regions are said to have increased the demand for prostitution and sometimes orchestrated its organization. Both academic and popular publications tend to describe this as an especially weighty issue, as those who come to bring stability and re-establish the rule of law are actually seen to encourage sexual exploitation and abuse (Higate, 2003; Martin, 2005).

R. de Wildt, *Post-War Prostitution*, Studies of Organized Crime 17,
https://doi.org/10.1007/978-3-030-19474-1_2

This chapter aims to contribute to a better understanding of this hegemonic discourse by elaborating upon the academic debate on prostitution. The two stances that dominate this debate origin from the so-called "sex wars"—a popular term for the feminist debates regarding prostitution and pornography in the late 1970s and early 1980s (Segrave, Milivojevic, & Pickering, 2009, p. 2). On the one hand, abolitionists (also referred to as radical feminists or prohibitionists) view prostitution as gender-based violence. On the other, "pro-sex-work scholars" put central emphasis on women's right to self-determination and to earn money in the sex industry. Both camps are driven by their own political agendas.

I will analyze both viewpoints together with their main critiques. They will be outlined and approached not as two opposing views on reality, but rather as two instrumental discourses aimed at achieving different goals. As the above examples illustrate, the abolitionist perspective tends to dominate the discourse on prostitution in the context of peacekeeping missions.

2.1 The Abolitionist Perspective

One body of academic literature contends that "trafficking in women for the purpose of sexual exploitation is a multi-billion dollar shadow market" in which "transnational networks and pimps prey on the dreams of women" (Hughes, 2000, p. 1). In this literature, women are generally portrayed as isolated trafficking victims and often referred to as "Natashas" (see also Denisova, 2001; Hughes & Denisova, 2001). "Natasha" is a nickname clients tend to use for Eastern European women involved in prostitution (Malarek, 2004). The term is adopted by scholars who, as observed by Zhang (2009, p. 181) in his review of studies on sex trafficking, generally portray trafficking victims as young, naïve women who assume that they will be waitressing, modeling, or bartending abroad, but find themselves violently forced into prostitution instead.

"Natasha-like stories" are articulated by abolitionist scholars such as Barry (1979), Hughes (2000), Raymond (1998, 2004), and Denisova (2001). Some abolitionists are critical of the attention that is being given to these extreme accounts, which emphasize deception and violence. Matthews (2008, p. 39), for instance, poses that such dramatic stories mask the fact that some women also become involved in the prostitution business knowingly. However, abolitionist scholars consider such knowledge insignificant; their central argument focuses on the non-existence and irrelevance of free choice in prostitution. Let us consider these two central claims in more detail.

Free choice is considered *non-existent* because woman's decision to enter the sex industry is always informed by economic, social, and personal constraints. Women involved in the sex industry are believed to have limited employment possibilities as a result of class, age, gender, and location restrictions, as well as low (educational) skills. Economically speaking, prostitution is then perceived as one of few limited possibilities—if not the only possibility—to make a living (Aronowitz, 2001, p. 167, 170; Jeffreys, 2009, p. 20; Matthews, 2008, p. 30). The subsequent argument of social constraint lies in structural power relations: structural male domination and female subordination legitimizes that men buy, and women sell, sexual services (Hughes, 2000, p. 635; Matthews, 2008, p. 30; Miriam, 2005, pp. 13–14). Abolitionists do not perceive a woman's decision to sell sex as a free choice, since the decision is informed by asymmetrical power relations and centered around the desires of "clients, pimps and entrepreneurs" instead of "the sexual interests of the women involved in prostitution" (Matthews, 2008, pp. 300–331).

To a certain extent, these two lines of thought are supported by scholars who are not necessarily involved in the heated debate about prostitution, but observe how gender inequality has led to a "feminization of migration." Ehrenreich and Hochschild (2002, p. 5), for instance, observe "increasing migration of women from poor countries to rich ones" (or, as I will argue in Sect. 3.2.6, to places with a temporary increase in economic activity, such as during peacekeeping missions). In these relatively affluent places, migrant women tend to take up caregiving work as maids, nannies, or sex workers. These types of work are considered feminine, yet local women are not able or willing to perform such tasks. The striking inequality in global wages means that migrant women fill in the "care deficit" (Ehrenreich & Hochschild, 2002).

Alongside these economic and social constraints, abolitionist scholars argue that on a personal level, a history of physical and sexual abuse and neglect can channel women toward the sex industry (Matthews, 2008, p. 31). Farley (2003, p. 256) suggests that most women involved in prostitution have experienced sexual abuse in their childhood, stating that "familial sexual abuse functions as a training ground for prostitution" (Farley, 2003, p. 255). As a result of these economic, social, and personal factors, feminist abolitionists hold that "engaging in prostitution cannot be seen as an expression of 'free choice'. Rather, prostitution is something that people turn to when they run out of choices" (Matthews, 2008, p. 31).

The notion of free choice is, moreover, considered *irrelevant*, since sexual violence and exploitation are believed to be imperative elements of prostitution. Abolitionists describe the experiences of women involved in the sex industry as "abusive, degrading, and harmful to their health and well-being" (Hughes, 2000, p. 653). Melissa Farley (2006, pp. 109–10) argues that "prostitution is sexual violence that results in massive economic profit for some of its perpetrators." Janice Raymond (1995) extends this argument by claiming prostitution is "like being paid to be raped." In presenting exploitation as such a central element of prostitution, women's "choice" to engage in the sex industry is considered irrelevant, as it leads to their victimization nonetheless.

2.1.1 Conflating Prostitution with Human Trafficking and the Battle Against Both

Based upon the arguments that women's consent to engage in prostitution is irrelevant and that women in prostitution are exploited and seldom free to leave the sex industry, abolitionists take the stance that prostitution and trafficking are fundamentally interrelated. As stated by feminist Leidholdt (2004, p. 167), "[S]ex trafficking can accurately be viewed as globalized prostitution while generic prostitution often is a practice of domestic trafficking." Consequently, abolitionists call for an end to prostitution and the inequality it perpetuates between men and women (Pateman, 1988), maintaining that "[s]ex must be based in intimacy" and "cannot be purchased, legally acquired, or seized by force" (Barry, 1979, p. 267, 270; see also Matthews, 2008; Pateman, 1988). Abolitionist scholars therefore oppose the legalization of prostitution.

This opposition to legalization is rooted in both symbolic and practical reasons (Weitzer, 2007). Raymond (2003, p. 322) provides an example of a symbolic objection in stating that "legalization of prostitution sends the message to new generations of men and boys that women are sexual commodities and that prostitution is harmless fun." She suggests that legalization of prostitution normalizes the exploitation of women by men, rendering it socially acceptable (see also Farley, 2004, p. 1088). Practically speaking, abolitionists propose that legalization increases prostitution and trafficking alike by "inviting them [clients] to spend their money" (Farley, 2004, p. 1088; Raymond, 2003).

Abolitionists argue in favor of the criminalization of clients of prostitution, claiming that this policy decreases the demand for commercial sex—which, according to abolitionist scholars, equals human trafficking (Farley, 2003; Leidholdt, 2004; Raymond, 2003).

2.1.2 *Critique for the Abolitionist Perspective*

The abolitionist understanding of prostitution and human trafficking for sexual purposes has been criticized for being based on a moral mythology that has "important real-world consequences" (Weitzer, 2010, p. 15; see also Zhang, 2009). This claim is made concrete through seven core critiques that I have summarized from critical discussions of the abolitionist approach. These critiques include: (1) the resolute representation of those engaged in prostitution as victims; (2) the conflation of prostitution and human trafficking for sexual purposes; (3) the representation of facilitators and clients of prostitution as the source of evil; (4) the moral argument that sex should be based in intimacy; (5) the lack of empirical proof for these aforementioned claims; (6) the use of questionable statistics about the scale of human trafficking and; (7) the alleged dangers of legalizing prostitution and favor of prohibitionist measures.[1] This section will be dedicated to examining these critiques.

The *first critique* is that those engaged in prostitution are resolutely represented as victims. Abolitionist scholars suggest that those engaged in prostitution should

[1] Weitzer (2007) has identified and debunked various core claims regarding human trafficking for sexual purposes by those campaigning against it in his article "The Social Construction of Sex Trafficking." My summary takes these claims into consideration, but I have organized it differently so as to encompass other critiques of the abolitionist perspective as well.

be considered victims of the circumstances that led them to the sex industry and, once involved in it, victims of exploitation and abuse. Inherent to this argument is the assumption that women never make the informed decision to engage in prostitution. Several scholars criticize this assumption, as it supposedly denies women any form of agency (Segrave et al., 2009, p. 4; Weitzer, 2007, pp. 452–453). As argued by Siegel (2011, pp. 262–263), prostitution can be "a career path chosen by women themselves [...] in order to improve their economic situation to support their families and children back home, to experience adventures, or to combine pleasure with travelling and doing business." The discourse of victimhood ignores women's motives for considering the sex industry (Andrijasevic, 2007, p. 87, 90) as well as their right to self-determination (Derks, 2000, p. 10; Segrave et al., 2009, p. 4) and ability to practice it. This leads to a lack of understanding regarding trafficking and prostitution (Andrijasevic, 2007; Siegel, 2011). Furthermore, it can spur undesired rescue operations of women who opt to return to the prostitution business after having been "saved" (Weitzer, 2007, p. 453).

Grand generalizations that "prostitution in and of itself is an abuse of a woman's body" (Dworkin, 1993, p. 3) are likewise considered fallacies. In reference to various studies on the experience of violence amongst women involved in sex work, Weitzer (2012, p. 18, 26) explains that victimization is a variable instead of a constant. The extent to which women encounter violence, for instance, depends on various factors, including the type of sex work that women conduct and their geographical location (Weitzer, 2012).

The *second criticism* of the abolitionist perspective maintains that unilaterally describing women engaged in prostitution as victims does not do justice to their motives and experiences. According to this criticism, prostitution and human trafficking are not inextricably linked. In their study of empirically based literature on human trafficking, Gozdziak and Bump (2008, p. 9) conclude that abolitionists fail to distinguish between human trafficking for forced prostitution, on the one hand, and voluntary migration (legal or irregular) for sex work, on the other (see also Zhang, 2009). Cheng (2008) argues that this failure causes global and local contexts, which generate the need for and the (constrained) agency of migrants, to remain unseen. According to Cheng, various global, regional, and local structures cause women to migrate, for instance in order to engage in prostitution abroad. Some women subsequently encounter labor exploitation or abuse. Yet these experiences are much more layered and complex than the abolitionist rhetoric suggests in presenting all women engaged in prostitution as victims of human trafficking for sexual purposes and organized crime.

Thirdly, in claiming that "pimping and procuring [...] rank about the most complete expressions of male hatred for femaleness" (Barry, 1979, p. 86), abolitionists portray men who facilitate prostitution or pay for sexual intercourse as caricatures or "folk devils" (Weitzer, 2007, p. 452). This relates problematically to empirical findings that women can sometimes only realize their migration plans with the help of human smugglers or traffickers. In her research among women engaged in street prostitution in Italy, Andrijasevic (2007, p. 91), for instance, found that women are not always forced into illegal migration by traffickers. On the contrary, women from disadvantaged areas often ask for assistance in realizing their plans to engage in prostitution abroad; these women, amongst other migrants, need help with illegal border crossings. Therefore, women regularly contact people who can facilitate their intended journeys. Not many women will be able to arrive in a new country free of debts or agreements on how to pay back the costs of the assistance they have received. Although traffickers are generally considered responsible for the exploitation of women involved in out-country prostitution, Andrijasevic (2010, p. 3) instead relates the sources of exploitation to immigration and employment regulation in the European Union. Such macro-level socio-economic inequality and power struggles remain unseen if the emphasis is placed on gendered power struggles alone.

Likewise, critics question the portrayal of those who purchase commercial sex as being the "personification of evil." While some clients use violence to obtain sex or seek the most vulnerable women in order to receive low costs of service (Cauduro, 2009, p. 17; Church, Henderson, Barnard, & Hart, 2001), there is no empirical evidence to suggest that such behavior is omnipresent (Weitzer, 2007, p. 452). Moreover, in her study on clients of prostitution in the Netherlands, Shiboleth (2015, p. 74) found that clients can sometimes have different roles and may help women if they suspect them to be coerced or to have encountered violence by facilitators of prostitution.

The *fourth critique* questions the claim that sex must be based in intimacy. This moral argument is critiqued since it assumes that sex is perceived and valued in the same way by everyone worldwide. Kempadoo (1998, p. 5) argues that people might very well be able to separate the sexual act from love and intimacy, irrespective of their involvement in sex work. Moreover, this moral argument is considered ethnocentric. In his book *The Transformation of Intimacy*, Giddens (1992) poses that romantic love is a modern Western invention that is under severe strain from both temporal and spatial domains. The pursuit of romantic love was far from usual in other times and remains so in various places. Furthermore, a multitude of studies show that commercial sex is not about sexual intercourse per se (Lucas, 2005; Sanders, 2008; Seib, Fischer, & Najman, 2009). The social aspects of sex work can be just as important for clients, especially regulars, who seek intimacy and emotional connectivity through prostitution (Weitzer, 2010, pp. 32–35).

The previous concerns with the abolitionist understanding of prostitution all relate to the *fifth critique*, which points to the absence of empirical data for the claims that abolitionists make about prostitution. Weitzer (2005, p. 3) suggests that "writers typically recount horror stories about victims […] to provoke the reader's abhorrence of prostitution. The most disturbing instances of abuse are presented as typical." Likewise, Zhang (2009, p. 185) highlights the absence of empirical studies in the discourse on human trafficking and worries that "imagination seems to have taken the place of sound empirical studies." Bold claims about prostitution are instead based on anecdotes, and inconvenient findings (i.e., counterevidence) are often ignored (see also Agustín, 2007; Sanghera, 2005).

A *sixth critique*, one that is also methodological, relates to abolitionists' claims regarding the scale of trafficking for sexual exploitation. Hughes (2000, p. 625) estimates "the value of the global trade in women as commodities for sex industries

[…] to be between seven and twelve billion dollars annually." Denisova (2001, p. 30) states that "nearly 2 million women and children annually become 'merchandise.'" However, the total count of victims—and profits—of human trafficking for sexual purposes is impossible to measure due to the underground nature of the phenomenon (Goodey, 2008; Kempadoo, 2003; Shelley, 2010; Weitzer, 2007, 2012; Zhang, 2009). Reliable statistics on the scale of human trafficking do not exist; there are only "guesstimates." Nevertheless, activist groups campaigning against human trafficking can benefit from giving high estimates so as to attract attention for their cause from the media, donors, and policymakers (Weitzer, 2007, p. 455).

The final and *seventh critique* relates to policy. Abolitionists argue that the legalization of prostitution unjustly legitimizes the male demand for commercial sex, which causes an increase in the demand for prostitution and an expansion of the prostitution business in general (Hughes, 2000, p. 637, 639; Hughes & Denisova, 2001, p. 43; Jeffreys, 2009; Raymond, 2001, p. 9). Abolitionists thus argue in favor of the criminalization of clients of prostitution. Criminalization of clients is believed to cause a decrease in the demand for commercial sex, which for abolitionists equals human trafficking (Farley, 2003; Leidholdt, 2004; Raymond, 2003). However, Weitzer (2007, p. 457) puts forward that "rather than being a magnet attracting migrants into a country, it appears that legal prostitution may help reduce trafficking due to enhanced government regulation and oversight of the legal sector." He underlines this point by referring to reports on human trafficking in the Netherlands, where prostitution is legalized, that have shown a decrease of trafficking cases in the legal Dutch prostitution business (Altink & Bokelman, 2006; Transcrime, 2005).

Furthermore, Segrave et al. (2009, p. 4) suggest that prohibitionist measures, such as the criminalization of clients of prostitution, do not decrease prostitution at all. With reference to the prohibition of prostitution in contemporary Sweden, they even pose that prohibition only increases illicit activities – a stance that is echoed by Murray (1998), who posits that the prohibition of prostitution attracts organized crime.

2.2 Pro-Sex-Work Scholarship

In opposition to the abolitionist understanding of prostitution, a pro-sex-work scholarship has emerged. Pro-sex-work scholars first and foremost see those engaged in prostitution as agents instead of victims; women's right to self-determination lies at the core of this discourse. Prostitution is acknowledged "as a matter of personal choice and a form of work" (Doezema, 1998, p. 38).

Pro-sex-work literature has adopted the term "sex worker" in order to underline that prostitution is a form of labor (Brennan, 2004, p. 23); "[i]t is a term that suggests we view prostitution not as an identity—a social or a psychological characteristic of women, often indicated by 'whore'—but as an income-generating activity" (Kempadoo, 1998, p. 3). Since prostitution is identified as a form of work, pro-sex-work scholars argue that the women involved deserve the same human rights and civil liberties as other workers. The abuse and exploitation of sex workers is thus interpreted as a violation of these rights (O'Neill, 2001, p. 331; Segrave et al., 2009, p. 5).

Empirical studies by pro-sex-work scholars explain out-country prostitution from the perspective of migration, as suggested by Andrijasevic (2007, pp. 97–98; see also Oude Breuil, 2008, 2009), or as a personal choice and career path, as proposed by Siegel (2011, p. 263, 266; see also Agustín, 2007; Brunovskis & Surtees, 2008; Davies, 2009; Janssen, 2007; Siegel, 2005; Siegel & Bovenkerk, 2000). Pro-sex-work scholars put forward that examining prostitution from the angle of women's desire for both vertical mobility (e.g., wealth and well-being) and horizontal mobility (i.e., between countries) (Siegel, 2011) allows for a greater consideration of the motives that inform their decisions to (migrate and) get involved in the sex industry. This exploration of women's motives differs from the feminist abolitionist approach, in which the discussion about choice primarily centers on demonstrating that "free choice" in the context of prostitution is non-existent and irrelevant. Examining prostitution through the lens of women's desire for mobility acknowledges the influence of migration policies on their possibilities of realizing migration plans. Furthermore, this angle expands the discussion to include an understanding of exploitative labor relations in any form of prostitution, independent of whether women were initially coerced into working in the sex industry (Andrijasevic, 2007, 2010).

With regard to policy, pro-sex-work scholars generally condemn the criminalization of prostitution; they believe it is only expected to aggravate the problem, since prostitution will move out of sight (Murray, 1998; Segrave et al., 2009, p. 4). In line with qualifying prostitution as a form of work, pro-sex-work scholars instead argue for the legalization of prostitution, as well as better working conditions and protection for those engaged in sex work (Segrave et al., 2009, p. 7).

2.2.1 Critique for Pro-Sex-Work Stance

Critique of the pro-sex-work scholarship primarily focuses on those aspects of the pro-sex-work movement that tend to romanticize sex work and strongly emphasize the potential for empowerment that engagement in prostitution may entail. An example of this emphasis is provided by Wendy Chapkis (1997, p. 30), who argues that sex workers have the potential to challenge "confining notions of proper womanhood and conventional sexuality." Likewise, former sex worker and sex-positive feminist Annie Sprinkle (1998) states that women engaged in prostitution "challenge sexual mores." Weitzer (2009, p. 215) critiques these scholars, accusing them of highlighting success stories "to demonstrate that sex work can be edifying, lucrative, or esteem-enhancing" while neglecting to discuss the negative experiences of women in sex work. He suggests that sex work can indeed empower women, but that there is a great variety in experiences; empowerment is just one of them. Pro-sex-work scholars who tend to romanticize sex work thus face criticism similar to that of abolitionist scholars. The most favorable stories of empowerment are presented as representative, while counterevidence (e.g., stories of abuse) is ignored. Like the abolitionists, in this literature ideals overshadow empirical data (Long, 2004, p. 23; Segrave et al., 2009). This leads Zhang (2009) and Weitzer (2014) to make pleas for research on sex trafficking with a solid empirical foundation.

However, there are also numerous critiques on pro-sex-work scholars who have a less romantic view of sex work. Matthews (2008, p. 28) disagrees with pro-sex-work scholars' suggestion that entry into prostitution can be a way for women to take control over their own lives. Engagement in prostitution does not reduce the vulnerability of those involved, but instead "heightens and extends the range of victimisation," he argues. According to Matthews (2008, p. 37), women often experience feelings of guilt and remorse as a consequence of their engagement in prostitution; this can instigate the use of alcohol and mind-numbing drugs, which only make women more dependent and desperate. Moreover, he suggests, prostitution can have adverse effects on the children of those women who become involved, as their needs for care might be jeopardized and they could experience stigmatization.

Matthews (2008, pp. 29–33) furthermore critiques the notion that women enter prostitution out of "free choice," since this does not take into consideration the "social and structural processes in play." As outlined in Sect. 2.1.1, he considers the notion of choice to be false, as it ignores existing economic, social, and personal constraints. Moreover, he puts forward that acknowledging women's involvement in prostitution as a matter of "free choice" negatively impacts them, since it portrays them as fully responsible for engagement in an occupation that involves illegalities, social stigmatization, and marginalization (see also Jeffreys, 2009). Yet this approach is unclear as to why women who face stigma as a consequence of their involvement in prostitution can only be let off the moral hook by emphasizing that the decision to get involved was not their own. Such an approach reinforces the idea that selling sexual services is immoral, while women likely benefit more from an approach that counters the stigma in the first place (see also Weitzer, 2017).

Pro-sex-work scholars' suggestion that prostitution is a legitimate form of work has also been criticized. Feminist Carole Pateman (1988) puts forward that clients not only buy sexual services, but mastery of the body of a woman. This, she argues, will affect the woman's sense of self in ways incomparable to other occupations. Following on this critique, Matthews (2008, pp. 41–42) disagrees with the use of the term "sex worker," arguing that it fails to acknowledge the uniqueness of prostitution in comparison to other activities that relate to sex, such as stripping and telephone sex. Moreover, he considers "sex worker" to be no less stigmatizing than the term "prostitute" and that using the term therefore first and foremost reflects one's perception of engagement in prostitution.

Finally, with regard to policy, Lynellyn Long (2004, p. 22) criticizes pro-sex-work scholars' call for the legalization of prostitution, arguing that "irregular migrants rarely benefit from legalization since their status sets them outside the protections afforded to sex workers who are citizens." Legalization would thus create a divide between legal and protected sex workers, on the one hand, and illegal and unprotected sex workers, on the other (see also Raymond, 2004). Critics have moral objections to the legalization of prostitution as well: Raymond (2004, pp. 316–322) puts forward that "legalization/decriminalization of prostitution is a gift to pimps, traffickers and the sex industry" that makes the "social and ethical barriers to treating women as sexual merchandise" disappear. She contends that legalization will intensify the prostitution market and the exploitation and abuse it encompasses (see also Jeffreys, 2009).

2.3 Instrumental Goals

What can be learned from the struggle between these two discourses? And how can we avoid getting stuck in this struggle or simply siding with one over the other? I argue that both perspectives are not two competing views on reality, but rather instrumental discourses that not only reflect how people understand the world, but—more importantly—how they wish to shape it. The abolitionist and pro-sex-work perspectives thus have differing instrumental goals.

The two perspectives can be seen as ideologies that spread around the globe through what anthropologist Arjun Appadurai (1990) has deemed "ideoscapes." Ideoscapes are one of five "scapes" that he defines in order to grapple with interdependent dimensions of global flows of people, machinery, money, images, and in this case, ideas.[2] With regard to ideoscapes, Appadurai proposes that in the current global era, ideologies and counter-ideologies increasingly follow "non-isomorphic paths" and shape themselves differently in various national and transnational contexts (idem). As such, in the transnational context of peacekeeping missions, prostitution is primarily considered through the discourse of the abolitionist perspective, but let us briefly consider the instrumental goals of both ideologies.

On the one hand, the narrative of the pro-sex-work caucus is put forward by scholars who aim, first, to acknowledge the variety of experiences of women engaged in prostitution, and second, to focus on the structural inequalities that these women come to resist. Immigration and employment regulation in the European Union are examples of socio-economic inequalities and power struggles on a macro level that scholars can lay bare through the pro-sex-work discourse (Andrijasevic, 2010; Siegel, 2011). On a more practical level, activists rely on the pro-sex-work discourse in order to strengthen the position of those involved in prostitution. The instrumental goal of organizations and activists within the sex workers' rights movement is to acknowledge prostitution as a legitimate form of work, destigmatize involvement in it, and recognize the exploitation of women engaged in prostitution as a violation of labor and human rights.[3]

---

[2] The other "scapes" identified by Appadurai are ethnoscapes, technoscapes, financescapes, and mediascapes.

[3] The Global Network of Sex Work Projects (www.nswp.org) is a prominent organization that advocates for the rights of sex workers.

The abolitionist rhetoric, on the other hand, aims to make sure that fewer (or, ideally, no) women engage in prostitution. As mentioned, this discourse is specifically influential in publications on prostitution during peacekeeping missions. In this context, commercial sex is primarily portrayed as a matter of forced prostitution in which innocent and deceived victims are exploited by peacekeepers. As a consequence, prostitution is equated with human trafficking (Agathangelou & Ling, 2003; Higate, 2003, 2007; Martin, 2005; Mendelson, 2005; Murray, 2002; Rathgeber, 2002). In her description of dominant stories on the causes, consequences, and solutions to sexual violence in the Democratic Republic of the Congo, Autesserre (2012, pp. 206–210) explains the power of narratives that likewise "assign the cause of problems to the deliberate actions of identifiable individuals [...]; which include bodily harm to individuals [...]; [and] suggest a simple solution." She argues that such "simple narratives" have more impact and are therefore effective in prompting action. In other words, they are instrumental.

Examples of actors that can benefit from such narratives about post-war prostitution in line with the abolitionist rhetoric include aid agencies, the media, and policymakers. Aid agencies, which are critically typified as "the rescue industry" by anthropologist Laura Agustín (2007), can benefit from one-dimensional narratives, as this generally makes them more successful in receiving grants and projects (Agustín, 2007; see also Gould, 2014; Weitzer, 2007, 2014, p. 20). Worldwide donors often eagerly spend money on "helpless victims" of trafficking exploited in post-war prostitution businesses. This is most definitely the case in donor-darling Kosovo, where embassies and other donors have financed multiple large-scale initiatives aimed at the countering of human trafficking (e.g., through the organization of a yearly anti-trafficking month). Likewise, the media need straightforward stories that the public can grasp in a few headlines (van Stokkom, 2013). Often such popular publications are accompanied by narrow visual representations of women engaged in prostitution as completely powerless victims (Andrijasevic & Mai, 2016; Krsmanovic, 2016). Caritas Kosovo, for instance, disseminated a brochure whose front cover featured a drawing of a woman with a rope around her neck. Finally, policymakers generally welcome brief representations of the situation with concrete policy recommendations (Autesserre, 2012, p. 207). All these actors use the abolitionist rhetoric instrumentally and therefore do not bring more nuanced abolitionist narratives to the fore. While their claims are not necessarily fact-based, they do impact the ways in which prostitution in the context of peacekeeping missions is understood and dealt with. As Thomas and Thomas (1928, p. 572) articulated, "[I]f men define situations as real, they are real in their consequences." That is exactly the intention in this case, as the aim of the abolitionist discourse is to counter the prostitution business at large.

Individuals and groups who take the lead in presenting prostitution in the context of peacekeeping missions as a form of sexual exploitation (as well as those who, on the contrary, argue that prostitution is a form of empowerment) can be considered in line with Howard Becker's (1963) definition of "moral entrepreneurs." Becker coined the term "moral entrepreneur" in order to describe those who force a certain moral on others out of a humanitarian motive. They strive to achieve a better life for others and believe that their perspective will prevent exploitation and suffering.[4] When applied to the hegemonic discourse on prostitution in the context of peacekeeping missions, actors who conflate prostitution with human trafficking and call for the battle against both generally believe that this view can prevent further exploitation of women in the prostitution business. Notwithstanding this good intention, Becker (1963, p. 11) points out that those who need to be protected do "not always like the means proposed for their salvation." In lieu of empirical data regarding the situation of women engaged in prostitution during peacekeeping missions, it remains to be seen if these women identify themselves as victims—and, indeed, if they want to be saved. Empirical chapters five and six zoom further into this insider perspective by examining how these women themselves consider their experiences in the post-war prostitution business in Kosovo.

References

Agathangelou, A. M., & Ling, L. H. M. (2003). Desire industries: Sex trafficking, UN peacekeeping, and the neo-liberal world order. *Brown Journal of World Affairs, 10*(1), 133–148.

Agustín, L. M. (2007). *Sex at the margins: Migration, labour markets and the rescue industry*. London, UK: Zed Books.

Altink, S., & Bokelman, S. (2006). *Rechten van Prostituees*. Amsterdam, The Netherlands: La Strada International. Retrieved http://lastradainternational.org/lsidocs/247%20Rechten_van_prostituees.pdf

Andrijasevic, R. (2007). Beautiful dead bodies: Gender, migration and representation in anti-trafficking campaigns. *Feminist Review, 86*(1), 24–44.

Andrijasevic, R. (2010). *Migration, agency and citizenship in sex trafficking*. New York, NY: Springer.

Andrijasevic, R., & Mai, N. (2016). Trafficking (in) representations: Understanding the recurring appeal of victimhood and slavery in neoliberal times. *Anti-Trafficking Review, 7*, 1–10. https://doi.org/10.14197/atr.20121771

Appadurai, A. (1990). Disjuncture and difference in the global cultural economy. *Theory, Culture & Society, 7*(2), 295–310.

Aronowitz, A. A. (2001). Smuggling and trafficking in human beings: The phenomenon, the markets that drive it and the organisations that promote it. *European Journal on Criminal Policy and Research, 9*, 163–195.

Autesserre, S. (2012). Dangerous tales: Dominant narratives on the Congo and their unintended consequences. *African Affairs, 111*(443), 202–222.

Barry, K. (1979). *Female sexual slavery*. New York, NY: New York University Press.

Becker, H. (1963). *Outsiders: Studies in the sociology of deviance*. New York, NY: The Free Press.

Brennan, D. (2004). *What's love got to do with it? Transnational desires and sex tourism in the Dominican Republic*. Durham, NC: Duke University Press.

[4] Moral entrepreneurs can give rise to what Stanley Cohen coined a "moral panic," observing that every now and then, societies are seized by "waves of indignation about non-existing or relatively minor threats" (Goode & Ben-Yehuda, 2009, p. 48). He described such periods of moral panic as "a condition, episode, person or group of persons [that] emerges to become defined as a threat to societal values and interests" (Cohen, 1972, p. 1). However, the moral indignation over UN peacekeepers' engagement in prostitution in war-torn and other vulnerable regions where they are expected to do good is not so widespread as to be defined as a moral panic.

Brunovskis, A., & Surtees, R. (2008). Agency or illness – The conceptualization of trafficking: Victims' choices and behaviors in the assistance system. *Gender, Technology and Development, 12*(1), 53–76.
Cauduro, A. (2009). Review of the research studies on the demand for prostitution in the European Union and beyond. In A. Di Nicola, A. Cauduro, M. Lombardi, & P. Ruspini (Eds.), *Prostitution and human trafficking: Focus on clients* (pp. 5–21). New York, NY: Springer.
Chapkis, W. (1997). *Live sex acts: Women performing erotic labor*. New York, NY/London, UK: Routledge.
Cheng, S. L. (2008). Commentary on Hughes, Chon, and Ellerman. *Violence Against Women, 14*(3), 359–363.
Church, S., Henderson, M., Barnard, M., & Hart, G. (2001). Violence by clients towards female prostitutes in different work settings: Questionnaire survey. *British Medical Journal, 322*(7285), 524–525.
Cohen, S. (1972). *Folk devils and moral panics: The creation of the Mods and Rockers*. London, UK: MacGibbon and Kee.
Davies, J. (2009). *"My name is not Natasha": How Albanian women in France use trafficking to overcome social exclusion (1998-2001)*. Amsterdam, The Netherlands: Amsterdam University Press.
Denisova, T. A. (2001). Trafficking in women and children for purposes of sexual exploitation: The criminological aspect. *Trends in Organized Crime, 6*(3–4), 30–36.
Derks, A. (2000). *Combating trafficking in South East Asia: A review of policy and programme responses*. Geneva, Switzerland: International Organization for Migration.
Doezema, J. (1998). Forced to choose: Beyond the voluntary v. forced prostitution dichotomy. In K. Kempadoo & J. Doezema (Eds.), *Global sex workers: Rights, resistance, and redefinition* (pp. 34–50). New York, NY: Routledge.
Dworkin, A. (1993). Prostitution and male supremacy. *Michigan Journal of Gender & Law, 1*(1), 1–12.
Ehrenreich, B., & Hochschild, A. R. (2002). Introduction. In B. Ehrenreich & A. R. Hochschild (Eds.), *Global woman: Nannies, maids, and sex workers in the new economy* (pp. 1–13). New York, NY: Henry Holt and Company, LLC.
Farley, M. (Ed.). (2003). *Prostitution, trafficking and traumatic stress*. New York, NY: Routledge.
Farley, M. (2004). 'Bad for the body, bad for the heart': Prostitution harms women even if legalized or decriminalized. *Violence Against Women, 10*(10), 1087–1125.
Farley, M. (2006). Prostitution, trafficking, and cultural amnesia: What we must not know in order to keep the business of sexual exploitation running smoothly. *Yale Journal of Law & Feminism, 18*, 109–144.
Freschot, A. (2013). *Amoureuze en pikante geschiedenis van het congres en de stad Utrecht*. Hilversum, The Netherlands: Uitgeverij Verloren.
Giddens, A. (1992). *The transformation of intimacy: Sexuality, love & eroticism in modern societies*. Stanford, CA: Stanford University Press.
Goode, E., & Ben-Yehuda, N. (2009). *Moral panics: The social construct of deviance*. Hoboken, NJ: Wiley-Blackwell.
Goodey, J. (2008). Human trafficking: Sketchy data and policy responses. *Criminology and Criminal Justice, 8*(4), 421–442.
Gould, C. (2010). Moral panic, human trafficking and the 2010 Soccer World Cup. *Agenda, 24*(85), 31–44.
Gould, C. (2014). Sex trafficking and prostitution in South Africa. *The Annals of the American Academy of Political and Social Science, 653*(1), 183–201.
Gozdziak, E. M., & Bump, M. N. (2008). *Data and research on human trafficking: Bibliography of research-based literature*. Washington, DC: Institute for the Study of International Migration.
Henning, J., Craggs, S., Laczko, F., & Larsson, F. (2007). *Trafficking in human beings and the 2006 world cup in Germany*. Geneva, Switzerland: International Organization for Migration (IOM).

Higate, P. (2003). Gender and Peacekeeping. Case studies: The DRC and Sierra Leone. *Africa Portal*. Retrieved November 7, 2017, from https://www.africaportal.org/publications/gender-and-peacekeeping-case-studies-the-drc-and-sierra-leone/
Higate, P. (2007). Peacekeepers, masculinities, and sexual exploitation. *Men and Masculinities, 10*(1), 99–119.
Hughes, D. M. (2000). The 'Natasha' trade: The transnational shadow market of trafficking in women. *Journal of International Affairs, 53*(2), 625–651.
Hughes, D. M., & Denisova, T. A. (2001). The transnational political criminal nexus of trafficking in women from Ukraine. *Trends in Organized Crime, 6*(3–4), 43–67.
Janssen, M. L. (2007). *Reizende sekswerkers: Latijns-Amerikaanse vrouwen in de Europese prostitutie*. Amsterdam, The Netherlands: Het Spinhuis.
Jeffreys, S. (2009). *The industrial vagina: The political economy of the global sex trade*. London, UK/New York, NY: Routledge.
Kempadoo, K. (1998). Introduction: Globalizing sex workers' rights. In K. Kempadoo & J. Doezema (Eds.), *Global sex workers: Rights, resistance, and redefinition* (pp. 1–28). New York, NY: Routledge.
Kempadoo, K. (2003). Globalizing sex workers' rights. *Canadian Woman Studies/Les Cahiers de la Femme, 22*(3–4), 143–150.
Krsmanovic, E. (2016). Captured 'realities' of human trafficking: Analysis of photographs illustrating stories on trafficking into the sex industry in Serbian media. *Anti-Trafficking Review, 7*, 139–160. https://doi.org/10.14197/atr.20121778
Lahiri-Dutt, K. (2011). The megaproject of mining: A feminist critique. In S. Brunn (Ed.), *Engineering earth* (pp. 329–351). Dordrecht, The Netherlands: Springer.
Laite, J. A. (2009). Historical perspectives on industrial development, mining, and prostitution. *The Historical Journal, 52*(3), 739–761.
Leidholdt, D. A. (2004). Prostitution and trafficking in women: An intimate relationship. *Journal of Trauma Practice, 2*(3–4), 167–183.
Long, L. D. (2004). Anthropological perspectives on the trafficking of women for sexual exploitation. *International Migration, 42*, 5–31.
Lucas, A. M. (2005). The work of sex work: Elite prostitutes' vocational orientations and experiences. *Deviant Behaviour, 26*, 513–546.
Malarek, V. (2004). *The Natashas: Inside the new global sex trade*. New York, NY: Arcade.
Martin, S. (2005). *Must boys be boys? Ending sexual exploitation & abuse in UN peacekeeping missions*. Washington, DC: Refugees International.
Matthews, R. (2008). *Prostitution, politics & policy*. London, UK: Routledge.
Mendelson, S. E. (2005). *Barracks and brothels: Peacekeepers and human trafficking in the Balkans*. Washington, DC: Csis.
Miriam, K. (2005). Stopping the traffic in women: Power, agency and abolition in feminist debates over sex trafficking. *Journal of Social Philosophy, 36*(1), 1–17.
Murray, A. (1998). Debt-bondage and trafficking: Don't believe the hype. In K. Kempadoo & J. Doezema (Eds.), *Global sex workers: Rights, resistance, and redefinition* (pp. 51–64). New York, NY: Routledge.
Murray, J. (2002). Who will police the peace-builders? The failure to establish accountability for the participation of United Nations Civilian Police in the Trafficking of Women in Post-Conflict Bosnia and Herzegovina. *Columbia Human Rights Law Review, 34*(2), 475–528.
O'Neill, M. (2001). *Prostitution and feminism: Towards a politics of feeling*. Cambridge, UK: Polity Press.
Oude Breuil, B. C. (2008). Precious children in a heartless world? The complexities of child trafficking in Marseille. *Children & Society, 22*(3), 223–234.
Oude Breuil, B. C. (2009). Nachtblind. (On)zichtbaarheid van prostitutiemigratie in Marseille. In C. Brants & S. van der Poel (Eds.), *Diverse kwesties. Liber amicorum prof. Dr. Frank Bovenkerk* (pp. 125–141). The Hague, The Netherlands: Boom Juridische Uitgevers.
Pateman, C. (1988). *The sexual contract*. Stanford, CA: Stanford University Press.

Rathgeber, C. (2002). The victimization of women through human trafficking – an aftermath of war? *European Journal of Crime, Criminal Law and Criminal Justice, 10*(2–3), 152–163.

Raymond, J. (1995, December 11). Prostitution is rape that's paid for. *Los Angeles Times*. Retrieved http://articles.latimes.com/1995-12-11/local/me-12813_1_human-rights

Raymond, J. (1998). Prostitution as violence against women. *Women's Studies International Forum, 21*(1), 1–9.

Raymond, J. (2001). *Guide to the new UN trafficking protocol*. New York, NY: Coalition Against Trafficking in Women.

Raymond, J. G. (2003). Ten reasons for not legalizing prostitution and a legal response to the demand for prostitution. In M. Farley (Ed.), *Prostitution, trafficking and traumatic stress* (pp. 315–332). London, UK: Routledge.

Raymond, J. G. (2004). Ten reasons for not legalizing prostitution and a legal response to the demand for prostitution. *Journal of Trauma Practice, 2*(3–4), 315–332. https://doi.org/10.1300/J189v02n03_17

Sanders, T. (2008). Selling sex in the shadow economy. *International Journal of Social Economics, 35*(10), 704–716.

Sanghera, J. (2005). Unpacking the trafficking discourse. In K. Kempadoo (Ed.), *Trafficking and prostitution reconsidered: New perspectives on migration, sex work and human rights* (pp. 3–24). Boulder, CO: Paradigm Publishers.

Segrave, M., Milivojevic, S., & Pickering, S. (2009). *Sex trafficking: International context and response*. Devon, UK: Willan Publishing.

Seib, C., Fischer, J., & Najman, J. (2009). The health of female sex workers from three industry sectors in Queensland, Australia. *Social Science and Medicine, 68*, 473–478.

Shelley, L. (2010). *Human trafficking: A global perspective*. Cambridge, UK: Cambridge University Press.

Shiboleth, T. (2015). *Being a "John": A client's perspective on paying for pleasure*. Oisterwijk, The Netherlands: Wolf Legal Publishing.

Siegel, D. (2005). Recent trends in women trafficking and voluntary prostitution: Russian-speaking sex-workers in the Netherlands. *Transnational Crime, 4*(1), 4–23.

Siegel, D. (2011). Mobility of sex workers in European cities. *European Journal on Criminal Policy and Research, 18*(3), 255–268.

Siegel, D. (2015). *Het Zandpad, closing brothels or closing eyes? Utrechtse sekswerkers na de sluiting van het Zandpad*. Amsterdam, The Netherlands: Boom Lemma uitgevers.

Siegel, D., & Bovenkerk, F. (2000). Crime and manipulation of identity among Russian-speaking immigrants in the Netherlands. *Journal of Contemporary Criminal Justice, 16*(4), 424–444.

Sprinkle, A. (1998). *The forty reasons why whores are my heroes*. Gifts of Speech. Retrieved from http://gos.sbc.edu/s/sprinkle1.html

Thomas, W. I., & Thomas, D. S. (1928). *The child in America*. Oxford, UK: Knopf.

Transcrime. (2005). Study on national legislation on prostitution and the trafficking in women and children (Report to the European Parliament, 2005, 121). *European Commission*. Retrieved from http://ec.europa.eu/anti-trafficking/sites/antitrafficking/files/study_on_national_legislation_and_prostitution_en_6.pdf

Van Stokkom, B. A. M. (2013). *Mediaschandalen en punitief populisme*. Nijmegen, The Netherlands: Radboud University. Retrieved from http://repository.ubn.ru.nl/bitstream/handle/2066/124283/124283.pdf

Weitzer, R. (2005). The growing moral panic over prostitution and sex trafficking. *The Criminologist, 30*(5), 1–4.

Weitzer, R. (2007). The social construction of sex trafficking: Ideology and institutionalization of a moral crusade. *Politics & Society, 35*(3), 447–475.

Weitzer, R. (2009). Sociology of sex work. *Annual Review of Sociology, 35*, 213–234.

Weitzer, R. (2010). The mythology of prostitution: Advocacy research and public policy. *Sexuality Research and Social Policy, 7*(1), 15–29.

Weitzer, R. (2012). *Legalizing prostitution: From illicit vice to lawful business*. New York, NY: New York University Press.

Weitzer, R. (2014). New directions in research on human trafficking. *The Annals of the American Academy of Political and Social Science, 653*(1), 6–24.

Weitzer, R. (2017). Resistance to sex work stigma. *Sexualities, 1*, 1–13. https://doi.org/10.1177/1363460716684509

Whitworth, S. (2004). *Men, militarism, and UN peacekeeping: A gendered analysis*. Boulder, CO: Lynne Rienner Publishers.

Zhang, S. X. (2009). Beyond the "Natasha" story – A review and critique of current research on sex trafficking. *Global Crime, 10*(3), 178–195.

Fig. 3.1 Bill Clinton statue

Chapter 3
The Kosovo War and Its Aftermath

The photograph at the beginning of this chapter shows a three-meter-high statue of Bill Clinton, former president of the United States of America. The statue of Clinton welcomes those who enter Kosovo's capital, Pristina, through the main boulevard that also bears his name. His brass monument stands upon a pedestal surrounded by rows of modernist apartment blocks, typical of former socialist regimes, built by the Yugoslav government during the 1960s and 1970s. Graffiti on the walls of these buildings condemn the European Union Rule of Law Mission in Kosovo (EULEX), which currently aims to strengthen the local rule of law through deployment of European Union police officers, prosecutors, judges and other personnel.

The small urban square encapsulates various key elements of the recent history of Kosovo: its place within former Yugoslavia, the Kosovo War (which ended after a NATO intervention that was strongly supported by Clinton), and subsequent self-governance with the international presence of UN and European Union missions. Academic and popular publications alike generally agree that the prostitution business in Kosovo grew during this latter period due to internationals' demand for commercial sex (Amnesty International, 2004; Mertus & Bertone, 2007). However, before examining the alleged clientele of the sex industry in Chap. 4, this chapter considers the context in which the sex industry in Kosovo blossomed—a context shaped by the violent breakup of former Yugoslavia and subsequent international involvement.

The aim of the chapter is twofold. First, it provides necessary background information about Kosovo: the prelude to war, the violent conflict and its aftermath. The second aim is to investigate how these events shaped the context in which the prostitution business took flight. Certain characteristics of Kosovar society in the wake of war—those which likely favored the growth of the sex industry—will be deciphered.

R. de Wildt, *Post-War Prostitution*, Studies of Organized Crime 17,
https://doi.org/10.1007/978-3-030-19474-1_3

3.1 A Brief History of the Kosovo War and Its Aftermath

Academic publications of the war in Yugoslavia generally agree that it was neither alleged long-standing ethnic hatred nor the spirit of the uncontrolled "homo balkanicus" that caused the violence to escalate. In his ethnographic study during the outbreak of war in Serbia, Mattijs Van de Port (1994, pp. 103–108) observed that explanations for the violence were increasingly sought in such notions about the barbarian East, even amongst Serbs themselves. Tensions between ethnic groups obviously existed: Van de Port (1994, p. 80), for instance, describes how his Serbian respondents lost all sense of proportion when discussing "primitive" Albanians. Conversely, Albanians generally considered themselves to be peaceful in contrast to "the aggressive Serbs" (Mertus, 1999, p. 232). Yet academic publications conclude that these ethnic tensions, together with old myths about Kosovo, did not start the war.[1] During his travels through former Yugoslavia in the early 1990s, Glenny (1992) observed that various ethnic minority groups lived together in relative contentment.

Instead of centuries-old ethnic hatred, scholars argue that the war was "the result of recent hatreds fuelled by recent propaganda campaigns" (Mertus, 1999, p. 4). Mertus puts forward that Serbian political leaders remembered, refashioned, and retold stories about Kosovo and Albanians. With these stories, the Serbian leadership aimed to create feelings of insecurity and victimization amongst the public and eventually prepare them for war. The war in Kosovo could help to keep politicians in power as they promised to protect Serbs against their enemy. This conclusion has been supported by Žižek (2013, p. 38), who underlines the aspirations and actions of political leaders in igniting the Kosovo War by stating that "it's the political power struggle stupid" (see also Malcolm, 1999).

As the role of politicians has been identified as key in creating the conflict, I will take up this brief history of the Kosovo War some years before the rise to power of former Serbian president Slobodan Milošević, the most prominent employer of this propaganda strategy. I present the trajectory of the events leading up to and during the war that most observers generally agree upon. To provide a history of the Kosovo War nonetheless remains a highly politicized undertaking.

[1] Such myths in the prelude to war focused on the dominant discourse amongst Albanians and Serbs, which both claimed Kosovo to be their cultural and historical heartland. On the one hand, Serbs referred to the fourteenth century foundation of orthodox monasteries in the Kosovar cities of Peja/Peć, Graçanicë, Deçani, and Prizren, as well as the mythological death of Serbian Tzar Lazar during the Battle of Kosovo in 1389. Albanians, on the other hand, maintained that their Illyrian ancestors had inhabited the territory long before the arrival of Serbian tribes and that the Albanian national awakening took place in Kosovo during the League of Prizren, a city in the south, in 1878 (Malcolm, 1999; Mertus, 1999; Rogel, 2003; Vickers, 1998).

3.1.1 War and Its Prelude

The Socialist Federal Republic of Yugoslavia consisted of six republics under the leadership of Josip Broz Tito.[2] In the Yugoslav constitution of 1974, Kosovo was designated as an autonomous province within Serbia, one of these six Yugoslav republics. The official name of Kosovo at the time was "The Autonomous Province of Kosovo-Metohija." In Serbia, people still tend to use the name "Kosovo and Metohija." Albanians, on the other hand, refer to it as "Kosova" (Mertus, 1999, p. xviii).[3]

As an autonomous province, Kosovo de facto had a status almost similar to the six federal republics. The majority of Kosovo Albanians that inhabited the province, aside from a large minority of Serbs and various other smaller minority groups, had rights and possibilities that historical accounts described as unparalleled in the history of Kosovo (Malcolm, 1999; Mertus, 1999; Ramet, 1999). The University of Pristina provided education in Albanian, and Albanian literary and cultural institutes opened and established cultural ties with neighboring Albania.

However, the relatively well-educated Albanian population in Kosovo was disappointed that Kosovo did not receive republic status. Expressions of such political aspirations were considered a threat to the unity of Yugoslavia and therefore taboo (Malcolm, 1999, pp. 327–330). Kosovo Albanians who nevertheless voiced nationalist demands ran the risk of being arrested and jailed as political prisoners, which drove the Albanian nationalist movement underground (Mertus, 1999, pp. 17–22). Aside from political crimes, Kosovo Albanians were increasingly accused of crimes against Serbs and Montenegrins, such as the damaging of Orthodox Church properties and aggression against priests and nuns. In an interview with Mertus (1999, p. 22), Ibrahim Rugova, the Kosovo Albanian leader during the downhill slide to war, denied most of these accusations, but acknowledged that "some people were out of control" at the time. This statement, in combination with the ever-deteriorating economic situation in Kosovo compared to the Yugoslav average, caused both Kosovo Albanians and Kosovo Serbs to be dissatisfied with the province's social, political and economic circumstances (Ramet, 1999, p. 306).

This discontent led to unprecedented demonstrations on March 11, 1981, about a year after Tito's death. The protests started with Kosovo Albanian students calling for better food and general conditions at the University of Pristina, but developed into Kosovo-wide demonstrations over the weeks that followed. Kosovo Albanian students and workers alike protested against the overall poor social, economic and political situation in Kosovo (Malcolm, 1999, pp. 334–339; Ramet, 1999, pp. 306–307). Protestors carried signs stating "Kosovo Republic," "Improve Living Conditions for Students and Workers," and "Stop Repression, Free Political Prisoners" (Mertus, 1999, p. 30). Alarmed authorities declared a state of emergency

[2] The Socialist Federal Republic of Yugoslavia consisted of the republics of Serbia, Bosnia and Herzegovina, Croatia, Macedonia, Montenegro and Slovenia. Serbia included two autonomous provinces: Kosovo and Vojvodina.

[3] The term "Kosovo" is used throughout this book for simplicity's sake and because it is the term most commonly used in English-language publications.

Fig. 3.2 (**a**) Remnants of a house, (**b**) Monument of the Kosovo War

Fig. 3.2 (continued)

in Kosovo and brought in special units of the security police from other parts of Yugoslavia to disband the protests. However, the protesters' demands were depoliticized and largely ignored. Instead, the events unleashed a stream of accusations about Albanian nationalist sentiment. Academics in Belgrade published texts in which the history of Serbs in Kosovo was described as an unending struggle, while the popular press issued sensational stories on Kosovo Albanians raping Serbian women as well as stories on high Albanian birth rates, supposedly rooted in an ideology of building a large Albanian community (Malcolm, 1999, pp. 334–339; Ramet, 1999, pp. 306–307). Zivkovic (2001, p. 92) shows how poets further added oil to the fire by turning "Serbian grievances, imagined and real, into a poetically exaggerated metaphysics of national victimhood."[4] Kosovo Serbs increasingly migrated from the autonomous province to Serbia proper (Malcolm, 1999, pp. 334–339; Ramet, 1999, pp. 306–307).

Slobodan Milošević's rise to power at the end of the 1980s further escalated the tensions in Kosovo. On April 24, 1987, Milošević—protégé of Ivan Stambolić, the head of the League of Communists of Serbia—delivered an inflammatory speech in the Kosovar village of Fushë Kosovë/Kosovo Polje. Milošević spoke to a crowd of Serbs who were demanding protection from the Kosovar Albanian majority in Kosovo. Fighting broke out between the Serbian crowd and the local (largely Albanian) police. Historical accounts differ in their description of the origin of the fights: Kosovo Albanian reports suggested that Serbian protesters started throwing rocks at the police after careful orchestration by the Serb demonstration leaders, while Serbian press reported that the predominantly Albanian police had initiated the violence (Malcolm, 1999, pp. 341–347; Mertus, 1999, p. 142). However, the most important aspect of this event was not so much who initiated the fighting, but the way in which Milošević reacted to it—telling the Serbian crowd, "Nobody should dare to beat you." Observers of the disintegration of former Yugoslavia generally agree that these words initiated Milošević's rise to power and the escalation of Serbian nationalism (Rogel, 2003, p. 172; Malcolm, 1999, pp. 341–347; Zivkovic, 2001). Mertus (1999, p. 143) concludes that Milošević turned into "the protector of the Serbian nation." By the end of 1987, he had become president of the Serbian League of Communists (Ramet, 1999, p. 25; Troebst, 1998, p. 16).

---

[4] Matija Beckovic was a leading poet in Serbia, as well as a member of the Serbian Academy of Arts and Sciences and the president of the Serbian Writers' Association. Zivkovic (2001, p. 93) translated one of his texts to English in order to illustrate the "poetic hyperbolae" used by poets in Belgrade at the time. This specific text follows the popular proposition with regard to Kosovo at the time, which holds that a territory with Serbian graves is Serbian territory:

> According to our popular belief, the land where there are graves is not for sale. Householders without progeny, or those who feared that their descendants might sell the land would prevent this possibility by burying their dead in the yard. Both the buyer and the seller would balk at the grave. In the Kosovo graveyard the whole Serbian people have been buried and that's why Serbs can neither sell nor trade that land.

Milošević's priority was a clampdown on the autonomy of Kosovo (and Vojvodina, Serbia's other autonomous province). His measures included dissolving Kosovo's assembly and government, giving Serbia control over Kosovo's police, courts and civil defence, banning Albanian as a language of instruction from primary school to university level, and closing down Albanian media, sports and cultural associations. Arrests and home searches of Kosovo Albanians became routine, as did police violence. The overwhelming majority of Albanians employed by the state (e.g., in schools, hospitals, factories and public services) were fired from their jobs. They were replaced by Serbs, some of whom came from outside Kosovo as part of a resettlement program, as well as Montenegrins and moderate Albanians (Malcolm, 1999, pp. 341–350; Ramet, 1999, p. 308; Rogel, 2003, p. 173; Troebst, 1998, pp. 16–18).

The firing of Albanian doctors meant that Kosovo Albanian patients no longer received medical care in what were now Serbian public hospitals. Furthermore, the sacking of Albanian teachers put Albanian children out of education. An Albanian human rights activist reminisced how "in the nineties, the situation radically changed. Everything was dangerous. […] Education [in Albanian] did not take place in schools. Women and men, girls and boys didn't get so much education anymore. It was a security issue."[5]

In December 1989, writer Dr. Ibrahim Rugova became the leader of a newly established political movement that opposed the policies of Milošević. His Democratic League of Kosovo (LDK) was supported by an overwhelming majority of Kosovo Albanians (Troebst, 1998, p. 16).[6] Rugova's political program aimed at peaceful resistance to Milošević's actions. Furthermore, he lobbied for international political involvement in Kosovo and systematically denied the legitimacy of the Serbian rule by boycotting Serbian elections and establishing a shadow government, as well a parallel social system (Malcolm, 1999, pp. 347–349). As a part of this parallel social system, health clinics and schools were set up in private premises such as living rooms. The teachers and doctors involved were paid from a voluntary 3% levy on the incomes of the diaspora (i.e., Kosovar Albanians living in Western Europe and the United States).[7] Kosovar Albanian printing agencies were re-established, and small businesses surfaced (Malcolm, 1999, pp. 349–350; Troebst, 1998, p. 19). A Kosovo Albanian respondent who was educated in the parallel system from age 10 to 17 described the situation as follows:

> From that time, Ibrahim Rugova time, schools started to move into private houses. Albanian volunteers started to open their houses. Sometimes they used houserooms for school. I

[5] Interview with NGO1, March 13, 2013.

[6] In Albanian, the political movement is called *Lidhja Demokratike e Kosovës*, more generally known by its initials LDK.

[7] The tax raised amongst Kosovo Albanians in exile was named The Fund for the Republic of Kosovo (RFK), but was generally called the "Three-Percent Fund." The fund was registered as a charity organization in each country where it operated (Perritt, 2008, p. 89).

> remember at the beginning there were owners of a house who had only one room. And they gave the room for school, for pupils. In Pristina I had my lectures, like 2 h' class in Sunny Hill [a suburb]. Then I had to walk from Sunny Hill to another area, maybe in the center, for another 2 h' class, a different lecture. Also there were times when Serbian police came and arrested the owner of the house who opened the house for studying. Professors too had [bad] treatment in such situations. So this happened with all the institutions.[8]

In 1991, Slovenia declared independence without a high number of casualties; war broke out in Croatia (1991) as well as Bosnia-Herzegovina (1992), and Yugoslavia broke apart. Rugova urged the Albanians in Kosovo to be patient and refrain from violent resistance to Milošević's regime. Rugova sought to avoid large-scale bloodshed, pleading that it would just be a matter of time until the international community acknowledged that the issue of Kosovo's status was not merely an internal question of the Republic of Serbia (Malcolm, 1999; Rogel, 2003, p. 173). The Albanians in Kosovo refrained from taking up weapons, but in December 1995, Rugova's non-violent political path was discredited after the Dayton Agreement put an end to the Bosnian War without enforcing a final settlement on former Yugoslavia in which the interests of the Kosovo Albanians were acknowledged. Although the sanctions against Serbia were lifted, Milošević continued a regime of segregation in Kosovo (Malcolm, 1999, pp. 350–353; Ramet, 1999, p. 309; Troebst, 1998, p. 7).

During 1996 and 1997, support grew inside Kosovo for the more militant approach of the Kosovo Liberation Army (KLA).[9] One Kosovar Albanian man who joined the KLA at age 18 explained the sentiment that led people to take up arms. He was 10 when he wanted to play in the soccer field opposite his house in Fushë Kosovë/Kosovo Polje. The playground was for Serbian children. When the Serbian police caught him, they beat his hands so badly that his mother had to feed him by hand for a week. "You don't just wake up one day and pick up the guns. This feeling grows slowly over time."[10]

The KLA undertook a growing number of attacks on Serbian officials and police officers, as well as Albanian collaborators (Perritt, 2008, p. 8; Troebst, 1998, p. 12). Milošević tried to crush the armed resistance with his forces, which were now freed from the wars in Croatia and Bosnia. In March 1998, Serbian forces attacked KLA strongholds such as the home of Adem Jashari, one of the founders of the KLA, in the village of Prekaz. This battle resulted in the death of Jashari, along with nearly 60 of his family members including women, children and elderly people (Perrit, 2008, pp. 8–9; Troebst, 1998, p. 14).

The conflict spiraled out of control, as Milošević's violent response paradoxically strengthened the KLA. The insurgency was overwhelmed with Kosovo Albanian men and women volunteering to join their ranks and grew to several

---

[8] Informal conversation with FST1 on March 16, 2016.

[9] In Albanian, the Kosovo Liberation Army is called *Ushtria Çlirimtare e Kosovës*, abbreviated as UÇK.

[10] Informal conversation with KLA1 on February 2, 2013.

thousand fighters (Malcolm, 1999, p. xxvii; Perritt, 2008, p. 9; Ramet, 1999, p. 309). This widespread engagement with the KLA is illustrated by the story of Jeta, a kind-hearted Kosovo Albanian primary school teacher, who described how people became associated with the KLA irrespective of gender, profession, age and so on:

> Jeta left her job in the nineties in order to join the KLA with her best friend, Mira. Mira died in battle: "I saw pictures of her. She was blown away by a bomb and landed against a tree. […] She looked so beautiful." Mira's battalion buried her under the tree, and Jeta was able to travel there a month afterward. She dug up Mira's body, wrapped blankets around her and brought her to her mother so that she could have a proper grave. We visit Mira's mother sometimes; she lives between the memories of her deceased daughter. Pictures of Mira with friends or alone, up in the mountains with her weapon and uniform of the KLA, cover the walls of her little apartment. Mira's mother was proud when her daughter told her that she was joining the KLA. She even brought Mira ammunition once: "I was an old lady, almost 70 years old. Nobody would check me […]. And if they had stopped me, then I would have told them that I don't know how these things got there. I was not afraid." Mira's mother took the bus and hit guns and bullets in bags under her dress. The police searched the bus, but didn't disturb her. Mira's mother met Mira and handed over the artillery; it was the last time she saw her daughter alive. Mira was killed 2 months later at age 28.[11]

The growth of (support for) the KLA again triggered Serbian forces to start a campaign of systematic destruction of Albanian villages in the summer of 1998. Human Rights Watch (1998) reported that "[u]nder the command of Yugoslav President Slobodan Milošević government troops have committed extrajudicial executions and other unlawful killings, systematically destroyed civilian property, and attacked humanitarian aid workers, all of which are violations of the rules of war."

The international community threatened military action against Serbia, which eventually resulted in a ceasefire in October 1998. Both the Serbian forces and the KLA, however, used this scaling down of the fighting to recover and reorganize. Fighting recommenced in December 1998 (Malcolm, 1999, p. xxxiv; Perritt, 2008, p. 9). In his opening statement during the trial against six of Milošević's top advisors, prosecution lawyer Thomas Hannis later described the violence as follows:

> All across Kosovo, in a concerted and coordinated manner, the forces of the FRY [Federal Republic of Yugoslavia] and Serbia began their widespread and systematic attack on the Kosovo Albanian civilian population, going from one tiny village to the next and from one town to another, murdering, beating, robbing, looting, destroying businesses and mosques, and forcing out the Kosovar Albanians in front of them. They burned and destroyed villages or towns as they went in order to leave nothing behind for those expelled to return to. [A] typical pattern occurred in which the Serb forces would nearly encircle a town or village, leaving one avenue of escape. The VJ [Yugoslav Army forces] would commence shelling with artillery and heavy weapons. Then the MUP [Serbian Interior Ministry special police] units, including special units and volunteers, incorporated or otherwise attached to the MUP or VJ, would enter the town, force the people out, sometimes killing or raping as they did so, and often looting and then burning the abandoned houses. This kind of activity

[11] Informal conversations with KLA2 and KLA3 beginning in July 2012.

> understandably created an atmosphere of terror, and the inhabitants of neighboring villages seeing this happen and hearing the stories of the primary victims would join in fleeing to avoid a similar fate as that suffered by their neighbors. And so the massive convoys seen in the international media quickly came into existence from the end of March 1999, as thousands and thousands of Kosovo Albanians literally fled for their very lives.[12]

More than 800,000 people sought refuge in Albania, Macedonia, Montenegro, Europe and the United States (UNDP Kosovo, 2014).

Serbian troops took the passports and identity papers of Kosovo Albanians when they crossed the border. Municipal registrations of birth and landownership were destroyed. This was part of a larger ethnic cleansing campaign that sought to evict the majority of the Albanian population from Kosovo (Mann, 2005). Without proof of their identity, Kosovar Albanians would have difficulties returning (Malcolm, 1999, p. xxxix).

While the violence continued, the international community initiated a round of peace talks in Rambouillet, France, in February and March 1999. The Kosovo Albanian delegation aimed to secure Kosovo's independence, but reluctantly agreed to the Western plan, in which Kosovar autonomy within the Serbian Republic would be restored. Milošević did not sign the agreement. Some historians suggest that the American administration expected his refusal and therefore wanted the Rambouillet talks (Daalder & O'Hanlon, 2000, p. 89; Rogel, 2003). Milošević's "no" would allow them to present the Kosovo Albanians as "the good guys" and the Serbs as uncompromising. When Serbian forces continued to assault Albanian villages, the North Atlantic Treaty Organization (NATO) began airstrikes against targets in Serbia, Kosovo and Montenegro. The Clinton administration had a large hand in starting the airstrikes, without the approval of the UN Security Council, on March 24, 1999. The aerial bombardment initially intensified the cleansing operation of the Serbian forces on the ground, but Serbian forces were driven out in June 1999 (Malcolm, 1999, pp. xxxv–xxxviii; Perritt, 2008, p. 9; Ramet, 1999, pp. 317–318).

3.1.2 The Road to Independence

Milošević agreed to withdraw almost all of his forces from Kosovo and (at least temporarily) hand over the exercise of sovereignty in Kosovo to the UN in the Kumanovo Agreement, concluded on June 9, 1999. Security Council Resolution 1244 provided the constitutional basis for the presence of a NATO-led peacekeeping force (KFOR). It also authorized the UN to govern the area through a civil administration until the final status of Kosovo was resolved (Perritt, 2010, pp. 51–54). The mandate of the international administration "virtually suspended Yugoslavia's sovereignty over Kosovo" (Yannis, 2001, p. 32).

---

[12] Prosecutor v. Milutonivic, IT-05–87 trial transcript 060710IT at 452–67 (opening statement by Office of the Prosecutor) in Perritt (2010, pp. 47–48).

Serwer and Thomson (2008, p. 370), however, have observed that "the UN discovered that it would lead the civilian intervention in Kosovo only after the military-technical agreement ending the warfare was signed." UN Missions are not standardized; this ad hoc approach makes missions more flexible and allows them to fit local needs. On the other hand, however, it also hinders the swift setup of a structure with clear goals. Learning of their role only shortly before arrival, the UN needed time to settle down in Kosovo—even more so because the mandate of the UN Mission in Kosovo was unprecedented in the history of peacekeeping operations. The UN exercised all legislative and executive authority in Kosovo, needed to rebuild the judiciary as well as the public sector (e.g., civil and social services, education, roads, public transport and mass media) and was responsible for the creation of a legal framework within with all these tasks could be performed (Strohmeyer, 2001, pp. 46–47).[13] It took months to organize their mission, as did the NATO forces (Perritt, 2010, p. 52; Yannis, 2001, p. 34). In the meantime, Kosovo was left in a power vacuum. Original law and order had vanished, as the administration of Kosovo had been in Serbian hands (Judah, 2008, p. 93; Strohmeyer, 2001).

The KLA officially disarmed and disbanded (Perritt, 2010, p. 51). Former combatants returned to their homes and jobs. Others found employment in Kosovo's unarmed defense force (the Kosovo Protection Corps) or the newly established Kosovo Police Service.[14] The KLA initially filled the power vacuum that the withdrawn Serbian forces and authorities left behind (Perritt, 2010, p. 52), and their actions were well received by part of the Kosovo Albanian population. Such actions included cleaning mines and replacing Serb chiefs with Albanian workers in an electricity substation and brewery in the city of Peja/Peć (Perritt, 2010, p. 52). Yet some Kosovo Albanians held a simmering resentment toward the attitude of KLA leadership in the aftermath of the war. Returning refugees, for instance, thought they could return to the jobs they held before Milošević's rule, but these and other leading roles were now often held by former combatants (Perritt, 2008, p. 154).

This same summer of 1999, radical Albanians engaged in attacks against Kosovo Serbs in retribution for the suffering inflicted upon Kosovo Albanians by Serbs prior to and during the war. On a lesser scale, Roma and other non-Albanians were victimized as well.[15] Serbian houses were burned, and people abducted and killed (Judah, 2008, pp. 91–92; Mann, 2005). This led to an exodus of Serbs from Kosovo. Serbs who stayed behind often regrouped in Serbian enclaves in Kosovo or in four

[13] The UN needed to set up a mission with a similar scope in East Timor only three months later; this mission was called the International Force for East Timor (INTERFET). Strohmeyer (2001) analyzes the challenges the UN faced while constructing new judicial systems in both Kosovo and East Timor.

[14] The Kosovo Police Service gradually developed into a multi-ethnic police force that included Serbs and other Kosovar minorities (Yannis, 2001, p. 38).

[15] Kosovo had a relatively large number of small arms and light weapons as a result of the conflict (Arsovska, 2015, pp. 216–217). This likely further allowed for this kind of violence.

municipalities in the north (Yannis, 2001, p. 37; Judah, 2008, pp. 91–92). These four municipalities in the north of Kosovo today remain almost completely inhabited by Kosovo Serbs. Mitrovica North is the urban center of this area. The Ibar River splits the city of into a northern part inhabited by Serbs and a southern part inhabited by Albanians. As Judah (2008, p. 101) outlines, "de facto, the north remained under Serbian control."

A political advisor to the first Special Representative of the UN Secretary-General in Kosovo reported, "The UN and NATO powers were neither operationally nor mentally prepared for the scale of violence that engulfed Kosovo following the departure of Serb forces; the early responses of KFOR and UNMIK were inadequate" (Yannis, 2001, p. 37). UNMIK had prioritized traditional peace-building efforts, such as the facilitation of returning hundreds of thousands of refugees to Kosovo, but an administration of justice that could deal with the violence was lacking. As Strohmeyer (2001, p. 47) suggests, the events in Kosovo illustrate that the development of an administration of justice cannot wait in post-conflict settings. He argues that "in postconflict situations, criminal activity does not cease; in fact, it often flourishes. Moreover, evidence of violations of international humanitarian and human rights law can be destroyed, while the perpetrators of serious crimes remain at large." The swift establishment of a functioning judiciary—and therefore a sense of law and order—was inadequate in Kosovo.

The international community gradually managed to organize their missions. In anticipation of elections, UNMIK formed a Joint Interim Administrative Structure in February 2000.[16] This interim structure consisted of Rugova's LDK and a political party formed by the political wing of the KLA: the Democratic Party of Kosovo (Partia Demokratike e Kosovës in Albanian, using the abbreviation PDK). The PDK was led by Hashim Thaçi, the political leader of the KLA (Perritt, 2008, p. 153).

The first post-war elections were held in October 2000. In these elections (for members of municipal assemblies), LDK won a large majority of the votes. Similar results came out of the national elections in 2001, and a coalition was formed with LDK's Rugova as its president. The coalition governed for nearly four years; UNMIK held veto power over all their decisions (Judah, 2008, p. 95; Perritt, 2008, pp. 154–159).

In October 2005, former Finnish president Martti Ahtisaari was appointed Special Envoy of the Secretary-General of the UN for the Future Status Process for Kosovo. Ahtisaari delivered the draft of his plan for the future of Kosovo in February 2007. His plan, which proposed "supervised independence" for Kosovo, included the establishment of the European Union Rule of Law Mission in Kosovo (EULEX). EULEX would aim to strengthen the rule of law in Kosovo, and the mission was planned as two divisions. The Executive Division would employ international EULEX judges and prosecutors who would investigate, prosecute and adjudicate sensitive cases in Kosovo; such cases included those related to war crimes, terrorism, organized crime

[16] UNMIK Regulation 2000/I.

and high-level corruption, as well as other serious crimes such as human trafficking. The Strengthening Division would monitor, mentor and advise local counterparts in the fields of police, justice and customs (Judah, 2008, p. 114).[17] As UNMIK had increasingly transferred its executive power to local institutions, Ahtisaari argued in favor of an EU mission that was supportive in nature (De Wet, 2009, pp. 1–2).

The provisional government of Kosovo unilaterally declared independence on February 17, 2008, over the objection of Russia and Serbia (Perritt, 2010, pp. 111–220; Van der Borgh, 2012, p. 31).[18] Tens of thousands of Kosovo Albanians streamed through the streets to celebrate what they hoped was the end of a long and bloody struggle for national self-determination (Judah, 2008, p. 145). Most Kosovo Serbs, on the other hand, still regard Kosovo as a province of Serbia. They largely do not acknowledge the Republic of Kosovo and view themselves as citizens of Serbia (Van der Borgh & Lasance, 2013, p. 188).

In line with the Ahtisaari Plan, EULEX became fully operational in independent Kosovo in April 2009. Yet the work of both EULEX and UNMIK is under the scrutiny of the local population. Graffiti throughout Kosovo expresses frustrations toward both missions. Kosovo Serbs primarily accuse EULEX—and, to a lesser extent, UNMIK—of supporting Kosovo Albanians and the independence of Kosovo at large (De Wet, 2009, p. 3). At the same time, Kosovo Albanians regularly blame UNMIK and EULEX for not working effectively. A Kosovar police officer voiced such sentiment when he recalled the times when internationals were in charge of the police station where he was working:

> In the beginning the police station was managed by Ukrainian and Russian foreign police. Even if they had the capacities, then they would leave again after one year and than a new person would come in to take their place and they have to start all from the beginning again. But also they wanted to enjoy. See the region. Travel a bit.[19]

These critiques are echoed in the publications of various observers of the Rule of Law Mission in Kosovo. The European Court of Auditors (ECA, 2012, p. 6), for instance, considers that EULEX "has not been sufficiently effective [...] overall progress in improving the rule of law is slow" (see also Bennett & Saferworld, 2011; Radin, 2014).[20]

---

[17] http://www.eulex-kosovo.eu/?page=2,16. Accessed Feb 19, 2016.

[18] Today Kosovo is recognized by 116 countries, including most of the member states of the European Union and the United States of America. See http://www.kosovothanksyou.com/. Accessed Mar 16, 2017.

[19] Interview with KPO1, Oct 30, 2013.

[20] An analysis of the reasons why the EULEX mission is not considered to function effectively is beyond the scope of this book. Radin (2014), however, offers a compelling examination in his article "Analysis of current events: 'towards the rule of law in Kosovo: EULEX should go.'"

Fig. 3.3 Billboard about EULEX

3.2 Characteristics of Post-War Kosovo and the Growth of the Prostitution Business

It was against this backdrop that an allegedly small-scale local prostitution market transformed in the wake of the war into a large-scale industry with high demand for commercial sex (Friman & Reich, 2007; Terre des Hommes, 2010). Attributing the growth of the sex industry to the demand of international peacekeepers, as some suggest (Amnesty International, 2004; Mertus & Bertone, 2007), is one-sided. It clouds the influence of various features that characterized Kosovo in the years after the war and allowed for and shaped the development of the prostitution business. I have identified these features as follows: weak law enforcement, corruption, socio-cultural attitudes adopted during the (prelude to) war that did not simply disappear when hostilities came to an end, the existence of regional smuggling and trafficking rings, Northern Kosovo as a nexus point for smuggling and trafficking and, finally, the establishment of a peacekeeping economy. These features will be examined in the upcoming sections. The growth of the prostitution business cannot be traced back to any single one of them, yet together they provided a context that colored the development of the prostitution business.

3.2.1 *Weak Law Enforcement*

As indicated above, the period in the wake of the war was characterized by a virtual absence of law and order. Kosovo experienced high levels of ethnic violence (Judah, 2008, pp. 91–92; Mann, 2005) and crime. Various scholars have observed and analyzed the climate of impunity in the wake of the war (Judah, 2008; Strohmeyer, 2001; Yannis, 2001), largely attributing it to the UN's enormous and unprecedented task of establishing an administration of justice after the original Serbian-led administration had vanished. More specifically, Strohmeyer (2001) explains that the UN needed time to establish their mission because they had to deal with a scarcity of experienced local legal personnel, problems with the appointment of local judges and prosecutors, a damaged physical infrastructure and correctional system, and the establishment of a basic legal framework.

However, critique of the efforts of the international community in Kosovo was not restricted to the initial period when UNMIK was getting organized. As outlined above, EULEX, which was responsible for building and supporting Kosovo's rule of law institutions, also received criticism many years later. International staff attributed the far-from-optimal functioning of both UNMIK and EULEX to institutional problems within the missions. For one, it was unclear what role some of the staff served. "If you don't have a clear role, you get frustrated and focus on other things than work, like your free time," explained one former employee of EULEX.[21] A second institutional

[21] Informal conversation with EUL1, August 17, 2017. Inhabitants of Kosovo regularly complained

problem was that part of the international staff did not have the competence necessary for their position. A former UNMIK police officer explained, "There were people from different countries in charge of large units that supervised a lot of people, but [back home] their job was keeping elephants off railways."[22] This criticism of the competence of international staff is not unique to Kosovo. Comparable criticism has been voiced in relation to the hiring process of international staff in other post-war settings. In his memoir, former UN worker Kenneth Cain describes how he was hired as a UN lawyer at the mission in Somalia, although "I'm not a licensed lawyer in the U.S., but it's anarchy here, that distinction matters in Cambridge, not Mogadishu" (Cain, Postlewait, & Thomson, 2004, p. 109).

With regard to the hiring of military and police personnel, the UN state that "they come from nations large and small, rich and poor. They bring different cultures and experience to the job, but they are united in their determination to foster peace."[23] The statistics of the countries that indeed provide military experts, troops and police to UN peacekeeping missions, however, paint a less diverse picture. Worldwide, Bangladesh is the first country in the "Ranking of Military and Police Contributions to UN operations." Bangladesh is successively followed by Ethiopia, India, Pakistan, Rwanda, Nepal, Senegal, and Ghana. The first "Western" country is Italy, in 26th place. Developed countries do contribute more money to UN peacekeeping operations,[24] yet the fact that these countries only marginally contribute in sending UN peacekeepers negatively impacts UN peacekeeping missions in general, as UN peacekeepers from third-world countries tend to be poorly equipped and poorly trained. Former UN Secretary-General Ban Ki-moon, for example, expressed concerns over the inadequate equipment of peacekeepers in the Darfur region. Their lack of equipment hampered them from protecting civilians and aid workers as violence increased.[25] The 2015 documentary *Journey of a Thousand Miles: Peacekeepers* shows Bengali UN peacekeepers arriving in Haiti, without any knowledge of the country, to demonstrations against the UN presence.[26] Nevertheless, the UN cannot afford to turn down (even poorly equipped and trained) peacekeepers since most of their missions are understaffed. After a year, UNMIK police were still only at approximately 77% of their authorized strength and short of international personnel (Yannis, 2001, p. 37). Peacekeepers from developing countries, such as Moldova and Ukraine in the case of Kosovo, tended to be willing to fill the gap, since working abroad allowed them to earn many times their normal salary. At the same time, their countries benefited from sending troops, since they then received money from the UN (see also Vermeulen, 2016).

---

that internationals just seemed to be interested in having a good time, while internationals explained that this allegedly laissez-faire attitude was a consequence of the abovementioned vagueness of their tasks.

[22] Interview with UNM1, Oct 7, 2013.

[23] http://www.un.org/en/peacekeeping/resources/statistics/contributors.shtml. Accessed Mar 17, 2016.

[24] http://www.un.org/en/peacekeeping/operations/financing.shtml. Accessed Mar 17, 2016.

[25] http://www.timeslive.co.za/africa/2014/03/10/restrictions-poor-equipment-hinder-darfur-peace-mission-un-chief. Accessed Mar 17, 2016.

[26] See also Autesserre (2012) on the situation in the Democratic Republic of the Congo.

However, at times international staff from developed countries also lacked the necessary capacity to do their job well. This is illustrated by the following conversation with an international prosecutor from Northern Europe who worked in Kosovo for some months in 2005 and returned again in 2008:

Prosecutor: UNMIK did a terrible job. Files were in places covered with bird shit. [...] It is difficult to find good prosecutors. Most prosecutors that came did their first big case here. It is like a learning school.

RdW: Why is it difficult to find good prosecutors?

Prosecutor: The incentives are little. The payment is a bit better than in the home countries, but not a lot. And the prosecutors handled all kind of cases. Countries were also reluctant to send their good people away and pay for them.[27] Therefore the capacities of the people that came under UNMIK were pretty low.

RdW: Does EULEX have that problem as well?

Prosecutor: It is easier for EULEX since they have a clear focus. They do cases focused on organized crime by Albanians that might also impact Western Europe. [...] Red-light districts and so on are often managed by Albanians, and therefore the governments of Western Europe are interested in tackling crime coming from Albania, the Balkans. [...] This focus makes it easier for EULEX to find good prosecutors.[28]

The former colleagues to whom this international prosecutor referred largely came from Western Europe. In his experience, the capability of personnel from developed countries was thus not necessarily sufficient either.

The institutional problems within UNMIK and EULEX hampered the process of securing sound law enforcement.[29] I do not want to suggest that the absence of both rule of law and a coherent legal system caused the prostitution business to flourish. The climate of impunity, however, did allow the industry to develop in plain sight (in random coffee bars and motels) irrespective of its illegality.[30]

Bar owners regularly shared anecdotes that demonstrated their total disregard for law enforcement, especially with regard to the initial years after the war. The following story told by Bujar, a Kosovar Albanian bar owner who had started to facilitate prostitution in this period, is illustrative of this sentiment:

> There was an UNMIK police officer from Turkey just drinking a beer in my bar one night. A Macedonian guy was making trouble. He put his gun on the table. I beat him, took his gun and gave it to the Turkish police officer: "Solve it! Do something! You are a police

[27] The prosecutor is referring to countries having to pay for the prosecutors that work abroad, since they most often work in seconded positions.

[28] Interview with EUL2, Oct 29, 2013.

[29] Notwithstanding these critical notes related to the functioning of UNMIK and EULEX, international efforts in Kosovo did, of course, achieve positive results as well: UNMIK managed to build Kosovo's institutions and provided inhabitants with means to live, the Kosovo Police Service (KPS) was created, people were provided with documents (e.g., UNMIK passports), and a government was established, to name but a few (Judah, 2008, p. 95).

[30] Article 7: Law on public peace and order, Law No. 03/L-142. In case of force, the act could also fall under Article 171: Trafficking in persons, Article 241: Facilitating or compelling prostitution, and Article 169: Slavery of the criminal code of the Republic of Kosovo, Code No. 04/L-082.

officer!" He only stiffened up and said, "If you report this to the police, please don't tell them I was here."[31]

Bujar emphasized that international police officers such as the Turkish police officer in his bar primarily seemed to be occupied with keeping their position and enjoying themselves instead of performing their task. Consequently, bar owners did not fear law enforcement or public engagement in illegal business such as the facilitation of prostitution.

3.2.2 Corruption

Corruption still negatively influences law enforcement in Kosovo today. Transparency International, a worldwide movement that aims to diminish corruption, describes corruption as "the abuse of entrusted power for private gain."[32] According to their index, which ranks how corrupt public sectors of countries worldwide are seen to be, corruption is widespread in Kosovo.[33] The 2017 Kosovo corruption report likewise states that "[a] lack of transparency and accountability in Kosovo's public administration results in widespread corruption [...]. The judiciary, customs, public utilities and procurement sectors are the most-affected by corruption. While anti-corruption laws are strong, the judicial system is inefficient, leading to poor enforcement."[34] With the help of UNMIK and EULEX, Kosovo has indeed developed a solid legal framework targeting corruption. Yet in practice, corruption remains pervasive (Belloni & Strazzari, 2014).

Belloni and Strazzari (2014) argue that widespread corruption is a consequence of the simultaneous transition from socialism to democracy as well as from war to peace. With regard to the first point, they put forward that corruption is a resilient character of post-socialist countries in general. A special prosecutor working for EULEX described corruption in Kosovo along similar lines, explaining that it was part of "how things are done" in (former) socialist countries: "If you are in the hospital, then you might give something extra to the nurse so she will have attention for you [...]. That pattern is seen in many parts of society. And until a certain point, everybody takes part. It is almost difficult to avoid it. This practice in combination with low salaries makes corruption difficult to avoid."[35] Regarding the transition from war to peace, Belloni and Strazzari argue that the international community has

[31] Interview with Bujar, Oct 17, 2013.

[32] https://transparency.org/what-is-corruption. Accessed Mar 16, 2018.

[33] Kosovo is ranked 95 out of 176 countries. The lower a country is ranked, the less trustworthy and more poorly functioning its public institutions (i.e., police and judiciary) are considered to be. https://www.transparency.org/news/feature/corruption_perceptions_index_2016. Accessed Aug 11, 2017.

[34] Gan (2017).

[35] Interview with EUL3, Oct 25, 2013.

been reluctant to take action against strongmen whose corruption channels were often known, as this was believed to have a destabilizing affect (see also Zabyelina & Arsovska, 2013, p. 11).

The existence of corruption directly affected human trafficking and prostitution in Kosovo. For instance, as will be described in Sects. 5.6.2 and 5.6.3, corruption facilitated the journey of Eastern European women to Kosovo and allowed them to arrive in Kosovo in large numbers. Eastern European women were able to cross borders after border police and corrupt officials responsible for filing stay-and-work permits were bribed to provide these women with the necessary papers to live and work in Kosovo. Furthermore, corrupt police officers incidentally obstructed legal actions against those engaged in the facilitation of prostitution. This is exemplified by the 2013 arrest of the head of the anti-trafficking unit in Ferizaj/Uroševac. In exchange for money, this police officer warned bar owners engaged in the facilitation of prostitution before their premises were raided. Also in exchange for money, he would offer to help people who had been—or were afraid of being—arrested.[36] Corruption has made it difficult to prosecute people in the higher echelons as well. An international special prosecutor explained that at times, judges seem pressured to come to certain decisions: "Most positions, high positions, are through appointment. You have to know someone, somewhere. [...] You have to have connections. And if you don't have that, and if you're seen doing something against high officials, then basically your career is screwed."[37] This practice keeps higher officials allegedly involved in prostitution out of the hands of law enforcement.

Corrupt acts related to prostitution have been observed worldwide. Agbu (2008), for instance, describes corrupt policemen engaged in the trafficking of young women in Nigeria. Such observations have led Kevin Bales (2007), a professor of contemporary slavery, to analyze datasets on the link between corruption and human trafficking in each country, concluding that corruption is a significant predictor of trafficking. Zhang and Pineda (2008, p. 52) even go a step further in stating that "corruption is probably the most important factor in explaining human trafficking." My book does not aim to determine which causes of human trafficking and prostitution migration are most significant, but my observations do indicate that corruption has shaped the prostitution business in Kosovo.

3.2.3 *Socio-Cultural Attitudes*

As outlined above, shortcomings from the side of the judiciary and law enforcement (including corruption) allowed the prostitution business to flourish in plain sight despite its illegality. In the first years after the war, the Kosovar Albanian population

[36] Interview with EUL3, Oct 23, 2013; interview with EUL4, Oct 16, 2013; and interview with NGO2, Oct 2, 2013.

[37] Interview with EUL4, Oct 16, 2013.

tended to be indifferent toward official institutions in Kosovo, which further strengthened the idea that the law could be disregarded. I will argue that this attitude developed as a reaction to experiences in former Yugoslavia, especially under Milošević's rule.

As summarized at the beginning of this chapter, Milošević quickly abolished Kosovo's once-considerable autonomy between 1988 and 1990. Kosovar Albanians established a parallel social system in response to the abandonment of Albanian education, media, sports and cultural associations and the firing of the majority of state-employed Albanians (Malcolm, 1999, pp. 341–350; Ramet, 1999, p. 308; Troebst, 1998, pp. 16–18). This parallel system was primarily comprised of health clinics and schools in private premises such as living rooms; doctors and teachers were paid by funds raised amongst Kosovar Albanians in exile (Malcolm, 1999. pp. 349–350; Troebst, 1998, p. 19).

This parallel social system has some overlap with the shadow economies and networks described by anthropologist Carolyn Nordstrom as "the complex sets of cross-state economic and political linkages that move outside *formally* recognized state-based channels and networks" (2004, p. 106, emphasis original), but often cause state and non-state actors to become intertwined. These networks exist worldwide, but are often characteristic of war-torn societies with a prevailing distrust of state institutions that have a possible role in the conflict (see also Arsovska & Kostakos, 2008, p. 373; Nikolić-Ristanović, 2009, p. 118, 125–126). In Kosovo, however, these networks were not just global linkages of people providing goods and services with the aim of making a profit. Instead, a vast network of Albanians provided money from abroad to build basic institutions—albeit in an improvised form—that were once provided by the state. The goal was to provide a basic social system for the Kosovar Albanian population in Kosovo outside the Serbian loci of power.

Kosovar Albanians learned to trust each other and organize their daily lives through the parallel social system. As voiced by a Kosovar Albanian police officer, people became used to structuring their lives irrespective of the regime in charge, instead of primarily in line with the regime: "We used to live under the Yugoslavian regime. Even in that time Albanians had the last place in entire Yugoslavia. All the time Albanians were fighting with the state—trying not to pay taxes, trying not to give anything to the state, because the state was foreign, not ours. Then we had the parallel system. From 1989 until 1998 we had, for 10 years, a parallel system. Then when the war came and later when it was finished, the foreign administrative government came again and said, 'You have no right to independence.' So this is all influencing the mentality."[38] This indifference toward authorities was not so much born out of rebellion; rather, it was a mechanism to cope with the exclusion faced under Milošević's rule (see also Perritt, 2010, pp. 77–78).

People thus were not primarily focused on the legality of their actions as decided by the authorities, especially right after the war. They had become accustomed to arranging their lives through unofficial channels. In combination with the limited overall employment possibilities in Kosovo (unemployment averaged 43% from

[38] Interview with KPO2, Jan 8, 2014.

2001 until 2014), this experience created an atmosphere in which some people opportunistically took any chance possible to earn money while paying little attention to the legality of their actions.[39] This included taking chances in the prostitution business. The police officer further explained, "I meet people around and they say, 'Ooh, I don't know. Here is no work to do. Here is no money. I don't know, maybe it is a good idea to open a bar and having some girls that they want to work. [...] Many people come after the girls. And then I can sell drinks and if they want to fuck. [...] If they want they can go.' So I said, 'No! If you do that then you will be in charge of facilitation [of prostitution],' and I am trying to explain. 'Ahh,' they said. 'Come on! Why you tell me that? It's better to start and profit something.'"[40] This opportunistic attitude is reflected in the way bar owners described their initial involvement in the sex industry. After seeing the example of some of his friends, Bujar changed his *qebabtore* (kebab shop) into a bar, with numerous female waitresses involved in prostitution.[41] After Rrustem's brother passed away, Rrustem closed his car wash, taking over his brother's bar and his network for recruiting Moldovan women to work in the Kosovar sex industry.[42] The shift these two men undertook—from involvement in the informal economy to the crime of engaging in the facilitation of prostitution—did not seem to occupy their minds. Both men had worked in various informal businesses for years. Now that money could be earned in the sex industry, it was seen as just another opportunity to make an income. Whether it was inside or outside the criminal code was not a primary consideration because of the tendency of indifference—at least in the first few years after the war—toward official institutions in Kosovo and its initially weak law enforcement. In the words of a special prosecutor, "I don't think that the notion of a rule of law is very much alive here."[43]

3.2.4 Cooperation with Regional Smuggling and Trafficking Rings

People such as Bujar and Rrustem, who started facilitating prostitution in the wake of the war, often benefitted from existing human smuggling and trafficking routes in the Balkans. Human trafficking into and within the Balkans has been reported since the 1990s (Friman & Reich, 2007, pp. 1–3; Segrave, Milivojevic, & Pickering, 2009, pp. 20–21; Shelley, 2010, p. 184, 189–190), and Albania played a crucial role from the start (Bekteshi, Gjermeni, & Van Hook, 2012). Under the rule of Enver

[39] The unemployment rate in Kosovo averaged 43.37% from 2001 until 2014. The highest unemployment rate was 57% in 2001, and the lowest was 30% in 2013 (Trading Economics, 2016).

[40] Interview with KPO2, Jan 8, 2014.

[41] Interview with Bujar, Oct 17, 2013.

[42] Various interviews with SP1, observations during court hearings, and analyses of testimonies between January and November 2013.

[43] Interview with EUL3, Oct 23, 2017.

Hoxha, Albania had experienced one of the most oppressive communist regimes.[44] The regime's collapse in 1991 brought an end to Albania's isolation, yet the country found itself in political and economic chaos. The situation further deteriorated in 1997 when an elaborate system of pyramid investment schemes collapsed (King & Vullnetari, 2003). The World Bank estimated that a total of $1.2 billion USD worth of Albanian savings was lost—an amount that equaled half of the gross domestic product (GDP) of the country in 1996 (Arsovska, 2015, p. xii; Olsen, 2000, p. 24). Thousands of people consequently tried to leave Albania and resettle in "the West," and an estimated 600,000 Albanians were living abroad by the turn of the millennium. The majority of these people moved to Italy and Greece, often in a clandestine way (King & Vullnetari, 2003, p. 284). Against this backdrop, Albanian smuggling and trafficking rings proliferated. In cooperation with other ethnic groups from the region, Albanian criminal groups initially trafficked Albanian women to sex industries in Western European countries such as Italy. They later shifted their focus to the trafficking of Moldovan, Romanian and Bulgarian women (Arsovska, 2015, p. 199; Hysi, 2007, pp. 98–99). One Albanian respondent, who was smuggled to Italy during the Albanian exodus and witnessed the rise of Albanian involvement in the sex industry, recounted this trajectory as follows:

> The market in Italy had a need for prostitution: "Let's find it. Let's organize. Let's try and find a way. We go back and talk with people of large families. Talk with them. Say, 'Yes you have a daughter. She is in high school. I will take her to Italy. I will take care of her and maybe I will find someone to marry her.'" They took her and immediately put her [in street prostitution]. So this is the first step. [...] There was nothing in terms of possibilities [in Albania]. To the point that it was 'OK, fine, we are suffering. We have 50 years of suffering. At least my daughter will not suffer. Go in Italy." And the image from the television also—it was very strong. Beautiful Italy. You know, this Berlusconi channels. This was like a dream for them [...]. After 2 or 3 years, this created social problems in Albania. Fighting between families [of traffickers and victims of trafficking]. People were killed. So some clever guys had the idea that maybe in the east it's easier to recruit. [...] So they started to recruit girls from Moldova, from Romania, from Ukraine, from Serbia, also Bulgaria."[45]

Women, primarily from Romania and Moldova, were brought to Albania through Serbia and Montenegro or Macedonia. From Albania they were taken to sex industries in Western Europe (Hysi, 2007, pp. 100–101; Rahmani, 2006, pp. 81–85).

Around the same time, human trafficking routes started to run toward Bosnia and Herzegovina. Publications outline that Bosnia and Herzegovina became a destination country for human trafficking during the war and remained so in its aftermath (Jennings & Nikolić-Ristanović, 2009; Rahmani, 2006, pp. 86–88; Vandenbergh, 2007, p. 84). The majority of women who engaged in the prostitution business in Bosnia Herzegovina were from Russia, Moldova, Romania and Ukraine.[46]

---

[44] Enver Hoxha was the leader of the Albanian Party of Labour from 1941 until his death in 1985. He was succeeded by Ramiz Alia, who introduced some economic reforms and diplomatic ties with Western European countries (Partouns & Willems, 1991, p. 8).

[45] Interview with NGO2, Oct 2, 2013.

[46] These publications speak of human trafficking in Bosnia and Herzegovina; it would be interest-

Kosovo's burgeoning sex industry benefited from its proximity to these, and other, human smuggling and trafficking routes in the Balkans. Foreign women were arranged for the Kosovar prostitution business by cooperating with people involved in existing smuggling and trafficking routes. Police officers recalled the existence of a neighborhood in Hungary where women, primarily from Eastern Europe, were traded to sex industries in Serbia, Macedonia and other countries in the region. When the Kosovar prostitution business proliferated, this market soon serviced the Kosovar sex industry as well.[47]

This example is noteworthy for its cooperation between inhabitants of Kosovo, including Kosovo Albanians, and those of other ethnic backgrounds from the Balkans. As outlined in the first part of this chapter, the Kosovo War followed an increasingly poisonous atmosphere between Kosovo Albanians and Serbs (Malcolm, 1999; Mertus, 1999). When the violence escalated, a large part of the Kosovo Albanians found refuge in Albania (UNDP Kosovo, 2014). However, Kosovo Albanians involved in human smuggling and trafficking in the wake of the war did not necessarily cooperate with Albanians, but neither did they refrain from business with Serbs.

With regard to this interethnic cooperation, a Kosovar Albanian special prosecutor explained, "During the war, Albanians and Serbs worked very well together in weapons. They sold weapons that would kill their brothers. No moral. A Serbian parliament member even said, 'We know where our arms are, with the UCK.'"[48] Kosovo Albanians, Serbs and people of other ethnic backgrounds found each other in business during the war, and this continued in its aftermath. A professor in criminology at the public university in Mitrovica North noted that Serbs and Albanians involved in human smuggling and human trafficking after the war "are the best friends."[49] While this seemingly unlikely cooperation has been observed in other studies on Albanian organized crime (Arsovska, 2015, p. 142) and human trafficking in the Balkans (Andreani & Raviv, 2004, p. 68), it has not yet been explained.

Several officers referred to the financial gains springing from this cooperation, and one American police officer employed by EULEX attempted to explain it by stating, "Money is stronger than blood."[50] Of course the actors involved in human trafficking and smuggling cooperated in order to earn money. But people from Kosovo who participated in my research regularly referred to their shared background within former Yugoslavia in order to explain that, despite the ethnic tensions that were fuelled by political propaganda campaigns (Mertus, 1999,

ing to examine whether there have been instances of prostitution migration toward Bosnia and Herzegovina in the aftermath of the war as well.

[47] Interview with KPO3, Oct 8, 2013.

[48] Interview with SP1, Feb 26, 2013.

[49] Interview with ACA1, Apr 26, 2013.

[50] Interview with UNM2, Mar 18, 2013. A similar remark was made, for example, in an interview with EUL5, Sept 17, 2013.

p. 4; Žižek, 2013, p. 38) and wartime atrocities, some Kosovo Albanians and Serbs did not make such unlikely business partners.[51] Having been part of former Yugoslavia, it was mentioned that Kosovo Albanians and Serbs shared a "central European mentality: people that are quite closed, not easily entering in different relationships with people outside."[52] This mindset differs, for instance, from the allegedly Mediterranean mentality of Albanians from Albania and was said to bring Serb and Kosovo Albanian business partners together. Furthermore, having a shared history with a business partner is more important than having a shared ethnicity. Kosovo Albanians, Serbs and others who lived in former Yugoslavia tended to have most contact with their former fellow countrymen. A Kosovar Albanian policeman explained the importance of individual contacts over ethnicity in establishing cooperation within human smuggling or trafficking: "They trust someone that they will know, much more. They know that family. So they will not so much be afraid that he will be kind of a traitor. So they will be afraid with the ones that they don't know so much. Maybe he is undercover or something. Who knows? We have experience with Albanians—they work with the Serbians for this kind of crimes. It is not a problem."[53] The importance of cooperating with acquaintances was confirmed by Bujar, the bar owner, who declared, "You just deal with people you know."[54] For example, he always did business with the same person in Montenegro. The apparent or perceived shared mentality and, furthermore, the individual contacts between Kosovo Albanians and Serbs can explain the cooperation between people who are otherwise generally considered to be enemies.

A similar line of argumentation has been used to explain why Albanians from Albania are not necessarily the most likely companions of Kosovo Albanians. Driving around Kosovo, the omnipresent red Albanian flag with a black double-headed eagle in the center gives the impression that Kosovo Albanians and Albanians from Albania feel very united. However, in line with the findings of Arsovska (2015, p. 140), Albanians in Albania and those in countries that used to be part of former Yugoslavia often highlight their differences. The alleged differences between Albania Albanians and Kosovo Albanians were clearly summarized by a Kosovo Albanian respondent: "We are different. We had such a different education. There, in Albania, people can really speak and write and present, but here: no. Also, we have a difference in language.[55] And we are nationalist, and they only care about money. For instance, here people are against marriages with internationals, while in Albania they really like it. Even if they now could vote for reunion with Albania, than people wouldn't. It was different in the past, before Milošević

---

[51] See, for instance, interview with HTE1, Oct 8, 2013.

[52] Interview with NGO2, Oct 2, 2013.

[53] Interview with KPO2, Jan 8, 2014.

[54] Interview with Bujar, Oct 17, 2013.

[55] The respondent refers to the linguistic differences between the Gegs and the Tosks (Malcolm, 1999, p. 14).

times."[56] Apart from factual differences (e.g., linguistic differences between the Gegs, who live in northern Albania and Kosovo, and the Tosks, who live in southern Albania), most respondents from both Albania and Kosovo mentioned dissimilarities in mentality between Albanians from Albania, on the one hand, and countries from former Yugoslavia, on the other. Many suggested that Albanians from Albania were focused on money after years of isolation and poverty and were considered rough in their means to reach wealth.[57] These differences meant that Kosovo Albanians did not necessarily cooperate with Albanians from Albania in the arrangement of foreign women for the burgeoning post-war prostitution business in Kosovo. Some did cooperate—but not exclusively, and not as a preference per se.

3.2.5 Northern Kosovo as a Nexus Point for Smuggling and Trafficking

Fig. 3.4 Mitrovica

Clark (2014, p. 527) describes Northern Kosovo as "Serbia in miniature." When you cross the Ibar River to Mitrovica North, this description is reflected in the omnipresence of the Serbian flag, the payment in Serbian dinar, and the presence of Serb institutions. Kosovo Serbian leaders generally refuse to work with EULEX, as they are considered to promote Kosovo's independence (Judah, 2008, p. 148). While the

[56] Interview with HTE1, Oct 8, 2013.

[57] Interview with KPO2, Jan 8, 2014; interview with NGO2, Oct 2, 2013; interview with HTE1, Oct 8, 2013.

various Serbian enclaves throughout Kosovo cannot ignore the international and Kosovar authorities in Pristina, the international community still fails to exercise authority and establish law and order in the north of Kosovo (Yannis, 2001, p. 33; De Wet, 2009, p. 2; Lehne, 2012).[58] Likewise, law enforcement under the auspices of the government in Pristina has very limited control. It can be dangerous for Kosovo Albanians to go to the north, and local Kosovo Serbs are reluctant to work for either the Kosovo police or EULEX. This latter sentiment was explained by an international living in Mitrovica North:

> People are skeptical to local people who are working for the Kosovo police and EULEX. From an economic point of view, it is understandable [that people would want to work for the Kosovo police or EULEX, as the salaries are good], but they would never advertise it. A hand grenade was thrown into the house of a Serbian man working for the Kosovo police. It can be dangerous to work for them. The Wild West is not completely accurate. But there is some truth in there."[59]

The area tends to be described as a hotspot for crime. Lehne (2012, p. 5), for instance, states that "in the absence of effective rule of law structures, smuggling and other criminal activities flourish in the area [of northern Kosovo]." This view was echoed in conversations with Kosovo Albanians. A Kosovo Albanian police officer in Pristina explained, "So it is a place of no one. […] The Kosovar authorities, police, judges and prosecutors have no influence in that part. No possibilities to see what is going on concretely. […] They claim it is ours. But the criminals—it could be a heaven for them. Nobody is touching them."[60] The disputed area is known as an important route for the smuggling of goods, but it is used for the smuggling and trafficking of women as well. The police officer continued, "In the north, Serbs, and in the south, Albanians. They work together. Bring girls up and down."[61] Bujar, the bar owner, recognized these observations, explaining, "Most of the women went through Mitrovica. This was not so difficult. Only the Serbs were guarding these borders there, but not so much."[62] Northern Kosovo became a nexus point for the smuggling and trafficking of Eastern European women toward bars in various cities throughout Kosovo.[63]

3.2.6 *Economic Prosperity in the Wake of the War*

The final feature of Kosovo's post-war society that allowed for and shaped the development of the prostitution business is the fact that Kosovo's economy was thriving in the wake of the war. Engagement in the facilitation of prostitution was

---

[58] EULEX hosted a discussion on the problems with the rule of law on Mar 9, 2016 (European Union External Action, 2016).

[59] Interview with NGO3, May 8, 2013.

[60] Interview with KPO2, Jan 8, 2014.

[61] Idem.

[62] Informal conversation with Bujar, Nov 12, 2013.

[63] See Sect. 5.6 for a discussion of the various journeys Eastern European women took to Kosovo.

considered lucrative, as quite a few people, both internationals and locals, could suddenly afford to pay for commercial sex. How might one explain Kosovo's economic prosperity of Kosovo shortly after the war?

First, it was a consequence of what Rehn and Sirleaf (2002, p. 62) have deemed a "peacekeeping economy." The concept of "peacekeeping economy" refers to the "industries and services such as bars and hotels that spring up with the arrival of large [numbers of], foreign, comparatively well-paid peacekeeping personnel" (idem). It thus draws attention to the economic impact engendered by an international peacekeeping presence. Internationals stir economic activity that would otherwise not occur or would occur on a lower scale (Jennings, 2015). In Kosovo, 50,000 peacekeepers from 39 countries arrived to provide security.[64] Aside from these peacekeepers, the UN also employed over 5500 police and international civilian personnel. Between 300 and 400 NGOs were on the ground by the end of 1999 (Currion, 2010; Scott-Flynn, 2003), and over $3 billion of international aid and assistance was flowing in (Konxheli & Sahiti, 2012). In 2008, when both UNMIK and KFOR had reduced their staff, EULEX reached its maximum strength of 1950 international police officers, judges, prosecutors and customs officials. These numbers indicate the enormous influx of (relatively wealthy) people and money into such a small area as Kosovo. Inhabitants of Kosovo benefited from these economic developments in various ways: they became employed by UNMIK or the other international organizations that settled after the war, and they earned money by meeting the legal (e.g., restaurants and car washes) or illegal (e.g., sexual services and drugs) demands of internationals (see also Jennings & Nikolić-Ristanović, 2009).

Kosovo's economy was furthermore stirred by the remittances of the Kosovar diaspora (UNDP, 2012). The economy had strongly relied on remittance flows from the Kosovar diaspora since as early as the 1960s. In the years after the war, approximately a quarter of the households in Kosovo received remittances (Kosovo Agency of Statistics, 2013). As a consequence of the peacekeeping economy and remittances, locals had quite a bit of money to spend and thus became potential clients as well.

But locals were not the only ones who sought to benefit from the peacekeeping economy. As outlined in more detail in Chap. 6, foreign women were attracted to the economic prosperity and tried to benefit from it by engaging in commercial sex. As will be expanded upon in the upcoming chapters, the growth of the sex industry during the peacekeeping mission in Kosovo is thus related to international players setting foot there—but not, as popularly argued, simply because internationals demanded commercial sex. Instead, amongst other reasons, this relation is a result of the socio-economic impact of internationals' arrival.

---

[64] On June 9, 1999, Milošević agreed to withdraw almost all of his forces from Kosovo and (at least temporarily) hand over the exercise of sovereignty in Kosovo to the UN in the Military Technical Agreement between the International Security Force (KFOR) and the Governments of the Federal Republic of Yugoslavia and the Republic of Serbia (commonly known as the Kumanovo Agreement). See https://peacekeeping.un.org/en/mission/unmik. Accessed Nov 28, 2017.

Fig. 3.5 Shop outside Camp Bondsteel

3.3 No Business as Usual, But Booming Nonetheless

Together, the previously mentioned features of Kosovo society in the wake of the war allowed for and shaped the growth of the prostitution business in the context of the peacekeeping mission. However, I do not wish to imply that prostitution ever was or came to be seen as "business as usual."

Before the war, Kosovo could be depicted as a small and close-knit society. Families were largely controlling and would not accept involvement in prostitution from either men or women. In her examination of Albanian organized crime, Arsovska (2015, p. 204) underlines how prostitution traditionally goes against all traditional Albanian rules of human life as laid down in the Kanun of Lekë Dukagjini.[65] Prostitution did take place; however, it was rare and hidden. When I asked inhabitants of Kosovo about prostitution before the war, they often answered in a similar manner to one police officer, who stated, "Before the war, the market in Kosovo was very minimal. It did exist, but it was very minimal."[66] Furthermore, as outlined by a human rights activist, the places where commercial sex was offered were kept out of sight: "Before the war, the idea of a brothel and prostitution was with women who were from abroad, not Kosovar, and that was... I mean, it was taboo topic... If you just said 'brothel' it was like... They were whispering, saying, 'There is a brothel in this place,' but just whispering."[67] Some men therefore opted to visit brothels abroad, for instance in Poland or Macedonia.[68]

This critical attitude toward engagement in prostitution remained after the war, especially when it came to the women involved. People tended to be horrified at the idea that nowadays Kosovar Albanian women make up the majority of prostitutes in Kosovo. The (largely male) facilitators of prostitution are confronted with less stigma. Still, they generally preferred to present themselves as bar owners and did not specifically mention the prostitution part, especially in conversation with a woman. Arsovska (2015, pp. 204–207) suggests that nowadays, Albanian facilitators of prostitution, both from Albania and Kosovo, justify their acts by simultaneously referring to the subordination of women being culturally acceptable in many Albanian settings, on the one hand, and the Western media and values making prostitution more common, on the other. Such selective use of traditional and Western value systems can function as a neutralization technique for some. However, I argue that it was not just Western media and values that made prostitution more common. Rather, the fact that money could be earned

[65] The Kanun is "the body of 'customary law' under which Albanians, particularly the northern clans, have conducted their lives" (Cara & Margjeka, 2015, p. 174). These laws were passed on orally and first published in writing in 1913 by Albanian Franciscan Shtjefen Gjeçov (idem). Personal and social honor, as well as hospitality, are central principles in the Kanun. The laws codified in the Kanun are no longer widely in use, however, as communism, globalization, and modernization have affected traditional practices (Arsovska, 2015, pp. 63–66; Malcolm, 1999, pp. 17–19).

[66] Interview with KPO3, Oct 8, 2013.

[67] Interview with NGO1, Nov 8, 2013.

[68] Interview with Bujar, Apr 14, 2014; interview with NGO1, Nov 8, 2013.

from prostitution served as a justification for increased involvement in it, and the previously mentioned developments in post-war Kosovar society allowed for and shaped this booming business.

References

Agbu, O. (2008). *Re-visiting corruption and human trafficking in Nigeria: Any progress?* Retrieved Nov 11, 2017, from https://www.researchgate.net/profile/Osita_Agbu/publication/240626318_Re-visiting_Corruption_and_Human_Trafficking_in_Nigeria_Any_Progress/links/0deec5319877bad666000000.pdf

Amnesty International. (2004). So does it mean I have rights? In *Protecting the human rights of women and girls trafficked for forced prostitution in Kosovo*. London, UK: Amnesty International.

Andreani, A., & Raviv, T. (2004). *The changing patterns and trends of trafficking in persons in the Balkan Region: Assessment carried out in Albania, Bosnia and Herzegovina, the Province of Kosovo, the Former Yugoslav Republic of Macedonia and the Republic of Moldova*. Geneva, Switzerland: International Organization for Migration.

Arsovska, J. (2015). *Decoding Albanian organized crime: Culture, politics, and globalization*. Oakland, CA: University of California Press.

Arsovska, J., & Kostakos, P. A. (2008). Illicit arms trafficking and the limits of rational choice theory: The case of the Balkans. *Trends in Organized Crime, 11*(4), 352–378. https://doi.org/10.1007/s12117-008-9052-y

Autesserre, S. (2012). Dangerous tales: Dominant narratives on the Congo and their unintended consequences. *African Affairs, 111*(443), 202–222.

Bales, K. (2007). What predicts human trafficking? *International Journal of Comparative and Applied Criminal Justice, 31*(2), 269–279.

Bekteshi, V., Gjermeni, E., & Van Hook, M. (2012). Modern-day slavery: Sex trafficking in Albania. *International Journal of Sociology and Social Policy, 32*(7/8), 480–494.

Belloni, R., & Strazzari, F. (2014). Corruption in post-conflict Bosnia-Herzegovina and Kosovo: A deal among friends. *Third World Quarterly, 35*(5), 855–871. https://doi.org/10.1080/01436597.2014.921434

Bennett, C., & Saferworld. (2011). *Public perception of safety and security in Kosovo: Time to act*. London, UK: Saferworld.

Cain, K., Postlewait, H., & Thomson, A. (2004). *Emergency sex: And other desperate measures*. New York, NY: Miramax Books.

Cara, A., & Margjeka, M. (2015). Kanun of Leke Dukagjini customary law of northern Albania. *European Scientific Journal, 11*(28), 174–186.

Clark, N. J. (2014). Kosovo's Gordian knot: The contested north and the search for a solution. *Nationalities Papers, 42*(3), 526–547. https://doi.org/10.1080/00905992.2013.870147

Currion, P. (2010). *Strength in numbers: A review Of NGO coordination in the field case study: Kosovo 1999–2002*. Geneva, Switzerland: International Council of Voluntary Agencies.

Daalder, I. H., & O'Hanlon, M. E. (2000). *Winning ugly: NATO's war to save Kosovo*. Washington, DC: Brookings Institution Press.

De Wet, E. (2009). The governance of Kosovo: Security Council Resolution 1244 and the establishment and functioning of Eulex. *American Journal of International Law, 103*(1), 83–96.

European Court of Auditors. (2012). *European Union assistance to Kosovo: Related to the rule of law (special report no. 18)*. Luxembourg, Europe: European Court of Auditors.

European Union External Action. (2016). Discussion on rule of law in the North of Kosovo. *European Union External Action*. Retrieved Apr 5, 2016, from http://www.eulex-kosovo.eu/?page=2,11,402

Friman, R., & Reich, S. (2007). *Human trafficking, human security, and the Balkans*. Pittsburgh, PA: Pittsburgh Press.

Gan. (2017). Kosovo corruption report. *GANBACP*. Retrieved Aug 10, 2017, from http://www.business-anti-corruption.com/country-profiles/kosovo

Glenny, M. (1992). *The fall of Yugoslavia: The third Balkan war*. London, UK: Penguin.

Human Rights Watch. (1998). *Federal Republic of Yugoslavia: Humanitarian law violations in Kosovo*. Retrieved Feb 15, 2016, from https://www.hrw.org/legacy/reports98/kosovo/

Hysi, V. (2007). Human trafficking and democratic transition in Albania. In H. R. Friman & S. Reich (Eds.), *Human trafficking, human security, and the Balkans* (pp. 96–118). Pittsburgh, PA: University of Pittsburgh Press.

Jennings, K., & Nikolić-Ristanović, V. (2009). *UN peacekeeping economies and local sex industries: Connections and implications* (Microcon Working Paper no. 17). Retrieved from http://www.peacewomen.org/assets/file/Resources/NGO/PK_SexIndustries_MICROCON_2009.pdf

Jennings, K. M. (2015). Life in a 'peace-kept' City: Encounters with the peacekeeping economy. *Journal of Intervention and Statebuilding, 9*(3), 296–315.

Judah, T. (2008). *Kosovo: What everyone needs to know*. Oxford, UK: Oxford University Press.

King, R., & Vullnetari, J. (2003). *Migration and development in Albania (Working paper C5)*. Brighton, UK: Development Research Centre on Migration, Globalisation and Poverty.

Konxheli, D., & Sahiti, A. (2012). Assessment of foreign aid effectiveness based on Kosovo sectors. *Asian Journal of Business and Management Sciences, 2*(2), 27–33.

Kosovo Agency of Statistics. (2013). *Study on remittance in Kosovo*. Pristina, Kosovo: UNDP.

Lehne, S. (2012). *Kosovo and Serbia: Toward a normal relationship*. Washington, DC: Carnegie Endowment for International Peace.

Malcolm, N. (1999). *Kosovo: A short history*. New York, NY: New York University Press.

Mann, M. (2005). *The dark side of democracy: Explaining ethnic cleansing*. Cambridge, UK: Cambridge University Press.

Mertus, J. (1999). *Kosovo: How myths and truths started a war*. Berkeley, CA: University of California Press.

Mertus, J., & Bertone, A. (2007). Combating trafficking: International efforts and their ramifications. In R. Friman & S. Reich (Eds.), *Human trafficking, human security and the Balkans* (pp. 40–60). Pittsburgh, PA: University of Pittsburgh Press.

Nikolić-Ristanović, V. (2009). Trafficking in humans and illegal economy in war and post-war society. In P. C. van Duyne, S. Donati, J. Harvey, A. Maljevic, & K. von Lampe (Eds.), *Crime, money and criminal mobility in Europe* (pp. 117–141). Nijmegen, The Netherlands: Wolf Legal Publishers.

Nordstrom, C. (2004). *Shadows of war: Violence, power, and international profiteering in the twenty-first century*. Berkeley, CA: University of California Press.

Olsen, N. (2000). *Albania*. Douglas, UK: Oxfam.

Partouns, K., & Willems, L. (1991). Albanie en de CVSE: Too long ago, too far apart. *Helsinki Monitor, 2*, 8–12.

Perritt, H. (2008). *Kosovo liberation army: The inside story of an insurgency*. Chicago, IL: University of Illinois Press.

Perritt, H. (2010). *The road to independence for Kosovo: A chronicle of the Ahtisaari plan*. Cambridge, UK: Cambridge University Press.

Radin, A. (2014). Analysis of current events: Towards the rule of law in Kosovo: EULEX should go. *Nationalities Papers: The Journal of Nationalism and Ethnicity, 42*(2), 181–194.

Rahmani, L. (2006). Invisible routes: An exploratory study of changing patterns and trends in routes of trafficking in persons in the Balkan region. In N. Narli (Ed.), *Trafficking in persons in South East Europe: A threat to human security*. Vienna, Austria: National Defence Academy and Bureau for Security Policy at the Austrian Ministry of Defence.

Ramet, S. P. (1999). *Balkan Babel: The disintegration of Yugoslavia from the Death of Tito to the War for Kosovo*. Boulder, CO: Westview Press.

Rehn, E., & Sirleaf, E. J. (2002). *Women, war and peace: The independent experts' assessment on the impact of armed conflict on women and women's role in peace-building*. New York, NY: United Nations Development Fund for Women.

Rogel, C. (2003). Kosovo: Where it all began. *International Journal of Politics, Culture, and Society, 17*(1), 167–182.

Scott-Flynn, N. (June 2003). Coordination in Kosovo: The challenge for the NGO sector. *Human Practice Network Magazine*. Retrieved from https://odihpn.org/magazine/coordination-in-kosovo-the-challenge-for-the-ngo-sector/

Segrave, M., Milivojevic, S., & Pickering, S. (2009). *Sex trafficking: International context and response*. Devon, UK: Willan Publishing.

Serwer, D., & Thomson, P. (2008). A framework for success: International intervention in societies emerging from conflict. In C. A. Crocker, F. O. Hampson, & P. Aall (Eds.), *Leashing the dogs of war: Conflict management in a divided world* (pp. 369–387). Washington, DC: United States Institute of Peace.

Shelley, L. (2010). *Human trafficking: A global perspective*. Cambridge, UK: Cambridge University Press.

Strohmeyer, H. (2001). Collapse and reconstruction of a judicial system: The United Nations Missions in Kosovo and east Timor. *American Journal of International Law, 95*(1), 46–63.

Terre des Hommes. (2010). *Regional report on the implementation of the "UNICEF guidelines for the protection of the rights of child victims of trafficking in South Eastern Europe": Assessment of the situation in Albania, Kosovo and the Former Yugoslav Republic of Macedonia, 2010*. Geneva, Switzerland: Terre des Hommes.

Trading Economics. (2016). Kosovo unemployment rate. *Trading Economics*. Retrieved on April 4, 2016 from http://www.tradingeconomics.com/kosovo/unemployment-rate

Troebst, S. (1998). *Conflict in Kosovo: Failure or prevention*. Flensburg, Germany: European Centre for Minority Issues.

UNDP. (2012). *Kosovo remittance study 2012*. New York, NY: UNDP.

UNDP Kosovo. (2014). *Kosovo human development report: Migration as a force for development*. Retrieved from http://hdr.undp.org/sites/default/files/khdr2014english.pdf

Van de Port, M. (1994). *Het einde van de wereld: Beschaving, redeloosheid en zigeunercafes in Servië*. Amsterdam, The Netherlands: Babylon-De Geus.

Van der Borgh, C. (2012). Resisting international state building in Kosovo. *Problems of Post-Communism, 59*(2), 31–42.

Van der Borgh, C., & Lasance, L. (2013). Parallel governance and boundary strategies in Gracanica, Kosovo. *Nationalism and Ethnic Politics, 19*(2), 187–209.

Vandenbergh, M. (2007). Peacekeeping and rule breaking: United Nations anti-trafficking policy in Bosnia and Herzegovina. In H. Richard Friman & S. Reich (Eds.), *Human trafficking, human security and the Balkans* (pp. 81–95). Pittsburgh, PA: Pittsburgh University Press.

Vermeulen, M. (2016, January 20). *Waarom blauwhelmen bijna nooit Henk heten (en des te vaker Abdullah)*. De Correspondent. Retrieved from https://decorrespondent.nl/3905/waarom-blauwhelmen-bijna-nooit-henk-heten-en-des-te-vaker-abdullah/170144755-6d2f1ec8

Vickers, M. (1998). *Between Serb and Albanian: A history of Kosovo*. London, UK: Hurst.

Yannis, A. (2001). Kosovo under international administration. *Survival, 43*(2), 31–48.

Zabyelina, Y., & Arsovska, J. (2013). Rediscovering corruption's other side: Bribing for peace in post-conflict Kosovo and Chechnya. *Crime, Law and Social Change, 60*(1), 1–24.

Zhang, S. X., & Pineda, S. L. (2008). Corruption as a causal factor in human trafficking. In D. Siegel & H. Nelen (Eds.), *Organized crime: Culture, markets and policies* (pp. 41–55). New York, NY: Springer.

Zivkovic, M. (2001). Kosovo is the most expensive Serbian word: Political enchantment and Milosevic's rise to power. *Anthropology of East Europe Review, 19*(1), 91–97.

Žižek, S. (2013). NATO as the left hand of God? In S. Žižek & A. Hamza (Eds.), *From myth to symptom: The case of Kosovo* (pp. 17–33). Pristina, Kosovo: Kolektivi Materializmi Dialekt.

Fig. 4.1 Men in a bar

Chapter 4
Clientele of the Post-War Prostitution Business

Literature on the post-war prostitution business concludes that Kosovo would not have developed a significant sex industry without the influx of ready-made clients from the international community (Amnesty International, 2004, pp. 7–8; Friman & Reich, 2007; Terre des Hommes, 2010). The preceding chapter discussed the legal, socio-cultural and economic features that characterized Kosovo in the wake of the war and together shaped a context in which the post-war prostitution business could flourish. Therewith, attention has been drawn to more factors—not merely demand—that enabled the growth of the sex industry. Let us now turn to the clientele to examine if internationals indeed singlehandedly created demand for prostitution in Kosovo. Who were the clients of the nascent sex industry during the peacekeeping mission? And who makes up the clientele now that the peacekeeping mission is being dismantled?

So far, studies on clients of prostitution during peacekeeping missions have largely been conducted amongst peacekeepers themselves. Peacekeepers were asked about (their perception of) their colleagues' involvement in prostitution during missions in the Democratic Republic of the Congo, Sierra Leone (Higate, 2003, 2007; Higate & Henry, 2004), Liberia, Haiti (Jennings, 2008; Martin, 2005) and Bosnia and Herzegovina (Simic, 2012). Yet women involved in prostitution during the peacekeeping mission in Kosovo indicated that the clientele of the fledgling sex industry had always been more diverse than internationals alone. As a consequence of the aforementioned tendency to focus on peacekeepers as respondents who reflect on other peacekeepers' involvement in prostitution, clients other than internationals have not yet been considered in studies on prostitution during peacekeeping missions.[1]

In this chapter, I therefore shift my concern to women engaged in prostitution in the context of the peacekeeping mission in Kosovo. I asked these women to reflect

[1] Notable exceptions are Whitworth (2004) and Jennings (2014), who included several interviews with sex workers and victims of sexual exploitation and abuse in their study of the peacekeeping missions in Cambodia and Liberia and the Democratic Republic of the Congo, respectively. These interviews, however, again only examined women's experiences with peacekeepers as clients.

R. de Wildt, *Post-War Prostitution*, Studies of Organized Crime 17,
https://doi.org/10.1007/978-3-030-19474-1_4

upon the clients they were servicing, and they broadly identified three types of clients. These included internationals employed in Kosovo; Kosovo Albanians who live abroad and return to Kosovo with relatively large sums of money to spend during their holidays; and local men. The chapter is organized according to these three main categories of clients. Internationals are examined in the first section.

An analysis of the clientele of prostitution in the context of a peacekeeping mission, based on the lived experiences of the women involved, allows for three elaborations of the contemporary debate. First, it considers the experienced impact that internationals as clients have on women engaged in prostitution during peacekeeping missions. This debate has thus far been fueled by more general discussion about the rights and wrongs of prostitution, with echoes of the abolitionist perspective of prostitution as gender-based violence, on the one hand, and the liberal perspective that emphasizes the right to self-determination, on the other (Segrave, Milivojevic, & Pickering, 2009). Nevertheless, empirical findings about the actual experiences of the women concerned are largely lacking. Second, this approach reflects on the full range of clientele instead of being limited to peacekeepers as clients. And third, my ethnographic research amongst women involved in prostitution in Kosovo continued while the peacekeeping mission greatly decreased in staff. This long-term approach allows for an examination of the literature's suggestion (see Jennings, 2010) that peacekeeping economies are predisposed to become sex tourism economies and will continue to attract international clients beyond the life of the mission.

4.1 Internationals Employed in Kosovo

Fig. 4.2 Camp Bondsteel

Lorena, from the north of Kosovo, welcomed me in fluent English when I met her in the bar where she was working. The bar was located in a city close to Camp Bondsteel, the main U.S. military base in Kosovo. "My English is not so good," she unnecessarily apologized. "I cannot practice my English so much anymore, only sometimes with two American soldiers from Bondsteel. In the past, more people from Bondsteel came, but not so many anymore. […] I like American clients. They treat you with respect. […] But now the [international] customers are getting less and less because the soldiers leave Bondsteel."[2]

In a bar around the corner, Saranda was exchanging frequent texts with Flavio from Italy. Saranda used to work in Camp Bondsteel and later owned a bar in front of the camp. She met Flavio 12 years ago, and he quickly became her regular client. Saranda described Flavio as a true friend: "He was working in Bondsteel. Sometimes he helps me. The other day was my daughter's birthday. My daughter wanted to have a new iPhone. I told her I do not have the money for that. I mentioned all of it to Flavio and he brought a new iPhone when we met again."[3]

Flavio, and Lorena's American clients, were amongst the approximately 50,000 peacekeepers from 39 countries that arrived in Kosovo after Milošević handed over the exercise of sovereignty in Kosovo to the UN.[4] Aside from these peacekeepers, the UN also employed police and international civilian personnel; between 300 and 400 NGOs were established (Currion, 2010; Scott-Flynn, 2003) in part with international staff; and EULEX hired international police officers, judges, prosecutors and customs officials.[5] As in most peacekeeping missions (Jennings, 2014, p. 314), the majority of internationals working in Kosovo were men. As illustrated by the experiences of Lorena and Saranda, as well as those of Mimoza and Shqipe in Chap. 1, some of these men visited prostitutes during their employment in Kosovo.

As previously mentioned, studies generally focus on peacekeepers as clients (Higate, 2003; Simic, 2012). In Kosovo, however, the group of internationals-turned-clients has been broader than peacekeepers alone; one can also think of international police officers, civilian personnel, diplomats and relief workers. This observation is illustrated by a court case against a Kosovo Albanian man who allegedly facilitated prostitution in a Kosovo hotel. During this trial, indicted by EULEX, it became painfully clear that an international police officer employed by EULEX regularly purchased commercial sex[6]:

[2] Interview with Lorena, April 27, 2013.

[3] Interview with Saranda, September 19, 2013.

[4] http://www.un.org/en/peacekeeping/missions/unmik/background.shtml, accessed December 10, 2016.

[5] https://www.consilium.europa.eu/uedocs/cms_data/docs/missionPress/files/091214%20FACTSHEET%20EULEX%20Kosovo%20-%20version%209_EN.pdf, accessed December 10, 2016. See Sect. 3.2.6 for the exact number of employees.

[6] Indictment of the Eulex Prosecution Office, September 21, 2012, District Pristina, p. 3.

> I joined the EULEX prosecution unit when the case went to court. The Norwegian prosecutor asked the Kosovar judges for permission to listen to some telephone interceptions together. The first intercept was a conversation between the main suspect, Kustrim, and a friend. Kushtrim told his friend, "I have filled it [the hotel] with whores. I have got ten Serbian girls from Belgrade, two meters tall."[7] Kushtrim looked slightly embarrassed when he heard his voice through the courtroom speakers. Another telephone tap started to play. This time we heard loud music in the background and the voice of an Albanian woman. Kushtrim urged her to come downstairs because her regular international client was there: "Come, because the guy from EULEX has come and he is asking for you; come [swearing] if you want to make money, come."[8] The defendants looked at the EULEX prosecutor with a smug smile.[9] Her colleague, an international police officer, was fired from the EULEX mission as a consequence of being caught having sexual intercourse with an alleged victim of trafficking.

These are no exceptional cases. In online forums, internationals employed in Kosovo share their experience in the local sex industry: "Can any of you guys add an up to date report on the general situation in Kosovo and what the current P4P [Pay for Pleasure] scene is like. I am being contracted to work there and will be arriving in a couple of months, probably staying for 1 year. Any advice would be really appreciated."[10] This 2010 post is followed by reactions from internationals suggesting places to find commercial sex and attempts to meet up and go to brothels together. According to women involved in prostitution in Kosovo, these international men—employed by KFOR, UNMIK, EULEX, governmental (i.e., embassies) and non-governmental organizations—formed a large part of the clientele, specifically in the early years of the peacekeeping mission in Kosovo.

Various studies on prostitution in the context of peacekeeping missions also describe longer-term relationships between local women and international men (one or more), who maintain these women as a form of prostitution. Relationships of this nature were primarily observed in studies on the African continent. Based on research in the Democratic Republic of the Congo and Liberia, Jennings (2014, p. 319) explains that "in these relationships, the material expectations of the boyfriend, and the desired availability and behavior of the girlfriend, tend to be mutually understood." She observed that women have relatively stable relationships with these men for the time that the men are in the country. Likewise, and also with regard to the Democratic Republic of the Congo, Oldenburg (2015, p. 326) describes how women sometimes "engage in multiple relationships to pursue their aspirations." Some Kosovar women engaged in sexual relationships with internationals as well. These relationships, however, differ from those observed by Jennings and Oldenburg and therefore do not classify as prostitution. Let us briefly consider them for clarification.

---

[7] Intercept on April 4, 2012. Indictment of the Eulex Prosecution Office, District Pristina, p. 10.

[8] Intercept on April 5, 2012. Indictment of the Eulex Prosecution Office, District Pristina, p. 8.

[9] Observations in court in Pristina, September 16, 2013.

[10] Post from 2010 on the internet forum http://forum.cityxguide.com/topic/other-areas-67, accessed December 16, 2013. P4P refers to "Pay for Pleasure" and refers to any sexual services in return for money.

On the one hand, local women can be found to engage in occasional secretive sexual encounters with international men. Local women tend to keep these sexual endeavors confidential in order to avoid stigmatization for such "sexually promiscuous" behavior.[11] Likewise, international partners are generally inclined to keep these experiences to themselves, as the UN strongly discourages sexual relationships between UN staff and beneficiaries of assistance in their official code of conduct.[12] "Beneficiaries of assistance" refers to all nationals of the host country as well as refugees in the host country.[13] In practice, this means that sexual relationships between UN staff and local women are forbidden when they are exploitative or abusive according to UN standards. This is "determined on a case by case basis."[14] Self-evidently, UN staff do not go through this official process before a spontaneous one-night stand. Therefore, they tend to be careful in sharing their experiences widely afterward.

On the other hand, some women from Kosovo engage in serious long-term relationships with international men. Such public relationships generally end in marriage. I met various Kosovo Albanian women who married international men, started a family and joined them abroad. Although such marriages generally encompass a lifestyle that is out of reach for many ordinary citizens of Kosovo, marriage to an international is not a widely shared dream amongst the general population. Generally, marriage to a partner with the same ethnic background is preferred. This is reflected in the ways in which internationals complained in online forums about the approachability of local women in Kosovo: "Kosovo is truly the asshole of Europe. While I will not automatically rule out local Albanian women, they are very difficult to get, even when one promises to marry them."[15]

Internationals' perception of local women in Kosovo does not correlate with the findings of Jennings (2014) or of Higate and Henry (2004) in the Democratic Republic of the Congo and Liberia. Jennings (2014, p. 321) concluded that peacekeepers in the Democratic Republic of the Congo and Liberia "tended to have highly sexualized views of women." Similarly, Higate and Henry (2004, p. 491) found that "some local women were constructed as sexual predators." As women in Kosovo generally only engage in sexual relationships with internationals for fun and in secret, on the one hand, or as a long-term engagement resulting in marriage, on the other, they also do not allude to the successive relationships with sugar daddies, as these studies describe (see also Oldenburg, 2015). Instead, they more closely resemble the experiences of Bosnian women as described by Simic (2012, p. 121), who concluded that after the war, Bosnian women engaged in sexual relationships with peacekeepers as a result of "ordinary desires as sexual attraction, love, friend-

[11] See Sect. 6.6.2 on stigmatization.

[12] ST/SGB/2003/13. See UN Secretariat section 3.2 (October 9, 2003).

[13] ST/SGB/2003/13 (October 9, 2003, pp. 1–2).

[14] UNMIK (2011).

[15] Forum post, http://forum.cityxguide.com/topic/other-areas-67, accessed December 16, 2013.

ship and a sense of adventure." I thus do not classify these sexual relationships as a form of prostitution. When speaking about prostitution, I refer to the explicitly commercial sexual transactions between women and their clients as described in the beginning of this section.

4.1.1 Prostitution as an Unofficial Promise of "Mission Life"

Engagement of soldiers (and sailors; see Trotter, 2008) in prostitution is "almost something of a cliché" (Bickford, 2003). Historical studies describe how Asian "comfort women" were forced into prostitution by the Japanese military during World War II, as it would help maintain military morale and discipline (Hicks, 1997; Tanaka, 2002; Yoshimi, 2000); the sexual conduct of allied forces during the occupation of Japan (Tanaka, 2002); and prostitution in the proximity of U.S. military bases in peacetime in South Korea (Moon, 1997; Pollock Sturdevant & Stoltzfus, 1992), Japan and the Philippines (Pollock Sturdevant & Stoltzfus, 1992).

Similar stories of prostitution—as well as of sexual exploitation and sexual abuse—have accompanied peacekeeping missions that started to emerge after the Second World War.[16] This should come as no surprise. Peacekeeping tends to be a soldier's job, and therefore both military interventions and peacekeeping missions heavily rely on soldiers.[17] Allegations were made against peacekeepers and, as emphasized above, other internationals hired during peacekeeping missions, who exchanged money, employment, goods or services for sex. The location of their missions ranged from Bosnia and Herzegovina (Friman & Reich, 2007) and Cambodia (Whitworth, 2004) in the 1990s, to the Democratic Republic of the Congo (Higate, 2003, 2007; Higate & Henry, 2004) and Kosovo around the turn of the century, to the Central African Republic nowadays.[18]

The link between military interventions and peacekeeping operations, on the one hand, and prostitution, on the other, is so well known that Bickford (2003) argues that prostitution "can be seen as a hallmark of military service, something one expects to get as a soldier." But how can one explain the widespread involvement in prostitution of soldiers, peacekeepers and other internationals hired during peacekeeping missions? In attempting to understand the deeper underpinnings of the link

---

[16] Peackeeping missions have a wider variety of tasks (e.g., repatriating refugees and monitoring elections), but still rely heavily on soldiers (Simic, 2012, pp. 13–26; Whitworth, 2004).

[17] See Whitworth (2004, p. 3) for a critique of the observation that peacekeeping depends on "individuals (mostly men) who have been constructed as soldiers, and on the other hand, it demands that they deny many of the traits they have come to understand being a soldier entails."

[18] UN Doc A/59/710 (2005, pp. 7–8), UN Doc A/60/861 (2006), UN Doc A/62/890 (2008), UN Doc A/68/756 (2014), UN Doc A/69/779, UN Doc A/70/729 (2016).

between peacekeeping and prostitution, several studies point to the hypermasculine culture of military and peacekeeping missions (Enloe, 2000; Martin, 2005; Whitworth, 2004). These studies argue that an "ideology of manliness" amongst soldiers and peacekeepers produces tolerance for certain behavior, such as the purchasing of sexual services. Higate (2003, 2007) adds that the behavior of peacekeepers, their attitudes and the way in which they justify their behavior largely overlaps with sex tourists.[19] According to Higate (2003, p. 27), both internationals employed by peacekeeping missions and sex tourists "operate in conditions of sharp inequality and relative impunity, and therefore conduct themselves in ways they would never do within their home countries." Jennings and Nikolić-Ristanović (2009, pp. 20–21) likewise observe "that mission life itself was an excuse to act in ways that one would refrain from at home."

In an attempt to explain this difference in behavior, Higate (2007, p. 112) refers to the "privilege of temporality" that peacekeepers might experience. He argues that peacekeepers, and other men employed during peacekeeping missions, act while knowing that their time in the mission is temporary and that their involvement in prostitution (as well as sexual exploitation or abuse) will most likely not result in swift sanctions. This perspective is echoed in my research. Internationals employed in Kosovo suggested that it was easier to visit prostitutes on a mission than at home. When I asked for an explanation, an international police officer commented, "Sometimes when people live in another country, they search for the limits. Internationals based in Kosovo maybe take their car and drive fast and wild, something they would not do at home but they feel OK to do it here. People take advantage of that no friends and family are here. Mission life brings out the best of you… or the worst."[20] Here, the international police officer referred to the limited social control experienced while on a peacekeeping mission in order to explain why some internationals engage in behavior during missions that they would not engage in at home. With their family and friends far away, social control can only come from colleagues and, as outlined above, some studies suggest that there might be more tolerance for the buying of commercial sex amongst colleague soldiers (Enloe, 2000; Martin, 2005; Whitworth, 2004).

A more theoretically grounded explanation for the observed difference in behavior during missions can be derived from Mikhail Bakhtin's concept of "the second life of people" (1984). Bakhtin (1984, p. 6) describes how societies in medieval European countries "built a second world and a second life outside officialdom, a world in which all medieval people participated more or less, in which they lived during a given time of the year." In medieval times, Bakhtin argues, this second life was lived during carnival. The carnival created an alternative social space in which freedom and abundance ruled. All people were equal during this fragment of time, although in ordinary life they

---

[19] The link between prostitution in the context of a peacekeeping mission and sex tourism will be further explored in Sect. 4.2.1.

[20] Interview with UNM1, May 2, 2013.

were most clearly not. They could abandon their ranks and "escape from the usual official way of life" (Bakhtin, 1984, p. 8) because during carnival, everyday constraints were dismissed. During the carnival, people were free to behave as they pleased.

In his book *Cultural Criminology and the Carnival of Crime*, Presdee (2000) applies the notion of the second life to present-day transgressions. Presdee argues that an overly regulated (official) world has provoked a widespread desire to disregard rules and regulations. As a consequence, people engage in extreme, transgressive forms of pleasure such as joyriding, street crime and reality entertainment with real violence and real crime. Such contemporary transgressive behavior, however, does not fit in the official "first world." It emanates from the second life of people. In this irrational second life, people try to escape the rules of the rational legal world as they did during the carnival. However, as Presdee (2000, p. 46) questions, now that carnival has turned into a quasi-authorized event: "Where is 'the second life of the people' lived?" Presdee (2000, pp. 9, 81–85) suggests that expressions of the second life are no longer allowed during a specific time, as in the medieval days of carnival, but now reside in everyday life, where they emerge haphazardly. As an example, he mentions how people turn to the online world to secretly transgress by visiting websites about extreme violence and sex.

Psychologist and philosopher William James (Weenink, 2013; see also Collins, 2008) likewise recognized that people nowadays feel the need to dismiss the rules of the rational first world at times. He coined the term "moral holiday" in order to explain situations in which individuals allow themselves to enjoy the moment and temporarily let go of rules of conduct—in other words, to live their second life. On the one hand, Presdee (2000, p. 9) argues that people suspend conventional norms and enjoy disturbance, disruption and disorder in everyday life, in "the cracks and holes in the structures of official society." The moral holiday, on the other hand, suggests that people allow themselves to do so in an "enclave bounded in time and space" (Weenink, 2013, p. 1), in specific confined moments, after which they return to law and order. With this limitation in time, the concept of the moral holiday essentially returns to Bakhtin's interpretation of the carnival in earlier times, where rule breaking is confined to a certain time and place, and breaks away from Presdee's argument that transgressions can arise anywhere and at any time.

Examples of such enclaves bounded in time and space to which the concept of a moral holiday has been applied include joyous looting and vandalism during riots (Collins, 2008, p. 476, note 11; Martin, 1920) as well as "recreational" youth violence against strangers (Weenink, 2013). But it is applicable as well to mission life, which is characterized by being both temporally and spatially far away from home.

This perspective of mission life as a moral holiday in which the second life is lived is reflected in Jennings' observations amongst peacekeepers in Liberia and the Democratic Republic of the Congo (Jennings, 2014, p. 314). Jennings found that peacekeepers employed in these missions were sometimes "single for the mission." Echoing this idea, many women involved in prostitution in Kosovo told stories about encounters or long-term relationships with married internationals. Lorena, for instance, dated an American man who was employed at Bondsteel for several periods of a few months apiece. When they met in the bar where she was engaging in prostitution, he was wearing a wedding ring, but the ring was gone during his second mission in Kosovo; he also denied ever being married. Lorena's best friend asked several of the American man's colleagues if they knew about his marital status. All confirmed that he was "married back home."[21]

Mission life "allows" for such a suspension of conventional norms, for living a second life, because the peacekeepers and other internationals find themselves in what has been analyzed by anthropologists as a liminal phase. The concept of liminality was first developed by Belgian anthropologist Van Gennep (1960) and later taken up by anthropologist Turner (1969). In these initial works, liminality referred to the ambiguous condition people, especially in small-scale societies, find themselves in when in the midst of rites of passage or transition rituals, such as the initiation of youngsters into adult life. According to van Gennep, rites of passage consist of three phases: separation, liminality and aggregation. After leaving one group in the first stage, people find themselves in an ambiguous liminal phase of detachment before entering another group. As Turner (1969, p. 95) explains, a person in this liminal phase is "neither here nor there; they are betwixt and between the positions assigned and arrayed by law, custom, convention, and ceremonial." In the third phase, people are once again in a relatively stable position and are therefore expected to behave according to certain norms and standards. They integrate again into a structure with rules, whereas liminality can be seen as an "anti-structure."

The context here significantly differs from that of rituals in a small-scale society, but international peacekeepers, UN staff, diplomats and relief workers do seem to find themselves in a similar phase of liminality while working in peacekeeping missions in Kosovo. They are not at home, but not truly part of the society they find themselves in during a mission. Away from the scrutiny of their family and friends (and partially of the law, as will be argued in Sect. 4.1.2), this liminality creates freedom, which is at the heart of the idea of the second life. This feeling of freedom was quite literally expressed by an American legal advisor employed in Kosovo, who closed our conversation with the words, "I told you something about myself, but don't internationals always recreate themselves? [Laughing] So it's all like garbage, right?"[22] With this remark, the American legal advisor illustrated that, while on a mission, he felt that he could temporarily behave and be as he pleased.

[21] Interview with Rita, May 28, 2013.

[22] Interview with HTE2, October 24, 2013.

Fig. 4.3 Sign of Kosovo Force

4.1.2 UN Regulation of Prostitution during Peacekeeping Missions

The UN's response to the engagement of international employees in prostitution has become stricter throughout the years.[23] There was no coordinated legal reaction to or policy for such instances during initial missions in the early 1990s (i.e., in Mozambique and Bosnia and Herzegovina). This resulted in ad hoc reactions by UN officials, who largely condoned the behavior (Simic, 2012, pp. 39–69). One example of such a reaction can be found in the statement of the head of the UN Mission in Cambodia in 1993, who dismissed critique that peacekeepers were boosting the local sex industry by saying that "boys will be boys" (Whitworth, 2004, pp. 13, 17).

Yet the sexual escapades of UN personnel started to threaten the reputation of the UN at large (Simic, 2012; Whitworth, 2004). In 2003, the UN therefore attempted to regulate the sexual activity of their staff through the promulgation of the "Bulletin on Special Measures for Protection from Sexual Exploitation and Sexual Abuse." Although these special measures attempt to prevent and address sexual exploitation and abuse, they also include the regulation of prostitution and sexual relationships between "all staff of the UN, including staff of separately administered organs and programmes of the UN" and the local population.[24] In line with the abolitionist rhetoric, the special measures explicitly define prostitution as a manifestation of sexual exploitation. The bulletin states that the "exchange of money, employment, goods or services for sex, including sexual favours or other forms of humiliating, degrading or exploitative behavior, is prohibited."[25] Furthermore, sexual relationships with beneficiaries of assistance are "strongly discouraged."[26] Such relationships are believed to be "based on inherently unequal power dynamics." Therefore, they are said to "undermine the credibility and integrity of the work of the UN" (See footnote 25).

In 2004, the UN invited Prince Zeid Ra'ad Zeid Al-Hussein, Jordan's ambassador to the UN, to analyze sexual exploitation and abuse by UN peacekeeping personnel. The critical report that he published 1 year later became known as the Zeid Report.[27] The Zeid Report (UN, 2005, p. 8) concluded that "the reality of prostitution and other sexual exploitation in a peacekeeping context is profoundly disturbing to many because the UN has been mandated to enter into a broken society to help it, not to breach the trust placed in it by the local population." One of the key recommendations of the Zeid Report was that the UN should apply the rules of the special measures to all categories of UN peacekeeping personnel.[28] The General

[23] See Simic (2012, pp. 39–69) for an overview of the official UN responses to prostitution during peacekeeping missions.

[24] ST/SGB/2003/13. UN Secretariat (October 9, 2003).

[25] ST/SGB/2003/13. UN Secretariat (October 9, 2003, pp. 1–2).

[26] As outlined above, beneficiaries of assistance refer to the local population in the host country, including refugees.

[27] UN (March 24, 2005).

[28] UN Doc A/59/710 (2005, p. 4).

Assembly of the UN adopted this recommendation and broadened the reach of the zero-tolerance policy toward prostitution (and other sexual activities with local people) to include civilian police, military observers, members of national contingents, UN volunteers, consultants and individual contractors (Jennings, 2008, p. 15; Simic, 2012, p. 68). By doing so, the UN confirmed that they considered prostitution in the context of peacekeeping missions to be sexual exploitation.

The formal code of conduct developed by the UN Mission in Kosovo with regard to prostitution went a step further. UN as well as KFOR employees were not only forbidden to engage in prostitution, but premises where prostitution might take place were also out of bounds. UNMIK listed bars, brothels, strip clubs and nightclubs in which women were allegedly involved in prostitution in their "UNMIK Directive for Off Limits Premises." This off-limits list was constantly updated during its existence.[29] UNMIK stated that the off-limits list was "based on suspicion of prostitution (not necessarily with trafficked women) in such establishments that are fronted as legitimate businesses [...]. As a precautionary measure UNMIK staff are barred from visiting these premises that may be involved in the sex-industry."[30] Employees risked administrative and disciplinary actions if they did not comply with the directive.[31] The rationale behind this was that "by frequenting bars, brothels, strip clubs and night clubs, international representatives and by default their organization are condoning and supporting the sexual exploitation and slavery of women and contributing to the profits of organized crime."[32] With this statement, the UN Mission in Kosovo unilaterally depicted the Kosovar prostitution business in terms of exploitation, slavery and organized crime. They thus stigmatized the whole industry and, as will be argued in more detail later, left no room to consider engagement in prostitution in other terms than those of exploitation and victimization.

Paradoxically, the off-limits list was also being used by internationals in search of commercial sex. On the online forum mentioned above, peacekeepers recommended the list to those in search of sexual services:

> Search for "UNMIK Off-Limits Premises" Kosovo, or something like that. Anyway, if the UN is telling its people it's a NO GO Zone, you can bet it's the type of place you are looking for. Good list for Kosovo overall, but I was only in Pristina, downtown area, and didn't have a lot of free time to venture outside of town. [...] There were a half a dozen other places listed on the UNMIK list that were maybe a 20–25 min cab ride from downtown Pristina, I didn't have time to try them, hope you all have more luck. That list is the only item I found regarding establishments.[33]

---

[29] For an example of what the UNMIK Directive for Off Limits Premises looked like in March 2005, see UNMIK (January 31, 2005).

[30] UN Interim Administration Mission in Kosovo (2004, p. 17).

[31] The UN peacekeeping missions in Côte d'Ivoire, Liberia, the Democratic Republic of the Congo, Ethiopia, and Timor-Leste have also developed lists of no-go areas and premises. These places are allegedly frequented by women involved in prostitution and off-limits to UN personnel (Deen, 2005).

[32] UNMIK (January 31, 2005).

[33] Forum post, http://forum.cityxguide.com/topic/other-areas-67, accessed December 16, 2013.

Thus, the off-limits list in Kosovo, at best, did not completely reach its goal. Its dissemination was partially counter-effective, as it turned into a guide for some. The regulation of sexual abuse and sexual exploitation by the UN, which encompasses prostitution due to the conflation of prostitution and sexual exploitation, has been criticized for more than such questionable side effects. As outlined in the next section, some academics embrace the zero-tolerance policy of the UN toward prostitution, while others strongly critique it.

4.1.3 Evaluation of the UN's Zero-Tolerance Policy

Fig. 4.4 Skyline of Pristina

Sociologist Higate (2003, 2007); Higate & Henry, 2004) conducted empirical research on prostitution in the context of peacekeeping missions and is one of the most prominent advocates of the UN's regulation. Higate analyzed the peacekeepers' perspective on prostitution in the Democratic Republic of the Congo and Sierra Leone. His study did not include women involved in prostitution during these missions, but he found it "difficult to imagine that they are able to exercise any real choice about the ways in which their bodies can become units of sexual exchange" (Higate, 2003, p. 22). According to Higate (2007, p. 108), women only engage in prostitution in the context of peacekeeping missions because their possibilities to make ends meet are limited. He argues that peacekeepers, who pay for sex with local women, engage in an exploitative activity that springs from the stark inequalities between both parties (Higate, 2003, pp. 21–22). He defines this activity as a violation of human rights that undermines the overall credibility and effectiveness of peacekeeping missions. Higate's argument is largely shared by Sarah Martin (2005, pp. 1, 24), who conducted research amongst peacekeepers in Liberia and Haiti and defines women's bodies in these sites as "the only material asset they have to trade." She argues that "the difference in economic power between UN peacekeepers and local women makes it unlikely that there is any real choice in the relationship for the women involved" (Martin, 2005, p. 24). Both Higate and Martin therefore fully support the zero-tolerance policy of the UN and the conflation of sexual exploitation with prostitution that it entails. They also agree that the policy should become even stricter. Higate (2003, pp. 8, 60) would like to remove any "grey areas" that allow one to define prostitution as bona fide relationships and circumvent the rules. One example of such a "grey area" seems to be that the special measures strongly discourage sexual relationships, as opposed to blankly prohibiting them (as is the case with prostitution). Martin (2005, p. 27) suggests that standards similar to those of the UN should apply to militaries around the world that are not UN peacekeeping troops (e.g., peacekeeping troops of the African Union mission in Sudan).

While both studies provide valuable insight into peacekeepers' perspectives on prostitution, three points of critique can be made. First, both researchers accept the definition of prostitution as sexual exploitation. It is a line of thought that strongly echoes the abolitionist rhetoric (outlined in Chap. 2; see also Otto, 2007, p. 5; Simic, 2012, p. 55), which holds that free choice in prostitution is non-existent and irrelevant. Such a definition of prostitution makes it impossible to view local women involved as anything other than victims (Henry, 2013, pp. 132–33). It leaves no room to distinguish between "sex that is abusive, and sex that is labour, pleasure, survival, comfort, experimental or love" (Otto, 2007, p. 57). Thus—the second point—the studies condemn prostitution. Yet it remains unclear how further limiting the choices of these women, by prohibiting peacekeepers from being their clients, would improve their situation. Third, women involved in prostitution are portrayed as mere victims—a portrayal based on assumptions, as neither Higate nor Martin included women involved in prostitution in their research. As put forward by Zhang (2009) and Weitzer (2005) in their critical review of academic on sex trafficking, imagination contaminates knowledge.

Various studies have taken up the first two points of critique. Simic (2012) and Otto (2007) put forward that the UN fail to distinguish between consensual forms of sexual interaction, on the one hand, and sexual misconduct, on the other. Drawing on qualitative research in Bosnia and Herzegovina, Simic (2012, p. 167) argues that the definition of prostitution as sexual exploitation is over-exclusive and overprotective. She criticizes the definition for assuming, first of all, that all sexual activities between peacekeepers and local women have negative consequences and, second, that women lack the agency to make an informed decision about whether or not to be involved in prostitution with peacekeepers. In her theoretical work, Otto (2007, p. 35) goes one step further in arguing that the zero-tolerance policy toward prostitution 'denies women's sexual agency and will deprive many poor women of their livelihood.' This point is echoed by Jennings (2008, 2014, 2015), who conducted empirical research during peacekeeping missions in Haiti, Liberia and the Democratic Republic of the Congo. Jennings (2015, pp. 305–307) suggests that local women can try to benefit from the economic activity that occurs alongside a peacekeeping mission (i.e., the peacekeeping economy) by engaging in sex work. She argues that the zero-tolerance policy of the UN does not leave any space to acknowledge such agency to women. By removing a source of income upon which local women can depend in the context of peacekeeping missions, Jennings (2008, p. 64) suggests that "the zero-tolerance policy may make some people's lives more precarious." Moreover, Otto (2007, p. 35) worries that the policy will force prostitution underground, "making it more dangerous and increasing the risk of exploitation and even death." These alleged negative consequences of the zero-tolerance policy make Jennings (2014, p. 324) suggest that the policy was developed in order to safeguard the reputation of UN peacekeeping missions, instead of for the benefit of local people. She calls upon the UN to acknowledge and critically assess the direct socioeconomic impacts of their overall presence so that prostitution can be seen as a symptom of the larger political economy, instead of the consequence of some individual actors' behavior that can be dismissed (Jennings & Nikolić-Ristanović, 2009). Otto (2007, p. 57) argues in favor of the revision of the zero-tolerance policy "that is focussed on guaranteeing that those women involved in transactional sex enjoy safe and healthy working conditions and receive adequate remuneration, and ensuring that the stigma that often attaches to this work is actively challenged."

The latter studies first and foremost emphasize the importance of acknowledging as agents local women involved in prostitution in the context of peacekeeping missions. This stance substantially differs from the standpoint adopted by Higate and Martin, who identify these women as victims in need of protection. It is remarkable that these starkly opposing views, however, do not spring from qualitative research on the women at the center of this debate: those who are involved in prostitution in the peacekeeping context. With the exception of the later studies of Jennings (2014, 2015), who included several interviews with sex workers and observations in nightclubs in her research, all studies are based on interaction with peacekeepers and, in the case of Simic (2012), with Bosnian women who have no experience with prostitution.[34] Higate and Henry (2004, p. 495) note that "in the absence of data illuminating the everyday experiences of local women/men and their gendered relations with male peacekeepers, it is not possible to comment with any confidence on the experience of local women's security, even for those involved in prostitution."

In evaluating the impact of peacekeepers on post-war prostitution businesses, and the relevant UN policy in particular, researchers therefore appear to rely on the two dominant discourses on prostitution. Higate and Martin use arguments from the abo-

[34] Simic (2012, p. 6) argues that she "did not undertake empirical research into Bosnian women's experiences with prostitution primarily because of the difficulties involved in locating interviewees, since the Bosnian women prostitutes who worked during UNMIBH […] remain largely invisible because prostitution is illegal in BH." A plethora of studies have been conducted in countries where prostitution is illegal, including this one (see also Trotter, 2008). The illegality of prostitution in itself thus should not hamper the possibility of conducting ethnographic research amongst women involved in prostitution.

litionist rhetoric, while Simic and Otto refer to arguments posed by pro-sex-work scholars. Both discourses are functional in arguing for amendments to the zero-tolerance policy of the UN, whether in favor of tightening it or loosening it, but it remains to be seen if they do justice to the lived experience of women involved in prostitution in the context of peacekeeping missions. Do local women truly benefit from a prohibition of commercial sexual relationships with internationals, as suggested by Higate (2003, 2007)? Or does banning prostitution "push it underground" and "place women in danger," as suggested by Simic (2012), p. 163; see also Otto, 2007, p. 35)? I aim to contribute to filling that knowledge gap in the following chapters, which describe the lives of both international and local women involved in prostitution in Kosovo during the peacekeeping mission. Based on these ethnographic insights, I'll reflect on the zero-tolerance policy in the conclusion of this book.

4.1.4 Immunity or Impunity?

Despite the questionable aspects of the UN's zero-tolerance policy toward their employees' engagement in prostitution, internationals do not always face decisive action after breaching these rules. This does not only hold for those who purchase commercial sexual intercourse, but also for those who engage in sexual misconduct that is broadly acknowledged as such (e.g., rape, human trafficking for forced prostitution). Peacekeepers and other UN personnel occasionally face disciplinary actions, such as repatriation and the termination of working contracts, but criminal prosecutions remain rare (see also Higate, 2007; Simic, 2012).[35] When human trafficking for sexual purposes was allegedly at its height in the first few years after the war in Kosovo, Amnesty International (2004, p. 45), for instance, found that prior to 2002, 57 UNMIK police officers had been dismissed or repatriated. This included ten officers that faced allegations related to human trafficking. UNMIK police claimed that all of these officers would be disciplined or prosecuted in their home countries, but it could not be confirmed if this had actually occurred for any of them. Additionally, and more recently, the aforementioned international police officer who was caught having sexual intercourse with an alleged victim of trafficking was fired from the EULEX mission. However, unlike the local clients who were present in the hotel during the police raid, he was not indicted. The special prosecutor in charge of this case explained, "He got fired and sent home. Nothing else. Because of his immunity."[36]

[35] UN Doc A/59/710 (2005), pp. 7–8), UN Doc A/60/861 (2006), UN Doc A/62/890 (2008), UN Doc A/68/756 (2014), UN Doc A/69/779, UN Doc A/70/729 (2016).

[36] Interview with EUL4, May 2, 2015.

Immunity can hamper prosecution and lead to impunity of internationals (see also Higate, 2007; Simic, 2012).[37] The main purpose of granting immunity is to protect employees "against the unilateral interference by the individual government of the state in which they are located" (Nowicki, 2000, p. 8).[38] In Kosovo, UNMIK, KFOR and EULEX personnel all enjoy a form of immunity. This immunity varies from full immunity, whereby people are fully protected from host-state jurisdiction, to functional immunity, which ensures that people benefit from immunity with regard to acts performed in their official capacity or in the course of a mission.[39] Consequently, internationals are primarily subject to the criminal and disciplinary jurisdiction of the sending states (i.e., their home states). In theory, the immunity of internationals can be waived by the Special Representative of the Secretary-General (or by the High Representative in Brussels, in the case of EULEX personnel).[40] In a UN working paper on the accountability of international personnel taking part in peace support operations (Hampson, 2005, pp. 10, 15), however, it is noted that waiving the immunity of alleged perpetrators is rare (even if the act seems to be outside the scope of immunity) and doing so does not always end in prosecution. Moreover, Hampson (2005, pp. 15–16) concludes that effective exercise of criminal jurisdiction by home countries is often hampered by insufficient investigations, as well as by convictions that do not adequately reflect the seriousness of what has taken place. As a result, internationals employed by peacekeeping missions are rarely subject to criminal proceedings (see also Nowicki, 2000). Their working contracts might be terminated, but some are hired at other missions after being repatriated.[41]

[37] See, for instance, "Special Report No. 1 on the compatibility with recognized international standards of UNMIK Regulation No. 2000/47 on the Status, Privileges and Immunities of KFOR and UNMIK and Their Personnel in Kosovo", August 18, 2000, where the following is stated on page 7: "The Ombudsperson observes that the object and purpose of Regulation 2000/47 is to guarantee, by operation of law, broad immunity for the international civilian and security presences and for their international and local personnel. The Ombudsperson further observes that this grant of immunity creates an insurmountable procedural bar to any legal process in any territory at any time to KFOR and UNMIK as institutions, as well as to their property, funds and assets (Sections 2.1 and 3.1 of the Regulation, respectively) to locally recruited KFOR personnel in respect of words spoken and acts performed by them in carrying out tasks exclusively related to their services to KFOR (Section 2.3 of the Regulation) and to international and locally recruited UNMIK personnel in respect of all acts performed by them in their official capacity (Section 3.3 of the Regulation)."

[38] The necessity of immunity in the first years after the war was disputable in the case of Kosovo, since the UN themselves acted as a surrogate state in these years (Nowicki, 2000, p. 8; Hampson, 2005, p. 10). UNMIK, KFOR, and EULEX personnel were guaranteed broad immunity nonetheless.

[39] For a description of the immunity enjoyed by EULEX, see http://www.eulex-kosovo.eu/?page=2,23, accessed November 28, 2017. For a description of the immunity enjoyed by UNMIK and KFOR, see UNMIK (August 18, 2000).

[40] For an example of a notification of a request by local authorities in Kosovo to waive the immunity of a former EULEX staff member, see http://www.eulex-kosovo.eu/?page=2,10,341, accessed November 28, 2017.

[41] Interview with SUNM, the spouse of a UN employee who served in UN missions worldwide (including Kosovo, Timor-Leste, Haiti, and Liberia). See also UN Doc E/CN.4/Sub.2/2005/42 (2005, p. 20), where it is recommended that personnel found responsible for serious misconduct should not be employed in other peace support operations.

Irrespective of the question of whether clients of prostitution should face criminal proceedings, these events favor the positions of internationals over locals and create a sense of impunity with regard to the former. Such impunity is especially undesirable when it comes to internationals involved in sexual misconduct in the context of peacekeeping missions that is broadly accepted as such, including rape and human trafficking for forced prostitution.

Thus far in this section, I have investigated internationals' involvement in prostitution. However, as outlined in the beginning of this chapter, internationals that settled down in Kosovo after the war were only one of three main categories of clients as identified by women servicing them in post-war Kosovo. The next two sections are dedicated to two other sets of clients that constituted the demand of the prostitution business; to begin with: Kosovo Albanians who are living abroad.

4.2 "Schatzis" on a (Moral) Holiday

One day in the midst of summer, I was enjoying a coffee with a friend on a crowded terrace in Pristina. The tables around us were occupied by so-called "schatzis," the name teasingly given to people from the Kosovar Albanian diaspora; during the holidays they come back to Kosovo in large numbers. The waiter who was serving us knew my friend, and when he understood that I was doing a study on the prostitution business, he blushingly told us that a week before, he had been to a bar where the waitresses were also involved in prostitution. "My cousin came back from Switzerland and invited me and some other friends to this bar where women, you know… He said, 'Let's enjoy. I'm here for a few weeks. I'll pay! You know how the schatzis are. Eat, drink, party every day.'"[42]

A substantial number of people migrated from Kosovo in the 1960s, primarily young men with limited education who resettled in Germany and Switzerland as guest workers in search of temporary work. Migration from Kosovo further increased when tens of thousands of Albanians lost their jobs after Milošević came to power.[43] In this period, between 1989 and 1997, it was not only young men with limited education who migrated, but highly educated men as well. They went to Western Europe in order to search for employment and escape the Yugoslav military service (Dahinden, 2005; Vathi & Black, 2007). A third wave of emigration followed the outbreak of the Kosovo War. Between 1998 and 1999, more than 800,000 people fled Kosovo. A substantial part, but not all, of this group returned to Kosovo in the aftermath of the war; emigration continued after 1999, and it still happens today. These latter immigrants initially consisted of people who migrated for the goal of post-war family unification. Nowadays the group of emigrants is primarily composed of irregular or (temporary) legal migrants, the latter of which are often highly skilled and educated people who migrate through study or work

[42] Informal conversation with WAI1 in Pristina, July 1, 2011.

[43] See Sect. 3.1.1 for a description of the reasons why these Kosovo Albanians lost their jobs when Milošević rose to power.

arrangements (Dahinden, 2005; UNDP Kosovo, 2014; Vathi & Black, 2007). According to the Statistical Office of Kosovo, an estimated total of 703,978 Kosovars lived abroad in April 2011. This number consists of people that have migrated from Kosovo, as well as children born outside of Kosovo among the emigrant community (UNDP Kosovo, 2014).

These so-called "schatzis," or people from the diaspora, return to Kosovo in large numbers during holidays. They cause peak seasons in the sex industry in July and August, as well as in the weeks before and after the New Year. "I usually have clients from neighboring villages but also from the diaspora. I'm always happy with clients from diaspora. They respect you, sit and drink with you and give you tips. They also come in winter now. Not only in summer. That is really good for us," a Bulgarian woman involved in prostitution in Kosovo told me.[44] She and the majority of the others engaged in prostitution emphasized that they earned the most money from the schatzis nowadays, even though schatzis are not present year-round. The women explained that men from the diaspora tend to come to the bars with their (male) friends and family members and do not worry about the amount of money they spend during their holidays. Others suggested that schatzis are generous toward them because they pity their homeland: "The diaspora is more sensitive than the local clients. They respect us more. We have good conversations. We really talk. They also know we have suffered a lot. They are afraid that the daughters that are left behind have to do this kind of work. […] They give us five to ten euros of tips and give me more."[45] The diaspora accounts for such a large share of the women's income of the women that it made my respondent Elira state, during one of our weekly chats in the bar where she was working, "If the diaspora does not exist, then we do not exist" (See footnote 45).

Some women who otherwise work in Macedonia or Albania anticipate the presence of the diaspora and come to work in Kosovo during the holiday seasons. "I only stay here for the high season," explained Dea from Albania when interviewed in a bar some weeks before the New Year.[46] Sofija from Ukraine explained that she wanted to visit her daughter back home during the holidays, but her boss wanted her to stay "because of the busy periods."[47] Thus, there tend to be both more clients and more women involved in prostitution during the summer and winter holidays.

4.2.1 *Sex Tourism as an (Unintended) Consequence of Peacekeeping Missions?*

Jennings (2010) postulates that sex industries in the context of peacekeeping missions are prone to become (popular) destinations for sex tourists. She argues that prostitution has become a "survival or livelihood strategy" for some women in

[44] Interview with Aleksandra, December 2, 2011.

[45] Interview with Elira, March 16, 2013.

[46] Interview with Dea, December 2, 2011.

[47] Interview with Sofija, January 16, 2014.

countries emerging from a peacekeeping mission (idem, p. 235). These women are involved in prostitution businesses attuned to the needs of clients from abroad as a legacy of peacekeeping missions. Jennings, furthermore, observes that national authorities and international donors adopt pro-tourism policies in an attempt to stimulate the countries' economic growth—for example, this has been the case in Sierra Leone. She suggests that this development strategy might cause states to refrain from taking action against the sex industry. Taken together, these factors make Jennings (2015, p. 239) conclude that "a transformation of peacekeeping economies into sex tourism economies may be another long-term unintended consequence of peacekeeping missions."

At first glance, the behavior of some of the schatzis in Kosovo seems to confirm the potential for prostitution businesses to turn into sex tourism havens in the wake of peacekeeping missions. A closer look, however, challenges this suggestion—at least in the context of Kosovo. In my discussions with women involved in prostitution about the clients that they were serving, women never mentioned international clients other than those that were employed in Kosovo (i.e., peacekeepers, other UN and EULEX personnel, diplomats and relief workers) or were schatzis. Clift and Carter (2000, p. 6) define sex tourism as "travel for which the main motivation is to engage in commercial sexual relations." The clients of the women involved in prostitution in Kosovo never specifically come to Kosovo in order to engage in commercial sex; they arrive in Kosovo for other reasons, such as work or visiting family, and then engage in commercial sex. Clients from abroad, both internationals and schatzis, can thus only be seen as engaged in "sex in tourism" (idem, p. 9). Sex in tourism refers to sex as a byproduct of a journey. This difference is relevant, since the experience of women involved in prostitution in Kosovo suggests that people do not travel to Kosovo in order to engage in commercial sex. Kosovo, therefore, is not a sex tourism destination (yet), as the prostitution business is substantial as a byproduct of internationals' and schatzis' journeys at most.[48]

Of course it cannot be ruled out that my ethnographic research ended "too early" and that Kosovo will attract sex tourists in the future. Observations in premises that functioned as a meeting ground between women involved in prostitution and their clients, however, suggest that the Kosovar prostitution business will follow a different path. As will be outlined in more detail in the following section and chapters, the prostitution business nowadays largely seems to be targeted toward Kosovo Albanian men (both from the diaspora and living in Kosovo). For instance, bars engaged in the sex industry are often decorated with Albanian knickknacks, play traditional Albanian music and employ Albanian-speaking personnel. The overall atmosphere does not exude an international air at all. Therefore, the "comparative advantage" mentioned by Jennings (2010, p. 237)—that peacekeeping missions "generated a sex industry used to catering internationals"—can be largely dismissed.

[48] Jennings (2015, pp. 234–235) explicitly acknowledges the difference between "sex tourism" and "sex in tourism" as well. However, she argues that "there is a clear argument for suggesting that post-peacekeeping countries might be of particular interest to hard-core sex tourists" (idem, p. 237). I do not see that confirmed in Kosovo.

4.3 Local Clients

Peacekeepers have thus not been the only clients to instigate the expansion of the Kosovar prostitution business. Since its initial growth, clients of the sex industry in Kosovo have generally been more heterogeneous, including men from the international community, men from the diaspora and, as I will go into in this section, local men. Women involved in the prostitution business in Kosovo estimated that local men have made up the largest part of their clientele since the blossoming of the sex industry in the wake of the war.

The fact that Kosovar men are engaging in prostitution within relatively public premises in Kosovo is a new development. As outlined in the previous chapter, prostitution did occur before the war, but it used to be comparatively rare and hidden.[49] Two main reasons seem to have contributed to the increased local clientele. First, the "newness" of a public sex industry in Kosovo attracted local men. A police officer who had worked on human trafficking cases directly after the war explained: "You didn't see it before the war. Pretty girls dancing for you. Before the war you couldn't even imagine it. Maybe only in movies. Before the war, the system of occupation, the regime, didn't even let you think about that. The personal freedom was so limited. Even school was difficult. So you didn't think of that. […] It was something new. So everybody wanted to see it."[50] After the war, men simply did not have to make an effort to find an entertainment industry anymore (e.g., by traveling abroad or visiting more hidden brothels); they could find commercial sex offers all over Kosovo.

Second, many local men could suddenly afford to spend money on the sex industry in the wake of the war. As a Kosovar Albanian informant explained, "The years after the war were not the economically most challenging ones, with all the internationals spending money and the large amounts of international aid."[51] As outlined in Sect. 3.2.6, the arrival of the international community had a large economic impact. Inhabitants of Kosovo benefitted from the "peacekeeping economy" and remittances (UNDP, 2012).

Nowadays the Kosovar prostitution business cannot be imagined without the local clients that populate the establishments involved. The women that service these men noted that local clients differ in their attitudes vis-à-vis women involved in prostitution. Based on these descriptions, I have distinguished between three types of local clients of women engaged in prostitution in Kosovo. These emic types of clients differ from typologies of clientele in existing literature, which largely try to categorize clients' motivations for purchasing commercial sex. Vanwesenbeeck, De Graaf, Van Zessen, Straver, and Visser (1993), for example, differentiate between "the business client," "the adventurer," "the romantic," and "the misogynist." These

---

[49] Likewise, Whitworth (2004, p. 67) observed that prostitution could not be seen as a new phenomenon that had been brought to Cambodia as a consequence of the peacekeeping mission. However, she observed that there was a dramatic increase in prostitution during the peacekeeping mission and that it was much more open in nature then before the mission.

[50] Interview with KPO1, October 30, 2013.

[51] Informal conversation with RA1, September 25, 2013. The relative economic prosperity described is not a constant; Kosovo is currently one of the poorest areas of Europe.

categories of clients consider the purchasing of sex respectively as a commercial transaction, a way to deal with a sex addiction, a "girlfriend experience" in which the same woman is visited over a long period of time or, lastly, a possibility to exercise power over a sexual partner.[52] Since this research took as its point of departure the narratives of the women who are offering sexual services in Kosovo, I will not look into the personal reasons of clients for purchasing sex, and will depart from discussing the attitudes of local clients toward women engaged in prostitution as described by these women themselves.

Men can shift between the three defined categories. Therefore, these categories should not be seen as a rigid ordering of the clientele, but primarily as an insight into the spectrum of experiences that women have with men that visit establishments involved in the prostitution business. The categories apply to clients from the international community and the diaspora as well. Since the local clients make up the largest part of the clientele nowadays, however, the categories will be discussed here.

4.3.1 Those Looking for Commercial Sex

The first category of local clients consists of men that are looking for commercial sexual intercourse. As we were sitting at a table in the corner of a bar that primarily catered to local Roma men, an Albanian woman working there explained, "When you sit with a client, often they immediately ask to go somewhere. No conversation or anything. They ask you to go. We all know for what."[53] Women often complained about such directness of local clients. The majority of women did not like it if clients immediately asked for sexual services or started to have sexually suggestive conversations with them. Sofija from Ukraine, however, was an exception. She more than once mentioned that she was not interested in any communication with her clients: "I want to do my job quickly and then go on without losing much time by talking with a client or having sex for a long time. X [her boss] sometimes said, 'Sofija, take more time.' But I don't care."[54] Whether or not they employ small talk, the majority of local men visit establishments involved in the Kosovar sex industry with the objective of having sexual intercourse.

In line with international studies focusing on clients of prostitution, the group of clients looking for commercial sex seemed heterogeneous (Di Nicola, Cauduro, Lombardi, & Ruspini, 2009; Shiboleth, 2015). They were comprised of men of highly variable ages, educational backgrounds and occupations, and men in long-term relationships as well as singles.[55] However, this mixed local clientele did not necessarily mingle in the bars and clubs where they could meet women involved in

[52] See Flight and Hulshof (2009) as well as Zaitch and Staring (2009) for a critical analysis of the fourth ("misogynist") type in particular.

[53] Interview, April 14, 2013.

[54] Interview with Sofija, January 4, 2014.

[55] Observations and informal conversations with clients between 2011 and 2013.

prostitution. The premises that I visited in Kosovo either sought to attract relatively wealthy clients or seemingly less affluent ones. A group of young, prosperous-looking Kosovar Albanian men in suits and button-down shirts, for instance, enjoyed the pole-dance performance of a Moldovan woman in a club in a town close to the border of Albania. The young, beautiful woman had clearly invested time and money in her hair, makeup and dress. After the show, she joined the men on the soft red sofas; they bought her drinks and gave her tips. One man pulled her closer and started to touch her leg and arm.[56] A few kilometers down the road from the pole-dance club was an establishment that from the outside most closely resembled a large garage. Men from Kosovo and neighboring Albania made up the clientele. Most of them were wearing jeans; one group of men looked as if they just finished working on a construction site. They had dirt on their faces, hands and clothes, and one of them was dressed in the type of orange reflective vest often worn by construction workers. They were welcomed by a male singer who played traditional Albanian songs on a synthesizer. Some of the men started a traditional Albanian dance in front of the stage, forming an open circle and urging the women to join them. Until that point, the women had been sitting side by side behind a large table. One was doing her makeup while her colleague rested her head on the table between some empty cola bottles (See footnote 56). The latter observation illustrates that local clients of the post-war prostitution business in Kosovo did not primarily consist of the "nouveaux-riches," as suggested by Jennings and Nikolić-Ristanović (2009, p. 15), but men from all strata of society.

As will be outlined in more detail in Sect. 6.5.1, these clients usually did not have sexual intercourse with women in the premises where they met each other. The nightclubs, "musics" (large bars with live music are usually referred to as "musics" in Kosovo) and bars function as meeting grounds for women involved in prostitution and clients. If they come to an agreement on commercial sexual intercourse, a woman and her client either move to a hotel or an apartment.

4.3.2 *Those Finding Company*

A second group of local clients also visit bars and "musics," although they visit luxurious nightclubs to a much lesser extent. They differ from the first group of men in that these local clients do not necessarily seem to be looking for a sexual encounter. This rather substantial group predominantly consists of men above 50, but occasionally includes younger men as well. Like some of the clients studied in Italy by Cauduro, Nicola, Fonio, Nuvoloni, and Ruspini (2009, p. 52), these local clients primarily seek affection, comprehension and—I would like to add—company. When in a bar, they either invite the waitresses to sit and chat with them or they have a drink by themselves while looking around the bar. These clients are often the men populating bars with a sort of living-room-like atmosphere. These are bars with carpet on the

[56] Observations on December 6, 2011.

floor and tables surrounding a heater, with a dartboard and a television in the corner—they can be found all over Kosovo. The waitresses in these bars also engage in prostitution.[57] When clients order a drink, they can order a drink for the waitress as well. These drinks are more expensive, since clients are also paying for the companionship of the waitresses. Waitresses thus regularly sit with clients before making an agreement to have sexual intercourse. For this second type of client, however, companionship at the table seems to be the sole goal. The following observation in a bar is one of many examples of this kind of interaction—not necessarily sexual—between the women and their clients in these bars:

> Elira comes and sits with us. She immediately starts explaining about the older man with whom she had been sitting until now—he must have been in his 70s and was wearing the traditional white hat (*plis*). Elira says that he treats her very respectfully. He always tells her that he hopes that Elira will find a nice person. She mentions that she feels sorry for older people sometimes: "People always should treat older people with respect. This man is alone. His children live abroad. He comes to the bar sometimes to talk about his problems. But not very often." The two men at the next table are joking about Elira sitting with this old man. "Are you sitting with your father?" they ask her. The older man leaves quite quickly after Elira joins our conversation. When she sees that he is leaving, she stands up and greets him goodbye by giving him a hug. The man hugs her again and then leaves at a slow pace.[58]

In another bar, the television in the corner usually broadcast traditional Albanian music and dance, but the female owner switched the channel to a Turkish soap opera every evening. Whenever I entered the bar during the showing of the soap opera, a man in his 60s was watching the television from a table in the corner. He usually sat alone, although sometimes one of the waitresses joined him, and he normally left as soon as the soap opera was finished.[59] Thus, although the first and second types of clients largely visit the same premises, their objective is different: the second category of local clients in Kosovo is primarily looking for company.

4.3.3 Boyfriends

The third and last category of local clients that can be distinguished is that of the "boyfriends." Some local men from the first category (i.e., those looking for commercial sex) develop into the boyfriends of women involved in prostitution.[60] This happens to the extent that the overwhelming majority of the women who participated in this research mentioned being in a relationship. The nature of these relationships

[57] As will be outlined in more detail in the upcoming chapters, it is unusual for women to work as waitresses. Female waitresses in Kosovo are often involved in prostitution, although some trendy restaurants, nightclubs, and bars in the capital, Pristina, are notable exceptions to this unwritten rule: women work as waitresses and nothing else in these establishments.

[58] Observations on November 2, 2013.

[59] Observations on September 19, 2013, among other times.

[60] In some cases, bar owners or their family members (i.e., brothers or cousins) also develop into boyfriends.

differs substantially: some seem to be defined by the financial exploitation of the woman, while others counter such stereotypical images of relationships of women involved in prostitution, as the couples behave affectionately. Yet one feature does not necessarily preclude the other.

To start with the relationships in which financial exploitation seems to dominate: a plethora of studies examine such (financially) exploitative relationships between women involved in prostitution and their boyfriends (see, for instance, Hughes, 2000; Bullens & van Horn, 2000). Women engaged in prostitution are often characterized as victims of "loverboys" in discussions of their relationships. The term "loverboy" came into use in the Netherlands in the 1990s and is increasingly being used internationally in order to describe a working method aimed at the commercial sexual exploitation of women and girls. Characteristic of the technique of a loverboy is the means of recruitment and use of "grooming." Men and boys establish contact with a victim, seducing and charming her through (the promise of) a loving relationship, which is aimed at her exploitation in the prostitution business or another industry (Bovenkerk, Van San, Boone, Boekhout van Solinge, & Korf, 2006; Verwijs, Mein, Goderie, Harreveld, & Jansma, 2011).

A Serbian woman who had recently quit her work in the sex industry in Kosovo explained the relationships of her former colleagues with their boyfriends in similar terms: "Usually they have boyfriends who say that they will marry them, but never do and take their money in the meantime."[61] Women indeed shared various experiences with boyfriends who resembled loverboys: they mentioned how their boyfriends promised that they would be together in the future while taking large parts of their earnings in the prostitution business for months or years in a row. Vera's story is one such example:

> "A few months ago I met my boyfriend and he moved in with me. We had a good life together in Tirana." Vera tells me she is a singer, while she introduces her boyfriend as a manager of singers. After some months in Tirana, Vera's boyfriend arranged a job for her in a bar in Macedonia: "My boyfriend didn't work when I was in Macedonia. He arranged the job." Now her boyfriend has arranged a job for Vera in a bar in Kosovo. She stays in the bar for the "high season," when the diaspora is in the country, while her boyfriend lives in her flat in Tirana. "My boyfriend always helps me find a job. He also arranged the contract with this bar owner. The salary is very good! He takes the salary and arranges everything. Sometimes my boyfriend gives me money. If I need something, I call him. [...] He doesn't use me. He isn't the type."[62]

Vera mentioned that her Kosovo Albanian boyfriend had explained that they could live together in Tirana again after her job in Macedonia had finished. He then suggested that she also go to Kosovo. When we met, Vera was unsure as to how long she was going to work in the Kosovar prostitution business; her boyfriend made these decisions for her. The fact that her boyfriend was taking the money that she earned in the sex industry while promising her a future together closely resembled the working method of a loverboy.

---

[61] Interview with Mira, December 8, 2011.

[62] Interview with Vera, December 2, 2011. Vera is involved in prostitution; however, she preferred to present herself as a singer.

At the same time, these women's relationships with local boyfriends also differ from the traditional working methods of a loverboy on two points. The overwhelming majority of the women with local boyfriends in Kosovo had already been engaged in prostitution before they had a relationship. Women rarely entered the sex industry as a consequence of these relationships, whereas loverboys traditionally push women into the prostitution business (Bovenkerk et al., 2006; Verwijs et al., 2011). In the Kosovo case, women started to share the money that they had already earned with their boyfriends. Some women gave their earnings to their boyfriends directly, as Vera explained. Other boyfriends received money in exchange for services. For instance, this was the case for Vlora:

> Vlora, 20, from Albania was playing with her one-year-old son in the bar before it opened. Her boyfriend walked in; he is the brother of the bar owner. "The aunt of my boyfriend takes care of my son when I have to work. I earn around 300 euro per month and pay 200 euro for them to take care of him." Vlora teasingly stuck out her tongue at her son as he went into her boyfriend's car, and her working day started.[63]

A second difference from the traditional working method of a loverboy is that a substantial number of women were aware of the fact that their boyfriends were married men with families. Julia has such a Kosovar Albanian boyfriend: "He doesn't live with me because he has a family."[64] Aleksandra is in a long-term relationship with the married owner of the bar where she works[65]; Tanya has been dating the married cousin of her bar's owner for years, and 23-year-old Yana from Bulgaria told me, "I have had a Kosovar boyfriend for 4 years now. He has a wife and children, but I love him. […] We met in the bar. He was a client first."[66] These women do not have the illusion that their boyfriends will leave their families for them. Women experience a sense of being outcasts due to their involvement in prostitution. They might dream of having a traditional family, but at the same time they settle for the position of mistresses since this seems more realistic. These boyfriends do not necessarily promise a shared future, but shared moments and having someone to love. "Loverboys" are thus not exactly the issue here—rather, these are abusive relationships.

The fact that boyfriends benefit financially and sexually (i.e., free sex without a condom) does not mean that the relationships cannot fulfill any (emotional) desire of the women involved (see also Bovenkerk et al., 2006). Tanya from Moldova, for instance, was critical of the behavior of her boyfriend at times, but said, "I need to be with someone" in the empty and rather lonely life that she felt she was living in Kosovo.[67] The women mentioned it was important to have someone to love and emotionally engage with; they defined these relationships as serious commitments.

---

[63] Interview with Vlora, November 17, 2011.

[64] Interview with Julia, November 30, 2011.

[65] Interview with Aleksandra, December 2, 2011.

[66] Interview with Tanya, November 23, 2011, and interview with Yana, November 23, 2011.

[67] Interview with Tanya, November 23, 2011.

At the same time, some women are involved in relationships that contradict more stereotypical images of associations between women engaged in prostitution and their boyfriends dominated by financial exploitation and abuse. These relationships instead appear affectionate, and the women and their boyfriends both speak about each other tenderly. Inga from Moldova and Mentor from Kosovo were involved in such a relationship. They had become acquainted in the bar where Inga was working, and Mentor was a regular client initially. However, they started to fall in love and told each other about these feelings after some meetings. Inga and Mentor continued meeting in the bar; the bar owner did not allow them to meet somewhere else because he did not want to lose income over their sexual encounters. Since Inga worked in a high-class bar, clients normally paid 100 euro for sexual intercourse. These earnings were split between the bar owner and the woman who had met up with a client. Mentor stated the following about these proceedings: "Inga told me that she loved me and that for her it wasn't a problem, but I had to pay because she was working at the bar of another person. I was always thinking that her boss was forcing her to use me."[68] Inga and Mentor agreed that he would only pay 50 euro every time they met. Inga paid the other 50 euro, but she would eventually get that money back as her earnings. Mentor wanted the other women in the bar to know that their relationship was sincere: "I have given her money to buy clothes, too, or something else, in order to make the other girls understand that I wasn't just sexually using her but that we loved each other" (See footnote 68). Eventually, Inga had to go back to Moldova, and Mentor stayed in Kosovo with his wife and two children. Months after her departure, the couple was still in contact, and Mentor emphasized that his feelings had not changed.

Inga was aware of Mentor's marital status and thus not necessarily engaged in the love affair with the plan of building a shared future. Yet Inga and women in similar relationships became involved in these relationships for a number of other reasons. In her study of the experiences of romance and relationships of Filipinas trafficked to U.S. military club areas in South Korea, Yea (2005, p. 465) observes that these reasons include emotional and financial support, practical benefits (i.e., assistance in meeting daily needs such as food and clothes) and provision of freedom, as boyfriends buy them drinks and time while at work. These reasons are echoed in the accounts of women in Kosovo who discussed their relationships with me. As outlined above, Inga enjoyed the time that she could spend with Mentor while at work; it meant that she had to spend less time with other clients. Lorena mentioned that her Kosovar boyfriend helped her financially by paying rent for her apartment.[69] Yet women put most emphasis on the emotional satisfaction that these relationships provided. Women who are engaged in prostitution in Kosovo tend to have limited contacts outside the sex industry. They long for emotional engagement with a boyfriend (and friends) that can make them feel like a regular person other than a (heavily stigmatized) prostitute.[70] Lorena, for instance, especially treasured

[68] Interview with SP1, February 5, 2013.

[69] Informal conversation with Lorena, June 2, 2013.

[70] See Sect. 6.6.2 on the stigma encountered by Kosovar women engaged in prostitution.

the day-to-day moments with her boyfriend during which they picnicked beside the river, fell asleep together or played card games.[71] And Shqipe valued the fact that she could always count on her boyfriend: "He is married. Albanian men never leave their wife. But I can see him whenever I want. Even if I call him in the middle of the night, he will come if I need him."[72]

Women do speak about the downside of their relationships as well. Boyfriends often limit their freedom of movement. Shqipe did not visit any bars except for the one where she was working, since her boyfriend would not like it; he called to check her whereabouts almost every hour.[73] Likewise, Lorena did not drink coffee outside her apartment or the bar where she was working, since her boyfriend did not want her to.[74] Women also disliked the violence that boyfriends could sometimes use against them. In line with the stories of some other women, Lorena shared that her boyfriend hit her at times. She recalled, 'I never want that to happen again. I have been through enough violence in the past. But the next day, my boyfriend was really sweet. I forgave him. He is not perfect, but I need someone. Everybody needs someone."[75] Those in relationships that do not seem to be dominated by (financial) exploitation thus know their shortcomings as well. The women involved in them are not oblivious to these negative aspects (i.e., their status as a mistress instead of a wife, constrained freedom of movement and occasional violence) but through these relationships, they negotiate their desire for emotional engagement.[76]

As acknowledged by Dragomirescu et al. (2009, p. 147) in their study of clients and trafficked women in Romania, love between a woman involved in prostitution and her client is not an isolated episode. Nevertheless, it is a relatively neglected aspect of studies examining relationships between clients and prostitutes. This gap in literature on prostitution might be linked to the bit of a taboo regarding romantic relationships between women engaged in prostitution and their boyfriends. Paying attention to the ways in which women negotiate the tensions between their love lives and their work and try to fulfill the desire to have an intimate relationship doesn't comply with the stigma attached to prostitutes or trafficked women as passive victims. Instead, it endows them with a degree of agency (see also Oldenburg, 2015; Yea, 2005).

---

[71] Informal conversations with Lorena, April 29 and May 21, 2013.

[72] Informal conversation with Shqipe, April 23, 2013.

[73] Informal conversations with Shqipe, May 9, 2013.

[74] Informal conversation with Lorena, April 27, 2013; informal conversation with Rita (May 15 and 21, 2013), a friend of Lorena's, who referred to "the idiot boyfriend of Lorena" and described how he limited her freedom of movement.

[75] Informal conversation with Lorena, May 21, 2013.

[76] While Dragomirescu, Necula, and Simion (2009, p. 144) found that some of their informants married clients, I have encountered only one such case in Kosovo. In this case, a woman married the police officer who helped her leave the bar where she was working in prostitution (interview with Mira, December 8, 2011). Another couple considered getting married, but eventually the family of the Kosovar man came between them. The stigma of having been involved in prostitution is simply too large in Kosovo, and the society is too small to keep such a past hidden.

4.4 Not Just Internationals

The relatively well-paid internationals dispatched in Kosovo in the context of the peacekeeping mission contributed to the growth of the post-war prostitution business not just by creating demand for commercial sex, but by stirring the peacekeeping economy, which enabled more local men to afford engagement in prostitution. Furthermore, Kosovo Albanians who live abroad return to Kosovo during the holidays in summer and winter, causing peak seasons in the sex industry.

The suggestion that the growth of the sex industry is a direct consequence of the demand of international peacekeepers is thus too simplistic. This chapter has shown that the clientele of the Kosovar sex industry has never solely consisted of internationals. Moreover, Chap. 3 elaborated on other characteristics of post-war Kosovar society that enabled the growth of the sex industry, including weak law enforcement, corruption, socio-cultural attitudes adopted during the prelude to war that did not simply come to an end along with the violence, and cooperation with regional smuggling and trafficking rings.

Now that the suggestion that internationals singlehandedly created the demand for prostitution has been debunked, let us consider the assumption that victims of trafficking for sexual purposes made up the supply of commercial sex. Chapter 5 focuses on narratives of the foreign women who arrived in Kosovo in the wake of the war.

References

Amnesty International. (2004). *"So does it mean I have rights?" Protecting the human rights of women and girls trafficked for forced prostitution in Kosovo*. London, UK: Amnesty International.

Bakhtin, M. M. (1984). *Rabelais and his world*. Bloomington, IN: Indiana University Press.

Bickford, A. (2003). See the world, meet interesting people, have sex with them: Tourism, sex, and recruitment in the U.S. military. *American Sexuality Magazine*. Retrieved March 21, 2008, from http://nsrc.sfsu.edu/MagArticle.cfm?Article=113&PageID=8&SID=59FE2D7C4E0B33976D4CE7400DFFAD37&DSN=nsrc_dsn

Bovenkerk, F., van San, M., Boone, M. M., Boekhout van Solinge, T., & Korf, D. J. (2006). *Loverboys of modern pooierschap*. Amsterdam, the Netherlands: Augustus.

Bullens, R. A. R., & Van Horn, J. E. (2000). Daad uit liefde: Gedwongen prostitutie van jonge meisjes. *Justitiële verkenningen, 26*(6), 25–41.

Cauduro, A., Nicola, A. D., Fonio, C., Nuvoloni, A., & Ruspini, P. (2009). Innocent when you dream: Clients and trafficked women in Italy. In A. Di Nicola, A. Cauduro, M. Lombardi, & P. Ruspini (Eds.), *Prostitution and human trafficking: Focus on clients* (pp. 31–66). New York, NY: Springer.

Clift, S., & Carter, S. (Eds.). (2000). *Tourism and sex: Culture, commerce and coercion*. London, UK and New York, NY: Pinter.

Collins, R. (2008). *Violence: A micro-sociological theory*. Princeton, NJ: Princeton University Press.

Currion, P. (2010). *Strength in numbers: A review of NGO coordination in the field case study: Kosovo 1999–2002*. Geneva, Switzerland: International Council of Voluntary Agencies.

Dahinden, J. (2005). Contesting transnationalism? Lessons from the study of Albanian migration networks from former Yugoslavia. *Global Networks, 5*(2), 191–208.
Deen, T. (2005, April 4). Politics: 'No Go' zones to prevent sex abuse by U.N. peacekeepers. *Inter Press Service News Agency*. Retrieved November 7, 2017, from http://www.ipsnews.net/2005/04/politics-no-go-zones-to-prevent-sex-abuse-by-un-peacekeepers/
Di Nicola, A., Cauduro, A., Lombardi, M., & Ruspini, P. (2009). *Prostitution and human trafficking: Focus on clients*. New York, NY: Springer.
Dragomirescu, D. A., Necula, C., & Simion, R. (2009). Romania: Emerging market for trafficking? In A. Di Nicola, A. Cauduro, M. Lombardi, & P. Ruspini (Eds.), *Prostitution and human trafficking: Focus on clients* (pp. 123–161). New York, NY: Springer.
Enloe, C. (2000). *Maneuvers: The international politics of militarizing women's lives*. Berkeley, CA and London, UK: University of California Press.
Flight, S., & Hulshof, P. (2009). Klanten van raamprostitutie. De vraag naar raamprostitutie in Amsterdam onderzocht.
Friman, R., & Reich, S. (2007). *Human trafficking, human security, and the Balkans*. Pittsburgh, PA: Pittsburgh Press.
Hampson, F. (2005). *Administration of justice, rule of law and democracy* (working paper). New York, NY: United Nations, Economic and Social Council.
Henry, M. (2013). Sexual exploitation and abuse in UN peacekeeping missions: Problematising current responses. In S. Madhok, A. Phillips, & K. Wilson (Eds.), *Gender, agency, and coercion* (pp. 122–142). Basingstoke, UK: Palgrave Macmillan.
Hicks, G. (1997). *The comfort women: Japan's brutal regime of enforced prostitution in the second world war*. New York, NY and London, UK: WW Norton & Company.
Higate, P. (2003). Gender and peacekeeping. Case studies: The DRC and Sierra Leone. *Africa Portal*. Retrieved November 7, 2017, from: https://www.africaportal.org/publications/gender-and-peacekeeping-case-studies-the-drc-and-sierra-leone/
Higate, P. (2007). Peacekeepers, masculinities, and sexual exploitation. *Men and Masculinities, 10*(1), 99–119.
Higate, P., & Henry, M. (2004). Engendering (in) security in peace support operations. *Security Dialogue, 35*(4), 481–498.
Hughes, D. M. (2000). The 'Natasha' trade: The transnational shadow market of trafficking in women. *Journal of International Affairs, 53*(2), 625–651.
Jennings, K., & Nikolić-Ristanović, V. (2009). *UN peacekeeping economies and local sex industries: Connections and implications* (Microcon working paper no. 17). Retrieved from http://www.peacewomen.org/assets/file/Resources/NGO/PK_SexIndustries_MICROCON_2009.pdf
Jennings, K. M. (2008). *Protecting whom?: Approaches to sexual exploitation and abuse in UN peacekeeping operations* (report). Oslo, Norway: Fafo.
Jennings, K. M. (2010). Unintended consequences of intimacy: Political economies of peacekeeping and sex tourism. *International Peacekeeping, 17*(2), 229–243.
Jennings, K. M. (2014). Service, sex, and security: Gendered peacekeeping economies in Liberia and the Democratic Republic of the Congo. *Security Dialogue, 45*(4), 313–330.
Jennings, K. M. (2015). Life in a 'peace-kept' City: Encounters with the peacekeeping economy. *Journal of Intervention and Statebuilding, 9*(3), 296–315.
Martin, E. D. (1920). *The behavior of crowds: A psychological study*. New York, NY: Harper.
Martin, S. (2005). *Must boys be boys? Ending sexual exploitation & abuse in UN peacekeeping missions*. Washington, DC: Refugees International.
Moon, K. (1997). *Sex among allies: Military prostitution in US–Korean relations*. New York, NY: Columbia University Press.
Nowicki, M.A. (2000). *Ombudsperson Institution in Kosovo* (special report no. 1). Pristina, Kosovo: Ombudsperson Institution Kosovo.
Oldenburg, S. (2015). The politics of love and intimacy in Goma, Eastern DR Congo: Perspectives on the market of intervention as contact zone. *Journal of Intervention and Statebuilding, 9*(3), 316–333.

Otto, D. (2007). Making sense of zero tolerance policies in peacekeeping sexual economies. *Sexuality and the Law*, 259–282.
Pollock Sturdevant, S., & Stoltzfus, B. (1992). *Let the good times roll: Prostitution and the US military in Asia*. New York, NY: New Press.
Presdee, M. (2000). *Cultural criminology and the carnival of crime*. London, UK: Routledge.
Scott-Flynn, N. (2003, June). Coordination in Kosovo: The challenge for the NGO sector. *Human Practice Network Magazine*. Retrieved from https://odihpn.org/magazine/coordination-in-kosovo-the-challenge-for-the-ngo-sector/
Segrave, M., Milivojevic, S., & Pickering, S. (2009). *Sex trafficking: International context and response*. Devon, UK: Willan Publishing.
Shiboleth, T. (2015). *Being a "John": A client's perspective on paying for pleasure*. Oisterwijk, the Netherlands: Wolf Legal Publishing.
Simic, O. (2012). *Regulation of sexual conduct in UN peacekeeping operations*. New York, NY: Springer.
Tanaka, T. (2002). *Japan's comfort women: Sexual slavery and prostitution during World War II and the US occupation*. London, UK: Routledge.
Terre des Hommes. (2010). *Regional report on the implementation of the "UNICEF guidelines for the protection of the rights of child victims of trafficking in South Eastern Europe": Assessment of the situation in Albania, Kosovo and the former Yugoslav Republic of Macedonia, 2010*. Geneva, Switzerland: Terre des Hommes. Retrieved from http://tdh-childprotection.org/documents/regional-report-on-the-implementation-of-the-unicef-guidelines-for-the-protection-of-the-rights-of-child-victims-of-trafficking-in-south-eastern-europe
Trotter, H. (2008). *Sugar Girls & Seamen: A journey into the world of dockside prostitution in South Africa*. Athens, OH: Ohio University Press.
Turner, V. (1969). *The ritual process: Structure and anti-structure*. London, UK: Aldine Publishing Company.
UN. (2005). *A comprehensive strategy to eliminate future sexual exploitation and abuse in United Nations peacekeeping operations* (The Zeid report). Retrieved from http://www.un.org/en/ga/search/view_doc.asp?symbol=A/61/858
UN Economic and Social Council. (2005, July 7). *Administration of justice, rule of law and democracy: Working paper on the accountability of international personnel taking part in peace support operations submitted by Françoise Hampson (UN Doc E/CN.4/Sub.2/2005/42)*. Retrieved from https://documents-dds-ny.un.org/doc/UNDOC/GEN/G05/148/03/PDF/G0514803.pdf?OpenElement
UN General Assembly. (2005, March 24). *Letter dated March 24, 2005 from the Secretary General to the President of the General Assembly (UN Doc A/59/710)*. Retrieved from https://cdu.unlb.org/Portals/0/Documents/KeyDoc5.pdf
UN General Assembly. (2006, May 24). *Special measures for protection from sexual exploitation and sexual abuse (UN Doc A/60/861)*. Retrieved from https://undocs.org/A/60/861
UN General Assembly. (2008, June 25). *Special measures for protection from sexual exploitation and sexual abuse (UN Doc A/62/890)*. Retrieved from https://undocs.org/A/62/890
UN General Assembly. (2014, February 14). *Special measures for protection from sexual exploitation and sexual abuse (UN Doc A/68/756)*. Retrieved from https://undocs.org/A/68/756
UN General Assembly. (2015, February 13). *Special measures for protection from sexual exploitation and sexual abuse (UN Doc A/69/779)*. Retrieved from https://undocs.org/A/69/779
UN General Assembly. (2016, February 16). *Special measures for protection from sexual exploitation and sexual abuse (UN Doc A/70/729)*. Retrieved from A/70/729
UN Interim Administration Mission in Kosovo. (2004, May). *Combating human trafficking in kosovo, strategy & commitment*. UNMIK. Retrieved November 28, 2017, from http://unpan1.un.org/intradoc/groups/public/documents/UNTC/UNPAN019190.pdf
UN Secretariat. (2003, October 9). *Secretary-general's bulletin. Special measures for protection from sexual exploitation and sexual abuse*. Retrieved from http://www.unhcr.org/protection/

operations/405ac6614/secretary-generals-bulletin-special-measures-protection-sexual-exploitation.html

UNDP. (2012). *Kosovo Remittance Study 2012*. New York, NY: UNDP.

UNDP Kosovo. (2014). *Kosovo human development report: Migration as a force for development*. Retrieved from http://hdr.undp.org/sites/default/files/khdr2014english.pdf

UNMIK. (2000, August 18). *Regulation no. 2000/47 on the status, privileges and immunities of KFOR and UNMIK and their personnel in Kosovo*. UNMIK. Retrieved from http://www.unmikonline.org/regulations/2000/reg47-00.htm

UNMIK. (2005, January 31). *Off limits list*. UNMIK. Retrieved from http://kosovo6b.tripod.com/March_2005_Off-Limits_List.xls

UNMIK. (2011). *Special measures for protection from sexual exploitation and abuse*. UNMIK. Retrieved from http://www.unmikonline.org/SiteCollectionDocuments/Conduct%20and%20Discipline%20FREQUENTLY%20ASKED%20QUESTIONS%20AND%20ANSWERS%20%2003%20JUNE%202011.pdf

Van Gennep, A. (1960). *The rites of passage*. Chicago, IL: The University of Chicago Press.

Vanwesenbeeck, I., De Graaf, R., Van Zessen, G., Straver, C. J., & Visser, J. H. (1993). Protection styles of prostitutes' clients: Intentions, behavior, and considerations in relation to AIDS. *Journal of Sex Education and Therapy, 19*(2), 79–92.

Vathi, Z., & Black, R. (2007). *Migration and poverty reduction in Kosovo* (working Paper No. C, 12). Brighton, UK: Development Research Centre of Migration, Globalisation and Poverty.

Verwijs, R., Mein, A. G., Goderie, M., Harreveld, C., & Jansma, A. (2011). *Loverboys en hun slachtoffers. Inzicht in de aard en omvang problematiek en in het aanbod aan hulpverlening en opvang*. Utrecht, the Netherlands: Verwey-Jonker Instituut.

Weenink, D. (2013). Decontrolled by solidarity: Understanding recreational violence in moral holidays. *Human Figurations, 2*(3).

Weitzer, R. (2005). The growing moral panic over prostitution and sex trafficking. *The Criminologist, 30*(5), 1–4.

Whitworth, S. (2004). *Men, militarism, and UN peacekeeping: A gendered analysis*. Boulder, CO: Lynne Rienner Publishers.

Yea, S. (2005). Labour of love: Filipina entertainers' narratives of romance and relationships with GIs in US military camp towns in Korea. *Women's Studies International Forum, 28*(6), 456–472.

Yoshimi, Y. (2000). *Comfort women: Sexual slavery in the Japanese military during World War II*. New York, NY: Columbia University Press.

Zaitch, D., & Staring, R. (2009). The flesh is weak, the spirit even weaker: Clients and trafficked women in the Netherlands. In A. Di Nicola, A. Cauduro, M. Lombardi, & P. Ruspini (Eds.), *Prostitution and human trafficking: Focus on clients* (pp. 67–121). New York, NY: Springer.

Zhang, S. X. (2009). Beyond the 'Natasha' story – A review and critique of current research on sex trafficking. *Global Crime, 10*(3), 178–195.

Fig. 5.1 Motel

Chapter 5
Foreign Women Engaged in Prostitution: Rethinking the Singular Image of Victims of Trafficking

Scholars like Mendelson (2005, p. 8) describe how the demand for commercial sex in the wake of the war in Kosovo was met by women from countries in Eastern Europe, who were forced into prostitution after being "sold as chattel, stripped of their passports, and forced to pay off bogus debts to their traffickers." This gloomy picture of prostitution in the context of the peacekeeping mission in Kosovo is sustained in other publications that condemn the "trafficking of foreign women from among the poorest (post-communist) countries" (Jennings & Nikolić-Ristanović, 2009, p. 9; see also Amnesty International, 2004; Jeffreys, 2009, p. 107). Their shocking accounts largely mirror dominant descriptions of the influx of Eastern European victims of sex trafficking into post-conflict Bosnia and Herzegovina (Haynes, 2009; Murray, 2002).

Studies on prostitution in the context of peacekeeping missions outside former Yugoslavia principally focus on the involvement of local women (Jennings, 2015; Simic, 2012). If foreign women are considered at all, they are singularly portrayed as victims of trafficking as in the above accounts (Martin, 2005; Murray, 2002; Rathgeber, 2002). Higate (2003, p. 44) seems to be an exception to this "rule" at first sight. Having observed women from Liberia and Guinea in the sex industry during the peacekeeping mission in Sierra Leone, Higate briefly describes these women as vulnerable refugees who try to earn money by having relationships with peacekeepers. However, he does not further include these women in his study, which is otherwise conducted amongst peacekeepers. Although he does seem to create space to consider foreign women as more than solely being victims of trafficking, he later disregards any form of agency of those women involved in prostitution during a peacekeeping mission by saying, following Spencer (2005, p. 171), that "[E]xchanging sex or sexual acts to obtain protection, assistance, food and non-food

R. de Wildt, *Post-War Prostitution*, Studies of Organized Crime 17,
https://doi.org/10.1007/978-3-030-19474-1_5

items is sometimes misunderstood as an expression of agency. These acts may appear to increase a woman's agency and her sense of control over her body as she is choosing to engage in sexual activity. However, these exploitative circumstances do not involve real choices" (Higate, 2007, p. 108). With this statement, foreign women engaged in out-country prostitution during peacekeeping missions remain depicted as nothing but one-dimensional victims.

The foreign women engaged in prostitution in the context of the peacekeeping mission in Kosovo and who participated in this research all shared experiences of (sexual) violence and exploitation, yet an exclusive focus on the victimhood of these women does not do justice to their experiences. The abovementioned unambiguous accounts essentialize suffering while ignoring less stereotypical and more complex aspects of their lives. These accounts, for instance, fail to describe how these foreign women resisted structural inequalities (Andrijasevic, 2007, p. 98), negotiated their situations and sought to achieve pleasure and fulfillment (Yea, 2005, p. 459). Nor does it pay attention to their own insider perspectives.

Paying attention to these aspects does not aim to exchange the abolitionist rhetoric that centres on victimization—and is echoed in Higate's statement above—for a pro-sex work rhetoric that emphasizes the agency of women. As demonstrated by other studies on prostitution (O'Neill, 2001; Oude Breuil, Siegel, Van Reenen, Beijer, & Roos, 2011), women involved in prostitution can be both agents and victims—or not victims at all. However, I do aim to explore the complexity of the experiences of foreign women who became involved in the prostitution business in Kosovo directly after the war. I thus aim to widen "the rather restrictive lenses" (Yea, 2005, p. 459) through which women engaged in out-country prostitution in the context of peacekeeping missions are generally viewed to include conceptualizations of it as labor or survival.

This chapter will do so through a discussion of the life trajectories of foreign women involved in post-war prostitution in Kosovo. Where did these women come from? Why and how did they come to Kosovo? What did the women expect before their departure, and what did they encounter after their arrival? And why did foreign women disappear from the scene around 2012, almost without exception? Before turning to the narratives of foreign women engaged in prostitution in the context of the peacekeeping mission, however, let us first take a look at the ethnic makeup of the sex industry in Kosovo in the wake of the war.

5.1 Countries of Origin

Since the evolution of the sex industry after the war, roughly three periods of time can be distinguished based on the ethnicity of the women involved in the prostitution business. In the first phase, from 1999 onward, the women engaged in the Kosovar prostitution business were primarily foreign, coming from Moldova,

Ukraine, Romania, Bulgaria, Albania and Serbia. The fact that Eastern European women were largely present in the Kosovar prostitution business mirrored global and regional developments: the collapse of the communist regimes of Eastern Europe and the subsequent shift toward market economies in the early 1990s led to widespread unemployment, the demise of social support systems, high levels of corruption and a steep decline in living standards in countries including Moldova, Ukraine, Romania, Bulgaria and Albania. In search of better economic and social opportunities, men and women from newborn states in Eastern Europe increasingly opted for work abroad. Prostitution migration from Eastern Europe—as well as human trafficking for sexual exploitation—proliferated (Petrunov, 2014; Shelley, 2010, pp. 49, 174–76; Surtees, 2008, p. 40). The violent disintegration of Yugoslavia, the subsequent establishment of peacekeeping missions and strict rules on immigration to the European Union (Friman & Reich, 2007, pp. 3–9; Surtees, 2008), made Kosovo a destination country for these Eastern European women.

In 2000 and 2001, the International Organisation for Migration (IOM), the lead anti-trafficking agency in Kosovo at the time, primarily assisted victims of trafficking from Moldova, Ukraine, Romania and Bulgaria.[1] These were also the main countries of origin in 2002, with the addition of Albania (Counter-Trafficking Regional Clearing Point, 2003, p. 143; Surtees, 2005, p. 255).[2] This by itself does not mean that Moldova, Ukraine, Romania, Bulgaria, and later Albania were the primary countries of origin of women involved in post-war prostitution in Kosovo. The IOM data, logically, does not provide any information about the nationalities of victims of trafficking who were not assisted, nor about the nationalities of women who were not identified as victims of trafficking. This makes the IOM data inherently incomplete for an analysis of the nationalities of the women involved in post-war prostitution in Kosovo.

Therefore, the countries of origin of the women who populated the prostitution business in the wake of the war have also been discussed with respondents, including bar owners, women engaged in prostitution, and police and government officials. These respondents mentioned the same countries of origin (i.e., Moldova,

[1] In 2000, IOM assisted 72 victims of trafficking from Moldova, 20 victims from Romania, 10 victims from Bulgaria, and 8 victims from Ukraine. The following year, these countries remained the primary source countries of assisted victims of trafficking in Kosovo. In 2001, IOM assisted 71 victims of trafficking from Moldova, 36 victims from Romania, 20 victims from Ukraine, and 4 victims from Bulgaria. These were all women and girls who voluntarily repatriated to their countries of origin; women who declined services and voluntary repatriation were not included in these numbers. A report by IOM, amongst others, states that women who refused assistance "are likely to have returned under trafficker's control and remain[ed] in Kosovo" (Counter-Trafficking Regional Clearing Point, 2003, p. 138). As will be discussed in more detail in this chapter, however, it cannot be ruled out that these women did not return to their countries of origin because they themselves did not want to be repatriated.

[2] In 2002, IOM assisted 32 victims of trafficking from Moldova, 20 victims from Ukraine, 19 victims from Romania, 9 from Albania, and 6 from Bulgaria.

Ukraine, Romania, Bulgaria and later Albania), but added Serbia.[3] The fact that IOM only assisted one Serbian victim of trafficking between 2000 and 2003 (Surtees, 2005, p. 255), while the abovementioned respondents mentioned that Serbian women formed a significant group, can be related to the fact that Kosovo had been a province of Serbia until the exercise of sovereignty was (temporarily) handed over to the UN at the end of the war. As a consequence, Serbs had always inhabited and traveled through Kosovo. The stories of Serbian women in Kosovo suggest that they generally did not need to rely on human smugglers or traffickers to come to Kosovo.

One bar owner stated that "Serbian women were less popular in Kosovo at that time [in the wake of the war]" because of the strong anti-Serbian sentiment.[4] Various other respondents, however, mentioned that Serbian women were popular amongst some Kosovar Albanian men because of their presumed "free spirit."[5] They explained that Serbian women had an image of being promiscuous and easy to sleep with, while (Kosovar) Albanian women were traditionally tightly controlled by their families (see also Arsovska, 2015, pp. 202–207) so that it was almost impossible to have sexual intercourse with them outside of marriage. This allegedly made Serbian women popular as girlfriends and sex workers, even shortly after the war. In this discourse, sexual morality is used as a way in which to construct Serbian women as "the other." As Espiritu (2003, p. 178) also observed amongst Filipino communities in the United States, a discourse on sexual morality can allow one to accentuate that one's own culture is (morally) superior.

The composition of the Kosovar sex industry changed in the years prior to Romania and Bulgaria entering the European Union in 2007 (Surtees, 2005, p. 255). This marked a second phase when it comes to the ethnic makeup of the Kosovar prostitution business. Bulgarian and Romanian women, including Moldovan women with Romanian passports, could easily travel to affluent Western European countries. As explained by a police officer, "They found a better deal in Europe" than in Kosovo.[6] As will be discussed later in this chapter, women preferred engagement in prostitution markets in Western Europe over Kosovo, almost without exception. They expected to be able to earn more money there and assumed it would be more developed than in Kosovo. From 2007 onward, Romanian and Bulgarian women found routes to the Netherlands (Siegel, 2012), France (Oude Breuil, 2014) and Italy (De Wildt, 2009), as well as other countries in the European Union (Petrunov, 2014)—they almost completely disappeared from the Kosovar sex industry. In 2011, during various visits to premises where prostitution was taking place in Kosovo, I encountered no Romanian women and only a few Bulgarians. In this period, the majority of the women still came from Moldova, Ukraine, Albania and,

[3] Interview with SP1, February 26, 2013; interview with EUL4, May 2, 2013.

[4] Informal conversation with Bujar, March 3, 2013.

[5] Interview with SP1, February 26, 2013.

[6] Interview with KPO4, March 27, 2013.

on a lesser scale, Serbia. However, the number of local women, including Kosovar Albanian, Roma, Ashkali and Egyptian women, steadily increased. Local women had been there since the initial growth of the industry, but now they were significantly larger in number.

Stricter regulations for foreign women to enter and work in Kosovo initiated a third phase in which Kosovar Albanian and Albanian women took the place of Eastern European women altogether in the Kosovar prostitution business. From 2011 onward, Eastern European women mentioned that it was increasingly difficult to obtain the obligatory permits to work and stay. One Moldovan woman explained, "These days it is difficult to get proper Kosovar papers, but when I arrived four years ago I just needed to do a health test and go to the Ministry with my boss. It was no problem and all arranged in 3 days. The papers are for 1 year, and after one year you can extend it again."[7] By the end of 2011, the women with whom I spoke all mentioned that the police had become stricter. If a foreign woman could not show her working permit, she was immediately sent back to her country of origin. All women could think of Ukrainian and Moldovan friends to whom this had happened. Albanian women did not experience these difficulties as a result of the strong bilateral relationships between Kosovo and Albania (Kursani, Haxholli, & Gjikolli, 2014, pp. 21–22); they could stay and work in Kosovo without much problem.

At the same time, figures from the Kosovar office of the National Coordinator Against Trafficking in Human Beings show that increasing numbers of girls and women from Kosovo and neighboring Albania had become involved in Kosovo's prostitution industry. The progress reports *Implementation of Strategy and Action Plan Against Trafficking in Human Beings* (Republic of Kosovo, 2009, 2010) show that women and girls from Kosovo formed the largest group of identified victims in 2008, 2009 and 2010, with Albanian women and girls being the second-largest group in 2010. Although the reliability of official statistics should always be questioned, given the underground nature of prostitution (Goodey, 2008; Kempadoo, 2003; Shelley, 2010; Weitzer, 2007; Zhang, 2009), these figures give some indication of broader trends. Since 2012, these local and Albanian women have been practically the sole providers of commercial sex. In 2013, during visits to premises where prostitution was taking place, I only met a handful of women from Ukraine, Moldova and Serbia; all other women came from Kosovo or Albania.

I will specifically reflect on the engagement of local women in the Kosovar sex industry in Chap. 6. In the current chapter, I will continue to explore the trajectories of foreign women, who made up the largest number of those involved in prostitution throughout the first two phases in the years following the war.

[7] Interview with Julia, November 30, 2011.

Fig. 5.2 Motel

5.2 Women's Narratives

Various researchers of prostitution (i.e., not specifically related to peacekeeping) have criticized the unambiguously victimization-centric accounts of women engaged in out-country prostitution that were mentioned in the introduction of this chapter. Weitzer (2014, p. 20) puts forward that "migration and trafficking are much more complex and variegated than the image popularized in the dominant discourse." He explains the popular image as a consequence of the "moral crusade against sex trafficking" in recent years (Weitzer, 2007, p. 447), recognizing the appearance of this crusade in anti-trafficking campaigns, which spread horror stories about prostitution and emphasize that it is intrinsically harmful (2007, p. 467). Andrijasevic (2007) examined anti-trafficking campaigns that were launched in Eastern Europe, concluding that the displayed images and messages are "highly symbolic and stereotypical constructions of femininity (victims) and masculinity (criminals) of eastern European nationals" (Andrijasevic, 2007, p. 24). Based on similar observations, Doezema (2000, p. 47) argues that "[w]omen who migrate for the sex industry can only be freed from violations of their human rights if they are first freed of their mythical constraints." Godziak and Bump (2008) show that myths indeed play an important role in the debate on human trafficking. They analyzed human trafficking literature and demonstrated that the absolute majority of journal articles are non-empirical, while many publications deliberately seem to have a certain moral agenda in mind (i.e., abolitionism; see also Sanghera, 2005, p. 4; Zhang, 2009). This was the impetus for Zhang's (2009) call for empirically based—instead of ideology-driven—research on human trafficking. Weitzer (2014), in addition, emphasizes the importance of micro-level research that documents the complexities in lived experience of those who are trafficked or migrated. Empirical research on alleged victims of trafficking, such as the foreign women engaged in prostitution in the context of the peacekeeping mission in Kosovo, is pivotal for countering the dominant, ideology-driven discourse on human trafficking and prostitution. Such empirical data should also take into consideration the less stereotypical aspects of women's experiences. This can be achieved through the description of life trajectories.

In the following sections, I will introduce three women who left their countries of origin and became involved in prostitution during the peacekeeping mission in Kosovo.[8] The narratives of these women, from Ukraine, Moldova and Serbia, respectively, illustrate the wide variety of reasons why women had to travel to Kosovo and why they became engaged in its sex industry. These narratives deliberately do not leave out the less sensationalistic aspects of their experiences. In doing so, I hope to work toward a more mundane understanding of the situation of foreign women engaged in prostitution in the context of a peacekeeping mission. The three narratives will be analyzed and contextualized throughout the remainder of the chapter; general themes and patterns are derived from the narratives and discussed chronologically. After presenting these narratives, I will consider the reasons for women to engage in out-country prostitution prior to their departure. This is followed by an analysis of recruitment methods, women's expectations of their destination and the different ways in which women traveled to Kosovo. In the final section, the described lived experiences of foreign women engaged in prostitution during peacekeeping missions will be compared with the dominant label of these women as victims of trafficking.

5.2.1 *Sofija: Prostitution Migration to Engage in a Luxury Lifestyle*

I first met Sofija on a Wednesday afternoon in November 2011. She had just woken up after a night of working. In her pajamas and with her wet hair wrapped in a towel, she lit a cigarette and comfortably seated herself on one of the white leather sofas on the ground floor of Motel New York.[9] Motel New York was established by Hans, from the Netherlands, and Edi, from Kosovo. Both men had met in the Netherlands,

[8] Cultural criminologists have made a plea for studying the more mundane side of everyday transgressions (Ferrell, Hayward & Young, 2008, pp. 85–87).

[9] Informal conversation with Sofija, November 16, 2011.

where they cooperated in the prostitution business.[10] Two and a half years after that first meeting, Sofija would explain to me how Hans and Edi started their business in Kosovo: "Edi first had a business in prostitution in the Netherlands. While he was involved in this business, he had a problem with the police. He was not able to go to the Netherlands anymore or even to visit his brother in Germany. Then Edi opened a business in Kosovo with his former Dutch business partner, Hans. He took one Ukrainian girl that was working in the Netherlands. She found other Ukrainian women to work in Kosovo."[11]According to the police, the men thus paved the road for Ukrainian women to come to Kosovo and engage in its prostitution business.[12] Hans and Edi's business in Kosovo solely employed women from Ukraine.

Sofija worked in Motel New York together with seven other Ukrainian women, amongst them her younger sister and a childhood friend. In the evening, the women drank and danced with their clients in the lobby that functioned as their living room during the day. Sexual intercourse took place in two designated "working rooms" upstairs. If both working rooms were occupied, the women would take their clients to their personal sleeping quarters a bit farther down the hall. The sleeping rooms were the only personal quarters of those women who worked and lived in the motel. Sofija decorated her room with colorful drawings and a picture of her son Yuri, as well as a poster of a bull on which she pinned foreign bills. Her king-size bed stood in front of the window, which had a view of the road between Pristina and the border with Macedonia. Outside, an old sign with a fading picture of the skyline of New York invited passing cars to take a break and stop at the motel.[13]

Back in Ukraine, Sofija used to work as a cashier in a supermarket. Her salary was 150 euro per month for 4 days of work a week. She worked from eight in the morning until half past 10 in the evening. Sofija also received 50 euro from the state; at the time, women in Ukraine were entitled to this monthly allowance if they had a child below the age of three and did not work. A single mother, Sofija explained that she therefore deliberately worked without a contract: "I wanted to work without papers because 150 and 50 euro is not bad in Ukraine. […] My mother paid part of my rent and also paid for food and clothes for Yuri."[14] Sofija got by without many problems. She looked back on her job with satisfaction, although she found the salary a bit low. Her situation did not leave room for luxury.

During various meetings in the years that followed, Sofija revealed more details about how she had quit her job and become involved in out-country prostitution after following the example of her childhood friend. "My friend came back from working in Cyprus and had money to build a house. I wanted that. I don't remember how she told me about prostitution exactly. It's not good to ask, 'What job are you doing there?' But she told me everything. […] She said it is just like sleeping with

[10] Interview with EUL4, May 15, 2013.

[11] Informal conversation with Sofija, January 4, 2014.

[12] Interview with KPO3, October 8, 2013.

[13] Observations in Motel New York, January 9, 2014.

[14] Informal conversation with Sofija, January 8, 2014.

your husband, but then you get money. I thought, it's easy money."[15] Sofija decided to join her friend in 2005. For a year and a half, Sofija alternated between working in prostitution in Cyprus and Lebanon and resting with family in Ukraine. She explained that she preferred working in Cyprus over her Arab clients in Lebanon, but that she needed the job in Lebanon as well because "[i]n Cyprus, even if you work for one day and leave, then you cannot come back for six months."[16]

In Lebanon, Sofija met Ali, who was from Syria. It was the beginning of a long friendship, during which Ali financially supported Sofija and her family. "We were friends. Well, first he was my client. We have a big difference in age. He was 75 and I was 25. He was very rich. His children were big, so he spent on me. Sometimes he sent money every week. He works with oil."[17] Sofija showed me a picture of herself on a donkey during a desert safari in Abu Dhabi, where she had gone with Ali for 3 weeks. Ali also paid for the complete education of Sofija's younger sister. Her whole family knew him, although she did not disclose that they had met through the prostitution business. "In Ukraine, everybody thinks that I worked in Spain or Italy to take care of grandparents. Sometimes people say, 'Can you arrange this job for me?' Or the neighbor said, 'Can you arrange this job for my wife?'" But Sofija did not want people to know about her involvement in prostitution and therefore rarely took other women along. "I always say, 'No, it is difficult with visa and not legal.'"[18]

Another friend recommended that Sofija work in Malta instead of Cyprus and Lebanon. Sofija decided to give it a try, but explained that she quickly regretted her decision. "Malta was very bad. The man, the owner, was bad. He took my passport so I couldn't leave and it was only 10 euro per client. I didn't dare to go to the police because I wasn't legal there."[19] In retrospect, Sofija thought that her friend had recommended that bar in Malta because her friend could only leave there if she brought another woman to work. After 10 months in Malta, Sofija managed to get her passport and left. She stayed in Ukraine for a year and a half to recover from her experiences until the childhood friend that had introduced her to working in Cyprus and Lebanon asked if she was interested in joining her in Kosovo.

Sofija started working in Motel New York in 2008. She traveled to visit her son, who lived with his grandparents in Ukraine, every other month and all summer. When she spoke about her engagement in prostitution, Sofija repeatedly mentioned that money earned in prostitution was "easy money." When I asked her what she meant by that, Sofija mentioned that her income through prostitution was beyond anything she could imagine outside the sex industry. First of all, Sofija and the other women could make money by selling drinks: they would earn three euro for every cocktail they sold. Clients that purchased a drink would also buy some time for the

[15] Informal conversation with Sofija, January 4, 2014.
[16] Informal conversation with Sofija, January 6, 2014.
[17] Informal conversation with Sofija, January 4, 2014.
[18] Informal conversation with Sofija, January 4, 2014.
[19] Informal conversation with Sofija, January 6, 2014.

women to sit with them.[20] This drinking system exists in bars all over Kosovo and is also observed in other countries such as South Korea (Yea, 2005). But most money was gained through sexual services. Sofija explained that the prices at Motel New York were relatively high. Women in other bars would have intercourse with clients for as little as 20 euro, but in Motel New York, the prices were as follows: "For one time it is 60 euro, maximum is 30 min. For two times, it is 110 euro. For one hour, it is 100 euro. If it is after 3:00, a client always has to pay 200 euro for two hours. [...] Sometimes they come around 5 min before 3. I say we are closed. Then, OK, I can come with him to a motel, but I have to be back by 5:00. It doesn't matter if it is shorter. He has to pay 200 euro for two hours. So it depends also on the time. It is good. He also loses time for driving and bringing me back."[21] These prices almost compare to prices reported in affluent countries such as the Netherlands (Siegel, 2015, p. 69). Sofija could keep half of these earnings; the other half went to Edi, the Kosovar Albanian owner of the motel. Sofija had three to four clients per night, which allowed her to "make like 5000 euro per month. It also depends on the time of the year. In summer and with Christmastime, you can earn more. One time, I was one month in June, and I earned 7000 euro. Normally I was not there in summer and Christmas. But [there were] more clients, so I could earn more."[22]

Sofija spent her money on holidays and other luxuries she could never afford in the past. In addition to buying an apartment and installing heating in the floor, she told me about the vacations she was able to take with her son: "I went on holidays with Yuri. He saw Egypt in cartoons. And I want him to see those things. I spent a lot of money. You only live once. I went on a lot of holidays. Took all of my family."[23] However, she also tried to restructure and change the lives of her family members through her earnings. She attempted to do so, first of all, by changing the power balance within her family. Her stepfather was addicted to alcohol; he was violent at home when he was drunk, which was almost every day. Sofija told her stepfather that she would buy an apartment for her mother if he would not stop drinking alcohol. Knowing that Sofija had the means to do so, her stepfather was afraid that his wife would leave him if he did not overcome his addiction and managed to stop drinking. This was an enormous relief for the family.[24] Likewise, Oldenburg (2015, p. 321) describes how earnings in the sex industry can transform kinship relations. Secondly, Sofija attempted to invest money in a bus and in so doing secure a middle-class income for the family. "I told my mother, 'I will buy one or two buses for 15 people.' It's good business. My stepfather can drive one. [...] He is a taxi driver at

[20] Informal conversation with Sofija, January 8, 2014.

[21] Informal conversation with Sofija, January 8, 2014.

[22] Informal conversation with Sofija, January 8, 2014. She mentioned the higher earnings in summer and around Christmas when the schatzis celebrate their holidays in Kosovo, as elaborated upon in Chapter Four.

[23] Informal conversation with Sofija, January 8, 2014.

[24] Informal conversation with Sofija, January 6, 2014.

night. Then he can just work in the day. [...] My mother is selling mushrooms in a bazaar. With the bus, my mother can stay at home."[25] By purchasing a bus as well as an apartment for her family members, Sofija believed that her family, including the generations to come, would never have to pay rent or do low-paid jobs again and thus have a good standard of living.

While sex work brought "something good," Sofija also mentioned the physical and mental strain of prostitution.[26] She explained her health worries and the problems and pain all the intercourse caused, especially to her genitals. But most of all, she said, it caused her to suffer emotionally. "They take off clothes, and then you put on condom. You see this body. Sometimes men with no teeth. Then I thought, 'Just do it.' But if you force yourself like that all the time, it is very hard. Sometimes they didn't shower or very little."[27] Sofija also mentioned finding it difficult to engage in romantic relationships with men: "I can't meet a boy. I only think he will want something. I feel so bad. I don't want anything."[28]

Sofija's story illustrates how women engage in prostitution migration in order to participate in the luxurious lifestyles they have seen on television. While sex work can have an emotional backlash on them, prostitution migration does allow women to alter their socio-economic position, as well as that of their families. In this way, prostitution migration can be a career path. Women express agency by informing each other about countries and specific establishments where earnings in prostitution are good. Countries with a peacekeeping mission can be an example of such places where relatively large amounts of money can be made.

5.2.2 Rita: Prostitution Migration to Escape a Precarious Financial Situation

The emotional distress Sofija mentioned meant that some women were reluctant to speak about prostitution explicitly. Rita, from Moldova, is one example of a woman who avoided touching upon her experiences with commercial sex, so I never pushed her to do so. Instead, we had lengthy conversations about her precarious financial situation. In her struggles to make ends meet, Rita had found herself committing to shady job offers in Italy, Kosovo and Dubai. We never discussed the details of what happened during these jobs, but such details are not the most important for understanding survival strategies in a dire economic situation. The next section is dedicated to Rita's story.

---

[25] Informal conversation with Sofija, January 8, 2014.

[26] Informal conversation with Sofija, January 6, 2014.

[27] Informal conversation with Sofija, January 4, 2014.

[28] Informal conversation with Sofija, January 9, 2014.

After her parents passed away and her only sister moved to Russia, Rita, then 20 years old, found herself without employment or a social network to sustain her. She decided to go to Italy, as she expected to have more possibilities to make a living there although her stay would be illegal. She chose her smugglers carefully, since "some smugglers fool people."[29] An acquaintance of hers, for instance, had driven around in the back of a van with blacked-out windows for 2 days. On the third night, the organizer of the trip told this acquaintance and the rest of the group to get out of the van. He pointed at a village, which was supposed to be in Italy, and told them to walk there. When the group approached the village, they saw Moldovan road signs and knew they had been deceived. The van had simply been driving around Moldova for days on end.

Rita asked around if people knew any smugglers with a good reputation and was referred to a trustworthy group. The smugglers took Rita on an arduous journey with lengthy walks through the night, rides in jam-packed vans and a trip on a boat, crossing a lake while dressed up as a fisherman, before the Hungarian police caught her. She had to spend 2 weeks in a Hungarian prison for illegal border crossing. After several other attempts, Rita managed to reach Italy, but she quickly came in contact with the police and found herself deported back to Moldova.[30]

Back in Moldova, Rita still felt that there was no future for her there. She welcomed the invitation of a Moldovan acquaintance working in Kosovo to come and join her. Rita arrived in Kosovo in 2003 with a close friend. Her first impression was not very favorable: "It was right after the war and there was absolutely nothing here. No beauty parlor for women, nothing. I thought, 'Shit, where did I end up?'"[31] Rita avoided speaking about the work that her acquaintance promised her in Kosovo, but regularly mentioned stories like the following: "They told Moldovan girls about being a waitress in Kosovo. But not what kind of waitress; they just have to tell them about the job that they will be doing. But yeah, otherwise they don't want it [she shrugged her shoulders and smiled]. Nobody really wants to do this job, so… But most girls knew what they would be doing."[32] A Kosovar friend of Rita's who used to work with her told me that Rita was initially deceived and promised a job as a waitress.[33] In Kosovo, it is unusual for women to work as waitresses; female waitresses are often involved in prostitution. Some trendy restaurants, nightclubs and bars in the capital, Pristina, are notable exceptions to this unwritten rule, but these are the only establishments where women work as waitresses and nothing else. After a few months in Kosovo, Rita and her friend returned to Moldova, but decided that Kosovo offered more opportunities to earn money and came back.

The two worked as waitresses in several bars in various Kosovar cities. After some years, Rita and her Moldovan friend opened their own bar. Their savings from

[29] Interview with Rita, May 28, 2013.

[30] Informal conversation with Rita, May 21, 2013.

[31] Informal conversation with Rita, May 21, 2013.

[32] Informal conversation with Rita, May 28, 2013.

[33] Interview with Lorena, a friend of Rita's, May 14, 2013.

their initial period in Kosovo allowed them to rent premises close to Camp Bondsteel. Camp Bondsteel is located in the small village of Sojevo, but the street that runs to the entrance of the military camp alone has six bars and nightclubs, a luxurious restaurant and a souvenir shop. International soldiers stationed at Camp Bondsteel formed the largest part of the clientele in Rita's new bar. Rita recalled that they "used to barbeque in front of the bar. There were always people. And everybody had money to spend."[34] Earnings were good, and so was life in general: "We were drunk every other night. I needed holidays to Moldova to rest from the partying."[35] Rita smiled as she shared endless anecdotes about the evenings primarily spent with American soldiers that she considered her friends.

One of their regular customers was an American soldier in his 50s. "He is older but a good guy. Calm. Funny."[36] He got along well with Rita's friend, and they decided to get married. The couple jointly moved to Dubai when the American man was transferred there, and Rita decided to continue running the bar by herself. It became increasingly difficult for foreign women to live and work in Kosovo as regulations regarding the granting of working permits became stricter, and Rita was afraid that she would have to leave and return to Moldova. When a Kosovar Albanian friend suggested they get married in order to avoid further difficulties with papers, she agreed. The marriage was "not really based on love, but more a good deal to stay around."[37] Rita's husband traveled to the United States in order to visit his brother after a year of marriage. He was supposed to stay for a month, but did not return for many years.

In the meantime, the clientele of the bar dramatically decreased in number. When I visited Rita's bar in the deserted strip outside Camp Bondsteel in 2013, the closed nightclubs next door and the pictures on the walls were the only reminders of the thriving times right after the war. The photos showed Rita dressed up as the devil at a costume party, two muscled and tattooed men in American flag T-shirts holding a beer and smiling at the camera, and many more images of people dancing, drinking and playing pool inside the bar. A Kosovar Albanian friend of Rita's walked inside and pointed at the people in the pictures: "This one is gone. This one is gone. This one is gone."[38] Almost all of the internationals who used to visit Rita's bar had left. The military mission was downsizing, and personnel had been sent elsewhere. Rita explained, "Now it is bad. There are less soldiers, and the soldiers here now have less salary. They of course don't want to return home and say, 'Sorry, I spent all my money in Rita's bar.'"[39] Rita felt lonely and had problems making ends meet again.

[34] Informal conversation with Rita, May 15, 2013.

[35] Informal conversation with Rita, May 15, 2013.

[36] Interview with Rita, May 28, 2013.

[37] Interview with Lorena, a friend of Rita's, May 14, 2013.

[38] Informal conversations in Rita's bar, May 21, 2013.

[39] Informal conversation with Rita, May 15, 2013.

Rita and I remained in contact when I left Kosovo for a few months. In the summer of 2013, she wrote me, "I am so so. Selling stuff from the bar and house, getting ready to leave Kosovo for right now. Business is slow, no way to pay my rent and live. I am tired of this kind of life [...] Got to go because I can't survive here anymore. Not funny. I don't know yet when I am going, big trouble with money. [...] I want to go to Moldova, relax my mind a little bit, and then look for some job elsewhere."[40] Rita left Kosovo shortly afterward. She tried to build a life with her sister in Russia and later in Moldova, but she didn't manage to make a living there. The tone of her messages became more and more depressing, and she posted a picture on her Facebook page with the caption: "Let me play you a song called: there is no fucking food in my bowl!"[41] Rita wrote that she was focused on short-term survival: "I buy some food. For a couple of days I am fine. But then I don't know."[42] She also had some health problems, but could not afford to go to the doctor for treatment.

A Ukrainian woman Rita had met in Kosovo contacted her after seeing Rita's Facebook posts about her problems. She told Rita that she could arrange a job for her in Turkey in summer. The conditions of the job were unclear, but Rita was told that she would be working as a receptionist at a spa. In the weeks before her scheduled departure, Rita was nervous about the nature of the job. She told me, "No news about how they are gonna pay me. How I am gonna work, work time, days off. Where I am gonna live. How it works with visa. I don't know anything yet."[43] Rita finally decided that she did not trust the job offer. Instead, she managed to arrange a job in Dubai, where she has been working in the entertainment industry since the summer of 2014.

Unlike Sofija, who engaged in prostitution in order to travel and engage in a luxurious lifestyle, Rita became involved in prostitution in order to access some of the most basic needs. Rita's story elucidates that prostitution migration can offer a solution to women who find themselves in a precarious financial situation. Visa requirements, border controls and policies with regard to working and living in another country can hamper women's desires to move and work abroad, yet staying in a country where they experience difficulties in making ends meet is not always an option. Women might therefore engage with human smugglers or traffickers or enter into strategic marriages in an attempt to overcome migration barriers. Furthermore, not-so-standard destinations, which are accessible but still offer opportunities to earn money, are considered. In the wake of the war, Kosovo was one such destination: border control was not strict, and the peacekeeping economy offered the potential to make a living.

---

[40] Facebook conversation with Rita, August 16, 2013.

[41] Facebook post, February 2, 2014.

[42] Skype conversation with Rita, March 21, 2014.

[43] Skype conversation with Rita, February 19, 2014.

Fig. 5.3 Motel

5.2.3 Mira: Leaving a Troubled Home and Sustaining Drug Use

The final narrative I will discuss illustrates that money is not always the primary reason that women engage in prostitution. Escaping a difficult home environment or drug addiction may be other important factors.

Mira looks well-groomed with her long, shiny black hair, carefully polished nails and neat clothes. Seeing her, one would not imagine that she rehabilitated from drug addiction and quit working in prostitution to sustain her need for heroin less than a year ago. Mira's addiction started in Serbia, where she was married to an abusive husband with whom she regularly used drugs. Mira's husband was violent with her, resulting in serious injuries and a miscarriage. She recounted, "One day my husband told me I had to meet a Serbian drug dealer from Kosovo to arrange some drugs for us. When I met this dealer, I told him about the violence used by my husband. The dealer told me this was not normal and offered to take me with him to Kosovo. If I accepted work in a bar in Kosovo, he could provide me with drugs whenever I needed. I decided to do it."

Mira crossed the mountains with the drug dealer and entered Kosovo. Upon their arrival, the dealer found her a job at a bar and a room to live: "My friend [the drug dealer] found me a job in a coffee bar. I could also live in a room in the basement of the bar, together with the other girls working there. We didn't have to pay for it."

Mira worked in the bar with four other girls. One of the girls was Serbian as well. "The day I arrived, the Serbian girl said to me in Serbian, 'Why did you come? You don't know what it is like.' An older waitress heard our conversation and told us to be silent or speak in Albanian. Then she took the Serbian girl to the kitchen. I don't know what happened there, but she had been crying when she came back in the bar."

When working in the bar, every girl was responsible for three tables. "We had to keep the guests at our tables company. After work, some of the girls would go with the clients [for sexual intercourse]. But only after working hours. The boss wouldn't let you go during work because you had to keep all the guests company. Sometimes he [the boss] would say, 'Go to that man. He has a lot of money. Let him order these drinks for you because they are expensive.'"

In the beginning, Mira was not free to leave the bar after her working day had finished. The bar owner would not let her go out because he was afraid she would be tempted to work for other bar owners: "The bar owner and his wife lived in front of the bar. He told his wife to check if we were in the bar or in our room. She would watch us through the window from her house all the time. She also had the key to our room and sometimes would come over. She was so jealous and wanted to know if the bar owner had affairs with the girls. The wife wasn't allowed in the coffee bar, so she wanted me to tell her what was going on there and what her husband [the bar owner] was doing. So she would come and ask questions all the time."

After Mira had been working in the bar for some time, the bar owner did allow her to go out. Sometimes Mira would go with clients after work. "If I slept with a client, then he would come over to the bar more often, so the bar owner wanted that. But I could keep the money I earned after working hours for myself."

While in the bar, the clients would pay Mira for their drinks, and she would give this money to the bar owner after working hours. The money earned by keeping the clients company in the bar was for her. "If clients asked me to accompany them, the price would start at 10 euros. If they took my telephone number and asked to meet later, then they would pay more to seduce me. This is not for sex, but just for the company. If we left together and had sex later, then he would pay again—young men maybe 20 or 30 euros, and if older men looked wealthy, I tried to ask more, maybe between 60 and 70." She spent most of it on drugs. "I didn't pay my friend [the drug dealer] for his help with finding me the job in the coffee bar. But I always bought my drugs from him. I took drugs from him all the time. Drugs are expensive, so all the money I earned went to my friend. […] Sometimes I had to buy some clothes and makeup, but that was nothing. All my money went straight to my dealer."

In the beginning, Mira could keep all the money she earned. After a while, however, the bar owner started trying to take her money. "He would say, 'I need money. Can I borrow something from you?' And then you wouldn't get this money back. When I didn't want to give him my money anymore, he started to treat me really bad and he started to yell at me." Mira decided she needed to get away from the bar. She managed to escape and went to the police.[44]

[44] Interview with Mira, December 8, 2011.

Mira's story demonstrates that sex workers do not always migrate for economic reasons. Mira's engagement in prostitution allowed her to sustain her drug addiction, but she had already managed to do so in Serbia. Mira eventually left Serbia and engaged in prostitution because she found herself in an abusive relationship. The will to leave a troubled home situation is another reason to engage in prostitution migration.

5.3 Reasons to Engage in Out-Country Prostitution in Kosovo

The narratives of Sofija, Rita and Mira underline that there is no "typical" reason for Eastern European women to engage in prostitution in the context of the peacekeeping mission in Kosovo. However, they hint at an array of intentions that can largely be grouped into three main reasons. First, an unsatisfying financial situation and, second, a troubled home can make women consider engagement in prostitution abroad. These are both push factors. Third, in the wake of the war, Kosovo was a relatively accessible market where large sums of money could be earned in prostitution. Women were informed about these possibilities through their social networks. This worked as a pull factor. These three aspects will be discussed in the following sections.

5.3.1 Economic Needs and Desires

Sofija and Rita's experiences illustrate particularly well that, in correspondence with studies on prostitution elsewhere (Agustín, 2007; Siegel, 2011), the desire to improve one's economic situation is a principal reason for foreign women to engage in out-country prostitution. In Rita's case, dire poverty and a lack of other options made her consider prostitution abroad. Her story resembles "survival prostitution" (Higate, 2003, pp. 15, 22) or "survival sex" (Muir, 1991; Preston-Whyte, Varga, Oosthuizen, Roberts, & Blose, 2000). Both terms refer to the selling of sex in order to meet subsistence needs such as food, clothes and shelter. The narrative that dire poverty urges women to engage in prostitution is widely accepted. Abolitionist scholars posit that women only engage in prostitution as a consequence of economic—as well as social and personal—constraints that leave them without other options (Aronowitz, 2001, pp. 167, 170; Matthews, 2008, p. 30; Jeffreys, 2009, p. 20). Rita's story illustrates that dire poverty is an indisputable incentive to engage in prostitution.

Yet Rita also knew prosperous times when her engagement in prostitution was not a matter of survival. During the heyday of the sex industry in Kosovo, Rita spent most of her earnings on barbeques, parties, fashionable clothes and presents for her niece. Moreover, Sofija's experiences show that the economic reasons for entering the prostitution business are not restricted to "survival prostitution" only. Women also engage in out-country prostitution in order to earn money and enjoy the luxurious lifestyle presented on the television and internet (see also Andrijasevic, 2007, pp. 97–98; Ehrenreich & Hochschild, 2002; Siegel, 2012, p. 258). It can allow women to purchase items that are commonly associated with modernity and therefore increase their prestige and position in society (Oldenburg, 2015, p. 324). According to Benjamin Barber (2007), this desire to consume, which is constantly fed by the media, is characteristic of late modernity. Barber argues that citizens nowadays are constantly being seduced to consume. This is no different for the women who engage in out-country prostitution: they move in order to fulfill the widespread desire to consume (Bauman, 1998).

However, in her study on sexual exchange for material gain in Durban, South Africa, Leclerc-Madlala (2003, p. 224) found that "women legitimate their behaviours by seizing upon the language of survival sex and locating their efforts to acquire luxuries within a paradigm of sexual exchange for subsistence purposes." Similarly, in her study amongst Eastern European women engaged in the sex industry in Italy, Andrijasevic (2010, p. 24) observed that "some of the women tried to rid themselves of stigma by portraying themselves as 'being forced' to sell sex out of an economic responsibility to their families." Some of the (foreign) women involved in my research mentioned the dire economic situation back home as the main reason to engage in out-country prostitution. This was especially the case during our initial conversations. When trust between us had grown after several meetings, women shared more layered and complex stories in which dreams of traveling and middle-class lives featured. There are a number of questions that arise from this observation: Why would women feel the need to justify their involvement in prostitution by making reference to being (economically) forced into the business? Is the narrative of prostitution in order to acquire luxuries less acceptable than that of dire poverty?

The answers to these questions relate to the emphasis that is put on women involved in prostitution as victims, which springs from the aforementioned moral crusade against sex trafficking. Weitzer (2007, p. 450) outlines that one of the core abolitionist claims of this moral crusade is that "prostitution is immoral, a threat to marriage and the family, or oppressive to women." Women can feel the need to justify their involvement in such an "evil" business by emphasizing that they didn't *choose* to do so. Thus, they try to remain on the "right" side of the distinction between "innocent victims," who are (economically) forced into prostitution, and "voluntary prostitutes," who are guilty of their own accord (Doezema, 2002, p. 42) and involved in immoral behavior—a dichotomy that is both artificial and harmful. It is artificial because survival and "consumerist" prostitution (Higate, 2003, p. 23) are ambiguous concepts that, as illustrated by Rita's story, are not mutually exclusive (Leclerc-Madlala, 2003, p. 224). It is harmful because it creates what Doezema (2002, p. 47) defines as "the whore/madonna division": "The madonna is the 'forced prostitute'—the child, the victim of trafficking; she who, by virtue of her victim status, is exonerated from sexual wrongdoing. The 'whore' is the voluntary prostitute: because of her transgression, she deserves whatever she gets." This distinction is a threat to the human rights of women. If a woman faces human-rights abuses, as Sofija experienced in Malta, the fact that she was not forced into the sex industry is irrelevant. As Oude Breuil et al. (2011, p. 35) outline, "being willing to engage in prostitution does not automatically mean consenting to be subjected to abuse of all kinds."

This emphasis on economic force is nonetheless reiterated in publications on sexual exchanges in the context of peacekeeping missions. In various publications, prostitution is portrayed as one of the last resources of women in the wake of war. Jeffreys (2009, p. 120) describes how "[i]n conflict zones women and girls become vulnerable to prostitution as a result of being separated from families and being reduced to penury by displacement and destruction of subsistence" (see also Martin, 2005). She argues that these women only engage in prostitution "in order to survive." The notion that prostitution in the context of peacekeeping missions is exploitative in its very essence is also institutionalized in the zero-tolerance policy of the UN, discussed in Chapter Four, which forbids peacekeepers to have sexual intercourse with women involved in prostitution. A "frequently asked questions and answers" sheet from UNMIK explains that "prostitution is not a victimless crime, as it is an act of sexual exploitation which abuses a position of differential power for sexual purposes. [...] Those who have the money to buy sex, have more power than those who sell their bodies to survive. [...] Buyers of sex can walk away; sellers of sex rarely can."[45]

Dianne Otto (2007) is critical of this emphasis on survival prostitution within peacekeeping economies. She argues that survival prostitution is a form of livelihood that involves a level of agency in most peacekeeping contexts. Otto puts forward that sex in itself is not harmful and that the zero-tolerance policy is driven by what Rubin (1984) defines as "sexual negativity." According to Otto, sex is not the problem; poverty is. She contends that the focus on sex "divert[s] attention away from the obligations of the international community to cooperate to address global inequalities in wealth and opportunity and ensure that humanitarian assistance leads to tangible and sustainable improvements in the lives of its recipients" (Otto, 2007, p. 25). Otto's critique primarily focuses on the policy level, but her analysis also lays bare the larger context in which women opt for prostitution. With regard to the latter, her argument rightly points out that the stories of Sofija, Rita and other women who took part in this research are also stories of "wrenching global inequality" because global inequalities in income are immense (Ehrenreich & Hochschild, 2002, pp. 2, 8). However, Otto does not consider the ambiguity of the concept of survival prostitution and the prevalence given to it.

Based on empirical research in the peacekeeping economies of Liberia and the Democratic Republic of the Congo, Jennings (2015) and Oldenburg (2015) do indeed critique the automatic assumption that prostitution in the context of a peacekeeping mission is survival prostitution. They observed that local women engaged in sex work or romantic relationships with internationals whereby the associated sexual intercourse "is exchanged not for one's own survival but for the fulfillment

[45] FAQ: SGB ST/SGB/2003/23, "Special Measures for Protection from Sexual Exploitation and Abuse." Prepared by UNMIK/CDT/03-06-2011.

of desires" (Oldenburg, 2015, p. 322)—desires that are often both material and, as discussed in Sect. 4.3.3, emotional.[46]

Jennings (2015) defines the sexual engagement of local women with internationals as a logical reaction to the exceptional situation created by the presence of the peacekeeping mission. She suggests that local women try to "get while the getting is good" (idem: 307), referring to the fact that local people will try to benefit from the peacekeeping economy as long as it lasts. Yet my data suggests that this also holds for women from other countries. As illustrated by the stories of Sofija and Rita, foreign women see the opportunities offered by peacekeeping economies. Countries with a peacekeeping mission, such as Kosovo, become opportune destinations for prostitution migrants to consider, similar to wealthy Western European countries (but also dissimilar to them; see Sect. 5.3.3).

Bujar, the bar owner introduced in Chapter Three, explained foreign women's attraction to peacekeeping economies thus: "But you know, it was not just the internationals who made that there was a lot of prostitution. Also there were really a lot of girls. Offering it to them. They had already arrived."[47] Bujar suggested that the prostitution business in Kosovo did not necessarily flourish after the internationals arrived, but that the business was already there, anticipating their arrival. The mere announcement of a peacekeeping mission seems to attract women—in the case of Kosovo, initially primarily foreign women. This alters Jennings and Nikolić-Ristanović's (2009, p. 10) conclusion on the link between peacekeeping and sex industries that "[o]nce created, demand prompts the supply of women." What Appadurai (1990) called the "mediascape" is underemphasized in their argument. Mediascapes refer to the electronic capabilities to both produce and disseminate information—such as television and the internet—that are widely available, as well as to the images of the world that these media create. Through these media, women inform each other about places where earnings in prostitution are good, such as Kosovo during the peacekeeping mission.[48] Supply in Kosovo thus went hand in hand with demand, as people already knew about the economic possibilities of a peacekeeping economy.

Women aimed to benefit from the peacekeeping economy for a range of reasons along the continuum from survival to consumerist prostitution. They are amongst the international players who Carolyn Nordstrom (2004) observed as inhabiting (post-)war zones or, in this case more specifically, peacekeeping economies. These international players are not "drawn into a national drama for a specific set of rea-

[46] In no way do I want to suggest that the relationships between local women and internationals are always rooted in potential financial gains. As outlined in Chap. 4, in Kosovo I encountered many relationships between internationals and local women in which the latter did not need the financial support of an international partner and the relationship was based on love, intimacy, and the alleged liberal spirit of internationals. The relationships of women engaged in the prostitution business generally did have a more explicit material foundation, however.

[47] Informal conversation with Bujar, April 14, 2013.

[48] Other scholars have also observed that those in the underclass use social media in order to inform one another about economic possibilities. See, for instance, Nagy (forthcoming, 2018) on the experiences of Central European Roma migrants in accessing social services.

sons unique to this 'locale,'" but are attracted to the economic possibilities that it offers (idem: 13). Peacekeeping economies thus have ramifications not only for peacekeepers and the local population, as suggested by Jennings and Bøås (2015, p. 283), but also for other international players, such as women engaged in out-country prostitution.

5.3.2 *Social Escapes: Going East or West When Home Is Not Best*

Aside from economic factors, there are also several social factors that influence women's decision to move abroad and engage in prostitution in Kosovo. As Mira's case has shown, women might want to leave abusive relationships or otherwise difficult home situations where care responsibilities or oppressive expectations loom (Ehrenreich & Hochschild, 2002, pp. 10–11). Generally, the notion that home is comfortable, safe and overall the "best" place prevails (Hannerz, 2002, pp. 218–220; Oude Breuil, 2008, pp. 224–225). This is especially so in debates about prostitution. Andrijasevic (2007, p. 26) has observed how images of wounded and dead women in anti-trafficking campaigns in post-socialist Europe try to warn women considering migration about the dangers of possible engagement in prostitution abroad, "encourag[ing] women to stay at home." Home, Oude Breuil (2014, pp. 132–133) argues, becomes a normative concept. It claims to be the "proper place of women" where sexuality belongs and safety and comfort is assured. Yet, like Mira, large numbers of people try to get away from their homes because they do not feel comfortable, free or secure there. They prefer the uncertainty of the alternative to the known but oppressive home, opposing the suggested binary between "the safe home" versus "the dangerous outside" world (Oude Breuil, 2014, p. 132).[49]

Rea illustrated this when she explained how the brothel where she was working felt safe in comparison to her family home in Albania. Her father had taken Rea from the latter and forced her into prostitution abroad several times. "Maybe it is difficult to understand, but for me this is a good place."

Middle-aged men occupied most of the other tables in the brothel, some of them briefly touching 18-year-old Rea as they passed by. She flashed them affectionate smiles, explaining, "I have a room upstairs, but the owner never allows men there. You have to go to the city with clients. The room is all mine."[50] Rea could not freely leave the brothel; she had to ask the bar owner for permission to do so. But she felt that at least she had a certain amount of control over the clients that she met, and she enjoyed having a private room on the first floor. This control provided Rea with rela-

[49] This fictional binary also features in other settings; one can think of refugees who escape a dangerous home toward an unknown future.

[50] Interview with Rea, December 2, 2011.

tive comfort (and possibly even a sense of security) in comparison to the not-so-safe home from which she was trafficked by her father.

However, women do not necessarily leave home because their situations are as dire as Mira's or Rea's. Hannerz (2002, p. 220) suggests that home can be perceived as boring, especially by young people who cannot always stand the continuity of home and instead dream of the world beyond. Bickford (2003) posits that exploring the world is something "those from the higher classes take for granted. [...] This is expected, and in many ways, 'necessary' to the creation of a 'well rounded' individual." However, Bickford also observes that not everyone can afford to travel—and those who cannot afford it are nonetheless constantly confronted with images of adventure, travel and other lifestyles. Appadurai (1990) pointed out how these images in the media spark people's imagination about alternative possible lives. Bickford applies this tension between imaginations and individual possibilities to an analysis of military recruitment in the United States. He finds that the United States' military promises travel, adventure and, unofficially, exotic sex to attract those from lower-class backgrounds who have no other means to travel but through a military career (see Sect. 4.1.1). Similar discrepancies between a (boring) home, where women do not feel that they are able to develop themselves (Agustín, 2005), and dreams of adventure can be observed in the stories of women engaged in prostitution. Sofija, for example, dreamed of changing her monotonous life in Ukraine for worldwide travel, such as a vacation to Egypt with her son after he had seen pyramids and the desert in the movie *Aladdin*. For the foreign women whom I encountered in the Kosovar prostitution business, the possibilities to realize their dreams were limited. Being smuggled or trafficked abroad was one of the few options available to them (see also Siegel, 2012). Siegel (2012, p. 258) puts forward that such "a possible push-pull combination relating to the gap between hopelessness and boredom on the one hand, and a sense of adventure and satisfaction of curiosity, on the other hand is rarely taken into consideration" in research on human trafficking and migration.

Many women have such dreams, but it takes courage to actually leave and try to realize them (Ehrenreich & Hochschild, 2002). Based on their study amongst potential victims of trafficking in Romania, Lăzăroiu and Alexandru (2003, p. 22) conclude that girls who are willing to go abroad, including those who go with human traffickers, are "more independent, rather open to experiments, and willing to accept uncertainty and risk." This is also illustrated by the story of Rita, who knowingly placed herself at risk in order to achieve her objectives. Rita had already experienced exploitation in similar situations, but decided that the potential gains outweighed the possible dangers (see also Friman & Reich, 2007, p. 150; Long, 2007, p. 22; Mertus & Bertone, 2007, p. 50). Women involved in the sex industry are thus not only considered naïve and deceived victims but, on the contrary, can also be seen as adventurous (Surtees, 2005, p. 263) and willing to venture into the unknown in an attempt to realize their socio-economic dreams.

Yet women rarely explicitly dreamed of going to Kosovo initially. Why did they opt for Kosovo nonetheless? This question will be considered in the next section.

5.3.3 *Accessibility of Possible Destinations*

Ehrenreich and Hochschild (2002, p. 6) point out that migrants typically "go to the nearest comparatively rich country, preferably one whose language they speak or whose religion and culture they share" in order to improve their socio-economic living conditions. The Ukrainian, Moldovan, Serbian, Romanian and Bulgarian women who took part in this research were not necessarily interested in going to countries similar to their own. They preferred something different because they were unhappy in their home countries. As outlined in the previous section, some of these women mentioned that they moved abroad out of curiosity to experience other, primarily more Western, lifestyles. However, the main objective for most women was to make money abroad. Therefore, the most important criterion for a destination was, indeed, that it should be one where money could be earned (see also Agustín, 2007; Petrunov, 2014, p. 163).

For the foreign women whom I interviewed in Kosovo, countries within the European Union were by and large the most popular destinations. Like Rita, women usually only settled for Kosovo after their attempts to enter the European Union had failed. A 28-year-old Moldovan woman who had been working in a Kosovar strip club for over 3 years explained, "I really wanted to go to Italy. I found someone in Moldova who could arrange false documents for me. I paid him 1000 euros for these documents and was supposed to pay him the same amount upon arrival in Italy. I traveled to Italy with four other girls, but we were stopped at the border with Bulgaria." With her false documents having been taken, the woman went back to Moldova and arranged to go to Kosovo instead, "but I still plan to go to Italy. Maybe I can arrange a Romanian passport when I'm in Moldova this summer. Romanians can travel to Italy, so that must work out."[51] Border control and visa restrictions are hindrances for these women in realizing their plans to migrate to a desired destination. Andrijasevic (2010) therefore rightly points out that the restrictive regulations of the European Union make women increasingly vulnerable to exploitation in the sex sector, as well as in other informal sectors. Regardless of whether it is done legally or illegally, it is challenging for these women to travel to the European Union by themselves. Such barriers urge them to contact smugglers or traffickers, or to accept offers of smugglers or traffickers who can help them realize their migration plans (Andrijasevic, 2010; Long, 2007, p. 22).

Yet even when traveling alongside a smuggler or trafficker, women do not always manage to reach the European Union. What then? Studies on the sex industry rarely discuss what happens to the women who don't make it to the European Union. My data suggests that women do not just give up; some, at least, will start to consider more accessible yet still advantageous "markets" outside Western Europe. Peacekeeping economies such as Kosovo create these opportune markets. During a peacekeeping mission, economic activities grow as a direct consequence of international presence (Jennings & Bøås, 2015, p. 282). At the same time, at least as

[51] Interview with WP2, November 30, 2011.

observed in Kosovo, it was relatively easy to work there because residence and labor regulations were still being developed or were not strictly implemented.[52] Peacekeeping economies, as in Kosovo, can thus become a satisfactory Plan B.

For a few women, however, Kosovo had been Plan A all along. Sofija and her sister, a graduate in information technology who failed to find sound employment in Ukraine, were examples of this, as were women who had experience in out-country prostitution or women from the social circles of these experienced women. Through their networks, these women understood the economic possibilities that a peacekeeping mission could offer and decided "to get while the getting was good" (Jennings, 2015, p. 307).

5.4 "Recruiting" Abroad

The previous section outlined the plethora of factors that informed women's decision to move abroad, whether specifically to Kosovo or elsewhere. These factors largely go unnoticed as a result of the overwhelming focus on the victimhood of these women. The next section will explore which types of actors informed foreign women engaged in the Kosovar sex industry about the possibility to go to Kosovo, as well as the manners in which contacts were established between recruiters and women.

First, facilitators of prostitution in Kosovo cooperated with people already involved in human smuggling or trafficking from Eastern Europe to the Balkans. The way in which the Kosovar prostitution business was linked with other regional markets (irrespective of the ethnic background of those involved) has been discussed in Sect. 3.2.4 and will therefore not be repeated here. In this initial phase, Kosovar facilitators of prostitution also placed advertisements as a way to recruit, and international entrepreneurs played a crucial role in the establishment of the industry. These actors will be discussed, followed by an examination of the working methods of the Kosovar men and foreign women who subsequently recruited women in source countries. The following sections show that popular stories of recruiters who abduct and force women into prostitution are the exception rather than the rule (see also Andrijasevic, 2010, p. 31; Gould, 2011; Zhang, 2011).

5.4.1 Recruitment in the Early Days of the Sex Industry

Shortly after the war, bar owners in Kosovo placed advertisements in Moldova, Ukraine and Romania in which they offered international job opportunities (see also Andreani & Raviv, 2004, p. 10). These advertisements could be more or less explicit about the job's relation to the sex industry. Sofija, for instance, told me that

[52] See Chap. 3 for a detailed analysis of the post-war context.

her friend initially got involved in prostitution after she took a job offer from an agency: "They said it is topless dancing for one song and serving. But then, when she was there, she understood you can only earn money if you go with clients."[53] In her search for a job, Rita reported that organizations in Moldova were still advertising for work abroad—not so much in the Balkans at the time, but in Turkey or Dubai, for instance. The job offers were in sales or the tourist industry, but Rita was skeptical about this: "I am not ready for bullshit. I just want a serious job and no blah-blah."[54] These sometimes misleading advertisements were allegedly used in order to recruit women for the Kosovar prostitution business in its initial phase directly after the war.

International "entrepreneurs" also played a crucial role in this initial phase when the prostitution business was becoming established. Motel New York, where Sofija was working, is one example: Hans, from the Netherlands, and his Kosovar Albanian companion Edi established the hotel when they spotted the economic possibilities of the peacekeeping economy. As discussed in Sofija's narrative, Hans and Edi hired Ukrainian women, just as they had done in the Netherlands. According to the police, they "founded the connection to Ukraine" in Kosovo.[55]

In cooperation with experienced (international) entrepreneurs, one benefits from their knowledge about the prostitution business. Some "starters" in the facilitation of prostitution made typical beginner's mistakes. For instance, Kushtrim, the bar owner who appeared in court in Sect. 4.1, explicitly spoke about prostitution over the phone. Businesses like Motel New York, on the other hand, had extensive organization structures, illustrated by the way in which Sofija described its management.

As a safety measure against possible criminal investigations, Hans and Edi made sure that they could not officially be linked to Motel New York; on paper, the Ukrainian women seemed to be in charge of the business.[56] Sofija officially "owned and managed" Motel New York for years. She explained how this came about: "Edi said, 'I have a problem. I need to put the business in someone else's name. I cannot put it in Katya [another employee], her name, because she drinks too much. Katya is not good. Can we put it in your name? It is only for six months. Then I will search for someone from Kosovo. A local.' I was stupid. The business was also in the name of my childhood friend, but only for two months. She was smarter." Sofija agreed to put the business in her name for 6 months, but this turned into years; all official contracts bore her signature. "One time when I came back from Ukraine there was a new girl. My signature was on the contract for this girl. I said, 'How is this possible? I was in Ukraine!' Edi learned my signature." She also sent money to Ukraine if other (former) employees asked for money transfers of their income, as Edi did

[53] Informal conversation with Sofija, January 4, 2014.

[54] The quote is from a chat session with Rita, February 17, 2014. Other conversations about companies in Moldova that offered jobs in Dubai, for instance, were held on March 21, 2014 and April 1, 2014.

[55] Interview with KPO3, October 8, 2013.

[56] Interview with EUL4, May 15, 2013.

not want to do this in his name. Because of these measures, he officially could not be connected to Motel New York after 2006.[57]

Sofija paid the price when Motel New York was raided by the police and closed down in the spring of 2012. While most of the women returned to Ukraine, Sofija was detained for the facilitation of prostitution and money laundering. The prosecutor in charge of the case understood that Sofija was only managing the business on paper and explained that she had put Sofija in detention because she wanted her to be a cooperative witness, "but she absolutely refuses to speak. [...] She protects the owners."[58] After 20 months in detention, Sofija finally broke her silence and reached a plea agreement with the prosecutor. When the agreement was accepted by the court, Sofija was ecstatic and told me, "It's like a dream. I can't believe it."[59] Then she was handcuffed and briefly brought to prison for the last time before being placed in a witness protection program and sent back to Ukraine.

The special prosecutor informed me that Sofija would have been released much sooner if only she would have agreed to speak out against Edi and Hans earlier.[60] Sofija did not give the impression that she was afraid of Hans or Edi. Indeed, she spoke about Edi in a friendly fashion: "Edi is a good man. He took us to the mountains, to Bresovica, to relax and also to clubs sometimes. With two cars we go. One time, when Katya drank too much, she fell from the stairs and broke two legs. She couldn't work or go back to Ukraine. Edi helped her to go to the hospital and have an operation."[61] Sofija explained that she hadn't refused to speak out of fear for Hans and Edi, but because the prosecutor had never invited her to speak about them: "I told you. They never asked me before."[62] The prosecuting team explained that they had always contacted the Sofija's lawyer, who was paid by Edi. He had likely never passed the request to Sofija since this would have harmed the case of Edi, for whom he was actually working.[63] The prosecuting team only spoke with Sofija directly after she had fired her lawyer because she had lost patience with the whole process. The court subsequently appointed a new lawyer to Sofija's case and helped her establish a plea agreement.[64]

After Sofija decided to speak, her younger sister in Ukraine received a call from an unknown man. "He said, 'Tell your sister to go to EULEX and say that she lied. If she goes in jail for 7 or 10 years, then every month she will have a salary of 500 euro.' But what he think? To get 500 euro to live in jail? Pfff." The man also mentioned that Edi's mother was sick and that Edi could not go to prison, but Sofija said that she was not intimidated by this phone call. "I don't know this man that called. No, I am not afraid. They don't have anyone in Ukraine. Also here I am not

[57] Interview with EUL4, May 15, 2013.

[58] Interview with EUL4, May 2, 2013.

[59] Informal conversation with Sofija in court, January 3, 2014.

[60] Interview with EUL4 and EUL5, May 2, 2013.

[61] Informal conversation with Sofija, January 6, 2014.

[62] Informal conversation with Sofija, January 9, 2014.

[63] Interview with EUL5, January 9, 2014.

[64] Informal conversations with EUL2 and EUL5 and observations in court, January 3, 2014.

afraid."[65] Eventually, Sofija went back to Ukraine; Edi went to prison, and Hans is still being investigated by Interpol. These events elucidate how the experience of international entrepreneurs helps establish elaborately organized prostitution businesses.

Once the prostitution business was more or less established, the recruitment of foreign women largely took place through direct contact between men involved in the organization of the sex industry in Kosovo, as well as women from major source countries who were already working there, on the one hand, and, on the other, women in Moldova, Romania, Ukraine and other source countries.

5.4.2 *Meeting a Man*

Similar to Mira's story, various women I interviewed had traveled to Kosovo after meeting a Kosovar man in their native country. Aleksandra from Bulgaria, for example, met her Kosovar boyfriend when she was working in a bar in her hometown. After dating him for a short period of time, he invited her to come to Kosovo where she could work in his bar. "I was pregnant with our now-8-year-old son when I arrived in Kosovo. I started to work in the bar of my boyfriend and he arranged housing for me on the floor above. We couldn't live together because my boyfriend is married and has two daughters."[66] The way in which love played a central role in Aleksandra's involvement in the sex industry resembles elements of the working method of a "loverboy." As discussed in Sect. 4.3.3, "loverboys" typically seduce and charm a victim through (the promise of) a loving relationship while seeking to exploit her in the prostitution business or another industry (Bovenkerk, van San, Boone, Boekhout van Solinge, & Korf, 2006; Verwijs, Mein, Goderie, Harreveld, & Jansma, 2011). Alexandra's boyfriend made her emotionally dependent on him in order to benefit financially by subsequently involving her in his prostitution business. Her boyfriend and his brothers had similar relationships with other Eastern European women before these women entered their family business in prostitution.[67] However, this doesn't mean that such relationships do not fulfill any emotional desires for the women involved (see also Bovenkerk et al., 2006) or that all affection shown by the men is necessarily "fake." Aleksandra shared family-like moments with her boyfriend and son on a regular basis, and her boyfriend spent the night with them almost half the week.

Arsovska (2015, p. 199, 242) points out that Albanian pimps were notorious for using the "loverboy" approach to recruit Albanian—and, to a lesser extent, non-Albanian—victims of trafficking for the sex industry. In the loverboy recruit-

[65] Informal conversation with Sofija, January 6, 2014.

[66] Interview with Aleksandra, December 2, 2011.

[67] Businesses in Kosovo, both in prostitution and in other illegal or legal sectors, are often organized with family members. With regard to human trafficking in particular, Shelley (2010, p. 121) has also observed that "Balkan traffickers operate within family groups."

ment method as described by Arsovska (2015, p. 200), the use of severe violence also played a central role. Albanian pimps would first seduce a woman and subsequently not hesitate to use violence to force her into prostitution. This is in line with the "violent entrepreneur model," which Shelley (2010, pp. 121–123) describes as typical for Balkan crime groups. Some of the foreign women who participated in my research also recounted violent episodes and testified in court about the use of violence in order to force them into prostitution. An Albanian woman from Serbia told the court that she had been raped and injected with heroin in order to make her engage in prostitution[68]; a Moldovan woman stated that she had been beaten up by a Kosovo Albanian bar owner when she refused to work.[69] I observed a bar owner aggressively dragging two Roma women from a medical health clinic when they wanted to stay there and talk a little longer instead of going to work in his bar. While these episodes illustrate that violence is used by Kosovar pimps in order to force women into prostitution, (the threat of) violence did not seem to play a crucial role in recruitment processes per se. Both international and national law enforcement officials in Kosovo mentioned that attempts to force women into prostitution by the use of violence did not seem to be as widespread as the images of aggressive Albanian pimps would lead one to believe. An international prosecutor who worked for EULEX mentioned, "I would not want to exclude that some of the images are slightly exaggerated."[70] While violence did indeed occur at the hand of recruiters, it does not appear to be a "standard operational procedure" for Kosovar pimps.

Instead of deceiving or forcing foreign women into the Kosovar prostitution business by using the loverboy method or violence, respectively, most women who entered the sex industry after meeting a Kosovar man did so after accepting a job offer that explicitly mentioned engagement in prostitution. One Albanian man, who had been living and running a prostitution business in Serbia, brought two Serbian women to a newly opened motel in Kosovo to work in prostitution. The prosecutor who later indicted the owner of the motel explained, "These Serbian ladies were tough. They were a bit older, professional. Probably they had experience in the business and knew where they were signing up for."[71] The Serbian women had likely agreed to work in the motel. They told the prosecutor that they regretted the motel's closure by law enforcement even though they had limited freedom to move while living there. The Serbian women could only leave the motel to get groceries or go to the dentist, and then only after the owner had allowed them to do so and unlocked the door for them. Yet the women seemed to accept these temporary poor living conditions because the motel allowed them to earn an income. Some weeks after the motel closed, the prosecutor observed how the women tried to make up for their loss of income. The prosecutor went to a luxury

---

[68] Interview with Vesna, March 20, 2013.

[69] A Moldovan woman told the court, "I was beaten up" (desk research, office of the special prosecutor, February 13, 2013).

[70] Interview with EUL3, October 25, 2013.

[71] Interview with EUL4, May 15, 2013.

swimming pool outside Pristina that was primarily visited by international police officers (and thus primarily men) and saw the Serbian women there "showing their wares" and searching for customers. The women initially came to Kosovo with a job offer from a man that would allow them to earn money, and they continued to do so when the original plan did not work out.[72]

In her analysis of human traffickers in Southern and Eastern Europe in 2005, Surtees (2005, p. 261) concludes that, unlike trends in surrounding countries, most recruiters for the Kosovar sex industry were men. She attributes this observation to the increasing number of women from Albania that became involved in the Kosovar sex industry. In Albania, most recruiters tended to be men (see also Surtees, 2008, pp. 44–45). Yet nearly all the Moldovan, Ukrainian, Romanian, Bulgarian and Serbian women in Kosovo with whom I spoke after 2011—some of whom had been involved in the Kosovar sex industry for up to 10 years—had originally been recruited by women from their native country. The next section reflects on this final recruitment method by women from source countries who were (previously) engaged in prostitution.

Fig. 5.4 Motel

[72] Interview with EUL4, May 15, 2013.

5.4.3 Female Friends or Family Members

Both Rita and Sofija made the decision to come to Kosovo after an invitation from a friend who was already working there. Likewise, the two Serbian women mentioned above brought three female friends from Serbia to work in the motel. Entrepreneurs in the Kosovar prostitution businesses often tried to motivate current and former employees to bring female friends or family members. An example of this came to the fore in a court case against the owner of a bar in which Moldovan women were engaged in prostitution. The son of the bar owner chatted with former employees on the internet. Interceptions of these conversations show the son asking a Moldovan woman who used to work in his father's bar, "How are you? Why don't you send other girls to work in Kosovo? It's good work?" The woman agreed to "recruit" women for his father's business in exchange for money for each woman that she managed to send. Over a period of approximately a year and a half, she received over 10 money transfers of 200 or 300 euro each. She was not the only former employee who received money from this bar owner; in the same timeframe, a total amount of almost 18,000 euro was transferred to five different women via Western Union. All of these women were former employees proven to be involved in recruitment.[73] In most businesses, both former and current employees were invited to recruit women from their native country.

The women did not consider recruiting to be a simple task, as is illustrated by Sofija's experience. Edi, one of the owners of Motel New York pushed Sofija and his other Ukrainian employees to invite young women from their network in Ukraine to come and work for him in Kosovo. But Sofija was reluctant to bring other women to Kosovo: "I cannot tell them what I do. And if they want to come, I don't want that."[74] She didn't want other people to know about her involvement in prostitution and possibly judge her for it. Fear of the "whore stigma" more often makes women secretive about their involvement in the sex industry (Andrijasevic, 2010, p. 98; Weitzer, 2012, p. 30). Consequently, women do not always disclose the true nature or destination of the work to the women they recruit. As will be outlined in more detail later, some women were not expecting work in prostitution when they departed, nor were they aware that Kosovo was their final destination.

Sofija said that she did inform the few women whom she recruited about the work that would be awaiting them. In order to limit the risk that people would judge her involvement in prostitution, she only confided in those close to her, such as her younger sister. "My sister really wanted to come. I initially told her I work in services. Every time I came home, she asked if she can come. But she was young—now she is 24, then she was 22." At one point, Sofija informed her sister that she was actually involved in prostitution, but her sister was still eager to earn a similar amount of money as her big sister. She joined Sofija at work in the motel in Kosovo. "When she first came, I talked with the clients. I say, 'Only you can do like this and this,

[73] Analysis of financial data at the prosecution office, May 2013.

[74] Informal conversation with Sofija, January 4, 2014.

and I will stand in front of the door and listen, and if you do something to her you have a problem.'"[75] Since women largely recruited among their own network in their country of origin, one often finds family members (e.g., sisters, cousins and occasionally mothers and daughters) and women from the same region working in the same bar. This also held true for Rita. When she planned to return to Moldova, Rita mentioned that she knew so many girls from her village who used to work in bars around Camp Bondsteel that "we will have a little base party there."[76]

Surtees (2008, p. 45) proposes that recruitment by women as described above "plays on the existing trust between friends and requires little effort or manipulation on the part of the trafficker." The aforementioned conversation between Sofija and her childhood friend, about how the latter experienced engagement in commercial sex, illustrates that it can definitely lower the barrier to entering the sex industry if a woman already knows someone who is involved (see also Gould, 2011, p. 537).[77] Yet it is not only about trust. Seeing or hearing about an example of someone from a similar socio-economic background earning enough money to buy a house or small business is another incentive to engage in prostitution migration and "be recruited." Sofija mentioned that the example of her childhood friend, who returned from Cyprus with enough money to build a house, gave her the idea to work in prostitution as well. Examples of success are strong; moreover, they are likely more convincing than the highly symbolic and stereotypical images of trafficking victims that lie at the core of posters and brochures warning about the dangers of trafficking and sexual exploitation abroad (Andrijasevic, 2007, p. 42; Siegel, 2011, p. 263). Such successful examples can also alter women's perceptions and attitudes toward sex as a commodity (Siegel, 2011, p. 258) that can help them purchase luxuries.

The term "recruiters" doesn't seem fitting for women, who invite friends and family members to join them in offering commercial sex in Kosovo. Recruiters are generally seen as offenders (Hughes, 2000; Shelley, 2010, p. 95), while the female recruiters described above often fluctuate between the roles of exploited victim, migrant prostitute, recruiter and facilitator of prostitution. Again, Sofija is a clear example of this. In her study on trafficking in Southern and Eastern Europe, Surtees (2008, p. 44) seems to feel a similar unease about simply labeling women as recruiters in the instance that they invite their friends and family members. She states, "Some recruiters were women who were encouraged by their recruiter/trafficker to invite their friends to work abroad also but were unaware of the intention to exploit. Their role in recruitment, therefore, was unintentional." This line of argumentation seems flawed, however. When speaking about Kosovo, all the foreign women were or had been working in the exact premises for which they were recruiting; therefore, these women were well aware of the circumstances of the work. Surtees (2008) again portrays the women as victims, this time of their circumstances or their own naïveté. By doing so, she reinforces the unambiguous binary between victims of

[75] Informal conversation with Sofija, January 4, 2014.

[76] Informal conversation with Rita, August 16, 2013.

[77] This conversation is described in Sect. 5.5.2.1.

trafficking, on the one hand, and evil traffickers, on the other. Yet—as I aim to emphasize throughout this chapter—the lived experiences of women are more complex. They are often both agents and victims, or not victims at all. Their involvement in prostitution, like the possible involvement of the friends and family members they recruit, is an attempt to improve their living conditions within the means available to them. As the story of Sofija illustrated, most of these women encountered exploitation in some form along the way, but that doesn't reduce them to singular victims without dreams, plans or agency.

5.5 Expectations

As outlined in the previous section, the various recruitment channels sometimes withheld the true nature of the work for which women were recruited. Bar owner Bujar explained that the women whom he used to employ did not always know that they were expected to work in prostitution beforehand: "They often thought they would be a waitress. In the first bar they found out that they also had to work in prostitution and pay back the costs of their travels."[78] The fact that their expected involvement in prostitution came as a surprise to some women is echoed in stories of women who immediately returned to their countries of origin upon arrival. A police officer recalled, "There was this case of a girl that arrived in an airplane. In the airplane they told her that she would have to go with clients—another older, more experienced Moldovan woman in the plane told her. She declared at the airport that she didn't want this and wanted to go back. She took the first plane back to Moldova."[79] Comparable stories, in which women did not know that they were to engage in prostitution, were told about women from other Eastern European countries, especially in the days immediately after the war when the prostitution business in Kosovo started to blossom.

Furthermore, before their departure, foreign women who engaged in prostitution in Kosovo were not always aware that Kosovo would be their final destination. Sometimes these women only knew that they would be heading to Italy or the Balkans. In some cases, this vagueness was an explicit strategy, since women were not expected to be enthusiastic about Kosovo as a destination. Rita explained, "Girls thought they were going to Italy or Serbia. In that time, everyone in Moldova thought that Kosovo was still at war. I hate it that they lied to these girls."[80] In other instances, traffickers simply had not decided upon a specific destination. Women were initially brought to bars in Serbia, for example. From Serbia they moved on to Kosovo, Bosnia-Herzegovina or Macedonia, depending on the people who showed interest in them. A Kosovar Albanian special prosecutor described this way of work-

[78] Informal conversation with Bujar, March 3, 2013.

[79] Interview with KPO3, November 8, 2013.

[80] Informal conversation with Rita, May 21, 2013.

ing as follows: "Eastern European girls, their first station was Serbia. A Serbian man would take the Moldovan girls to Serbia. He would take the girls to a motel in Serbia. Albanian men come and buy them. One girl told me she was held in a place where men would come and buy them. She said, 'Two or three times some men came, but they didn't buy me because I was ugly.' Then one Albanian man came and took all the girls—also her. He took her to Kosovo."[81] In such a situation, women had very little to no say in where they would be going next, and a clear destination was not decided upon prior to departure. Bar owner Bujar explained that his Moldovan former employee, who was also his mistress for 6 years, had this experience: "She left Moldova after a friend of hers invited her to come to Serbia and work with her somewhere. This friend was already working in Serbia and took more women from Moldova to Belgrade. She was sold from one person to the next, and then she kind of accidentally ended up in Kosovo."[82]

In 2004, however, Andreani and Raviv (2004, p. 10) assessed changing patterns and trends of human trafficking in the Balkan region and concluded that a growing number of women knew about their destination and the work expected of them there. In line with that observation, the vast majority of the foreign women who participated in this research knew that they would be working in prostitution in Kosovo. Sofija and Mira are examples of this: they made well-considered decisions to migrate for prostitution. In an attempt to explain that women in Eastern European countries are often well aware that their countries are primary source countries for women involved in prostitution, one Ukrainian woman told me the following joke from her home country: "Katya came across a job vacancy of a dishwasher in Italy. She applied, and upon arrival in Italy it turned out that she actually had to do the dishes."[83] With this joke, she tried to counter the discourse of naïve and easily deceived victims of trafficking. Instead, women tend to know more than is generally assumed and, like Rita, are aware of the possible risks attached to attractive or shady job offers.

In conclusion, it can be said that foreign women in Kosovo, especially those who did not arrive immediately after the war had ended, generally knew that they would be involved in prostitution. They often made a well-considered decision to engage in sex work. Yet some women knowingly obtained work in the sex industry but did not expect violence, coercion or limited wages (Andrijasevic, 2010, p. 38; Long, 2007, p. 56). The relevance of their expectations thus goes beyond whether women were aware of their expected involvement in prostitution beforehand, but also includes expectations regarding working conditions.[84]

[81] Interview with SP1, February 26, 2013.

[82] Informal conversation with Bujar, October 17, 2013.

[83] Informal conversation with ACA2, July 30, 2016.

[84] The working conditions of women involved in prostitution in post-conflict Kosovo will be discussed in Chap. 6.

5.6 Journey to Kosovo

Strict border controls and visa procedures often hinder the realization of women's migration plans. As outlined by Rita's story, it is challenging to cross borders that your passport does not allow you to cross. And once Kosovo is reached, the rules that apply to living and working there have to be dealt with. Until July 2013, when stricter visa requirements were applied to citizens of some countries (e.g., Ukraine and Moldova), border guards would inquire about the purpose of their stay in Kosovo. People were permitted to stay in Kosovo for up to 90 days, during which time it was forbidden to work. Applications for stays that exceeded these 90 days could be submitted with the Directorate for Migration and Foreigners in Pristina, and those who wished to work in Kosovo needed to have a work permit issued by the Kosovar Ministry of Labour and Social Welfare. Border police are trained to recognize potential victims of trafficking and prevent women and girls with suspicious reasons for traveling from entering Kosovo. A former member of the inter-ministerial working group on anti-trafficking recalled several such suspicious cases, including the following: "One time we had the case of a girl from Moldova who came to work in an internet café and was going to clean the computers. Ha ha! We said, 'Thank you, but we don't need this. We have 40% unemployment here!'"[85] In cases like these, women were not allowed to enter Kosovo and were sent back to their country of origin. This also happened to Sofija's sister during her first attempt to travel to Kosovo. She came by plane, but the Kosovar border control immediately sent her back to Ukraine, as they suspected her of being a victim of trafficking.[86] Nevertheless, she managed to enter Kosovo during her second attempt.

Human smugglers and traffickers generally know ways of bypassing the barriers to cross international borders. In some instances, they can also arrange paperwork to make staying and working in Kosovo legal (e.g., with the help of corrupt officials; see Sect. 3.2.2). The joint mention of human smuggling and trafficking here is not intended to add to the "constant slippage between 'illegal migration,' 'forced prostitution' and 'trafficking'" described by Anderson and Andrijasevic (2008, p. 138). Both terms are mentioned, since—as the journeys of the women described in this section will show—it is often unclear who has been trafficked and who has illegally migrated with the assistance of smugglers.

What is clear is that the women who participated in this research all cooperated with human smugglers or traffickers, since the middlemen knew how to deal with measures that control immigration. Andrijasevic (2010, p. 28) made similar observations in her study amongst women from non-EU countries in Italy, concluding that "restrictive visa policies and strict border controls produce conditions that exac-

[85] Online interview with HTE5, January 17, 2014.

[86] Interview with Sofija, January 6, 2014.

erbate migrant women's vulnerability to abuse and exploitation." Immigration and visa regulations mean that women cannot travel to their desired destination by themselves and often arrive with debts to smugglers or traffickers (see also Anderson & O'Connell Davidson, 2003, pp. 7–8). Women are thus not necessarily the victims of "evil" smugglers and traffickers, but of regulations that try to force them to stay in places where they do not see a future for themselves. Subsequent engagement with human smugglers and traffickers is a way to fight this global inequality and pursue a plan that is not supported by the way in which the world is organized.

This section outlines the three main ways in which foreign women traveled to Kosovo managed by third parties. This was done by illegally crossing borders over land, making use of holiday packages in the region, or through direct flights in cases where papers were falsely arranged beforehand. The section also reflects on the financial agreements made with these human smugglers and traffickers and, based on these, discusses the blurry distinction between human smuggling and human trafficking.

Fig. 5.5 Roundabout in Pristina

5.6.1 Illegal Border Crossings Over Land

In the first method, women traveled to Kosovo over land without approved travel documents (i.e., neither with a visa for the countries en route nor with a Kosovar permit to work and stay). The journey without obligatory documents was long, often dangerous and, as outlined by Andreani and Raviv (2004, p. 14), women were sometimes subject to violence, rape and malnutrition. Rita explained, "A lot of girls died along the way. It's a hard road. In cars that were driving too hard. Sleeping in the woods. Walking through rivers."[87] Constanta, a Moldovan woman who was working in Bujar's bar, made a disgusted face when she heard that Bujar and I were talking about illegal border crossing. "The road from Moldova was more walking than in a car. I don't want to talk about it. It gives me bad memories," she said and continued playing darts with a client.[88]

Women from Moldova who took this route would usually first travel to Romania. Subsequently, Moldovan and Romanian women would travel to Vojvodina, an autonomous province in the north of Serbia, and then to Belgrade. Women from Ukraine would also travel to Belgrade, but usually via Hungary (Andreani & Raviv, 2004, pp. 67–70, 264); Belgrade was mentioned as a nexus point by most respondents. Police, however, noted that other cities (e.g., Skopje in Macedonia and Budapest in Hungary) fulfilled this role—as central cities from which women continued their journey—during other periods of time.[89] Borders were crossed illegally by paying corrupt border guards or by making one's way through forests or other green passages.

Once in Serbia, many women would travel to Kosovo directly (i.e., without passing other countries) via Mitrovica in the northern part of Kosovo. As outlined in Sect. 3.2.5, ethnic Serbs predominantly inhabit the territory north of the Ibar, and they generally do not recognize the state of Kosovo and the authorities in Pristina; law enforcement under the auspices of the government in Pristina thus has very limited control. At the same time, Serbian authorities would not necessarily guard the border of a territory they considered their own and thus did not recognize. While many foreign women traveled from Serbia to Kosovo through the various unsecured routes between Serbia and North Kosovo, others used Kosovo's eastern border with Serbia.

An alternative route to Kosovo was from Serbia through Montenegro and Albania. Bujar, the bar owner, recounted that women who took this route had a "very hard" journey. His former Moldovan girlfriend traveled this way: "When she arrived in Belgrade, she was forced to move with people. From Serbia she was sold to a person in Montenegro. This person sold her to a person in Albania. And this person sold her to a bar owner in Prizren.[90] [...] It took 5 or 6 days, but it was very hard. They didn't know where they were at all, which country, nothing. Sleeping

[87] Informal conversation with Rita, May 21, 2013.

[88] Informal conversation with Constanta, September 25, 2013.

[89] Interviews with EUL5, September 17, 2013, and KPO2, January 8, 2014.

[90] Informal conversation with Bujar, October 17, 2013.

somewhere in the mountains."[91] Bujar and his ex-girlfriend later tried to trace her path by looking at maps. This was when she understood that her journey had taken her through Montenegro and Albania. When I asked Bujar why smugglers and traffickers would take this challenging route, he explained, "Some people didn't have contacts there in Mitrovica, but they did in Montenegro and Albania."[92] As outlined in Sect. 3.2.4, people prefer to deal with the people they know.

These two are the most common routes to Kosovo, taken by women who traveled without the approved travel documents. Individual experiences largely depended on the specific network of smugglers or traffickers that transported the women. This could be a network with direct lines from Moldova to Kosovo, as was the case for Rita. Such networks would usually bring women to Kosovo without losing much time en route (e.g., by working in premises for prostitution in Serbia), since the women were expected at a specific bar in Kosovo. But these could also be networks that would take women to Belgrade or other regional markets, and would leave the decision on the women's final destination to whoever showed interest in them. This is what happened to Bujar's ex-girlfriend.

Foreign women who traveled to Kosovo for the first time often took this route, over land, without approved travel documents. A work and stay permit would be arranged upon arrival in Kosovo. This subsequently allowed the women to legally travel (usually by plane) between their country of origin and Kosovo.

5.6.2 Using Holiday Packages

A second group of women used holiday packages to Montenegro, which allowed them to travel to the Balkans in a legitimate way. Once in Montenegro, women only had to cross the last borders to Kosovo illegally. Ukrainian women often took this route, including Sofija: "All girls come to Montenegro; different cities, but all Montenegro. We don't need visa for that. Many tourists go there. I booked a tour with a ticket and a hotel for one week for 300 euro. But then I didn't go to the hotel. Hans picked me up from the airport. I knew that he would pick me up and that I would go to the motel [in Kosovo where she would be working]. But Hans didn't speak so much English and no Russian, so we couldn't really speak. And he was fat and then for seven hours in the car through the mountains. I was a bit afraid, uncomfortable. [...] At the border with Kosovo I said, 'I am his girlfriend. I stay for some days.' It was OK. The next day, Hans told me to go to the police. Hans said, 'Don't tell the truth. Say you came here to visit someone for a few days and then you saw this job [at the motel] and you like it, so you come to stay and work.' So I did it like that."[93] One day, Sofija showed me the stamps in her passport. She had a visa for Egypt for herself and her son, various entry and exit stamps for Kosovo and an entry

[91] Informal conversation with Bujar, November 12, 2013.

[92] Informal conversation with Bujar, November 12, 2013.

[93] Informal conversation with Sofija, January 6, 2014.

stamp for Montenegro—but when we searched for it, there was no stamp for her entry into Kosovo that same day.[94] Since Sofija vividly recalled crossing the border and speaking with a border official, it seems most likely that Hans bribed the official, who let them enter Kosovo but did not stamp her passport.

Like Sofija, women booked a holiday package to a beach resort in Montenegro (e.g., Tivat or Budva). Citizens and holders of ordinary Ukrainian passports can enter Montenegro without a visa and stay for up to 90 days.[95] Unlike Kosovo, Montenegro is a popular holiday destination for Ukrainian tourists. Women arriving in Montenegro with a Ukrainian passport are therefore not necessarily suspected to be victims of trafficking or to be migrating in order to engage in prostitution, as is generally the case in Kosovo. Their statements—that they are coming for tourism—are therefore not met with skepticism, and furthermore, they can also show a hotel reservation at an actual tourist destination. Upon arrival at the airport in Montenegro, however, women did not go to a hotel, but illegally continued their journey to Kosovo. Kosovo was entered through unprotected green borders between Montenegro and Kosovo, sometimes via Albania. A former member of the Kosovar inter-ministerial working group on anti-trafficking explained, "There are many routes through Rugova.[96] Sometimes they just came through the mountains like contrabands. There are many roads. Some are not so bad. You can pass some of them by car."[97] Others bribed border officials on roads, who are generally presumed to be more corrupt than the border officials at airports.

As was the case for women traveling only over land, women could apply for the necessary work and stay permits with the Ministry of Labour and Social Welfare and the Directorate for Migration and Foreigners, respectively, once in Kosovo.

5.6.3 By Plane with Falsely Arranged Papers

Third, women arrived in Kosovo by plane. As long as their work and stay permits were in order, foreign women didn't encounter problems with traveling back and forth between their countries of origin and Kosovo. However, these documents could only be arranged in person in Kosovo. Women thus had to enter the country primarily via the abovementioned illegal routes when arriving for the first time. Once in Kosovo, the appropriate documents could be arranged, and women would be able to cross borders legally and travel by plane.

One group of women, however, managed to arrive in Pristina by plane the very first time that they traveled to Kosovo. This was possible if the owners of the pros-

[94] Informal conversation with Sofija, January 9, 2014.

[95] http://www.visit-montenegro.com/montenegro-visa-regimes/ukraine/, accessed November 28, 2017.

[96] Rugova is a mountainous region located in the west of Kosovo, bordering Montenegro and, to a lesser extent, Albania.

[97] Informal conversation with HTE5, January 16, 2014.

titution businesses where they would be working had arranged their work and stay permits prior to arriving. Arranging documents beforehand required the involvement of corrupt officials responsible for filing work and stay permits. As a special prosecutor outlined, these women had "official documents, but they are not arranged through the official way."[98] The indictment against a group of Kosovar Albanian men, who had dozens of Moldovan women working for them in various bars in Western Kosovo, illustrated the complicity of corrupt officials in arranging the appropriate documents:

> Upon recruiting a new Moldovan employee, the owner of the bar where the woman would be working collected her personal information (e.g., passport number, date of birth). The bar owner provided the director of the regional employment center, in the city where his bar was located, with the personal data of the woman in need of a work permit. The director filed the application and sent his son to bring the completed application forms to the directorate in the capital, Pristina. The son, a student and unemployed, handed the applications to a high official at the directorate in Pristina, together with an envelope. The envelope contained a bribe consisting of sums of up to 400 euro in cash or accessories, like a watch. The high official used his authorization to fix the work permit. The son picked up the work permit and brought it to the respective bar owner. The bar owner subsequently sent the documents to the woman in Moldova, as testified by one of the women who was found working in the bar on the night that the police raided the premises: "I came to Kosovo after my sister was in Kosovo and she told me that I could come to work in Kosovo. Then X [the bar owner] sent papers to me in Moldova and I came to work in Kosovo."[99]

Sometimes the arrival of women from Moldova, Ukraine and Romania was met with suspicion even if they had the correct papers, but in general, border officials allowed women to enter if they could show the required documents. As outlined by a police officer, "When they arrived, they arrived with the permits. All the papers; that they are coming to work as dancers, waitresses, singers in these places. So they [border officials] have no possibility to stop them. So they came much easier."[100]

Surtees (2008, p. 51) explains that arranging working contracts and legal documents, such as work and stay permits, can deliberately be used by bar owners as "a means of deflecting concerns about trafficking and masking the intended exploitation." She argues that in cases where women are deceived about the nature of the job, documents might help preserve the façade of a non-sex-related job. Work permits in Kosovo, namely, stated that a woman would be working as a dancer, waitress or singer. In her search for a job, Rita would likely have felt more secure about dubious job offers if she had been presented with such legal documents. Yet the women I encountered in Kosovo largely knew about the job that was awaiting them. Like Sofija, they entered the prostitution business in order to earn money and simply didn't need to be fooled into the sex industry with legal documents. Work and stay permits in Kosovo thus primarily seemed to be arranged because the bar owners had the contacts to facilitate them and could hence allow for a pleasant and less risky journey.

---

[98] Interview with SP1, February 13, 2013.

[99] Transcripts of police interrogation.

[100] Interview with KPO2, January 8, 2014.

Traveling by plane did not work out if women did not have the correct papers. Sofija's sister experienced this firsthand: "When my sister came, she was young. Edi said, 'She can come directly to Pristina. She doesn't need to go through Montenegro.' She was young and he was afraid she would change her mind. When my sister arrived in Pristina, she wasn't allowed to come in. They sent her with the plane back to Ukraine." Without the necessary documents to legitimize her arrival in Kosovo, Sofija's sister wasn't allowed to enter the country. Border police, trained to recognize potential victims of trafficking, prevented women and girls with suspicious reasons for traveling from entering Kosovo, especially if they were from known source countries.

Whether bar owners made women travel over land, both over land and by plane, or directly by plane with pre-arranged work and stay permits depended on their network. Bar owners with trustworthy partners along smuggling routes passing through North Mitrovica would take this route, while bar owners with contacts in Albania would opt for a route through Montenegro and Albania. Still other bar owners, with contacts at the directorates for the filing of work and stay permits, would arrange and secure these documents and invite women to come by plane.

5.6.4 *Paying for the Journey by Working in a Bar*

Most women did not have savings to finance the journey to Kosovo and agreed to reimburse the costs by working upon arrival. This was the case for Tanya, who had arranged to pay back the expenditures of her journey from Moldova to Kosovo to the bar owner who had invited her and covered the costs. She could earn the total sum of 600 euro through her work in the bar. Tanya started working in the bar on the day of her arrival and continued to do so every day for a year. She lived in a room above the bar, for which she had to pay rent to the bar owner, but she managed to pay off her debts after several weeks. When a colleague and friend of hers decided to move to a bar in another part of Kosovo, Tanya followed her. With her debts paid, she was free to move on.[101]

Tanya earned money in ways similar to the methods described by Mira, which are characteristic of prostitution as it takes place around coffee bars and clubs in Kosovo. First, women and girls can earn money by accompanying guests in the bar where they are working; a client pays the girl to sit with him by buying her expensive drinks. In some bars, women can earn more money if they dance, pole dance or sing. Second, women meet clients for sexual intercourse. Sometimes, this takes place in a woman's place of work and during working hours, as was the case for Sofija. In other instances, women meet clients from the bar for sexual intercourse after working hours. A woman and a client can agree on a place to meet after the bar has closed, or a client can ask for her telephone number and establish a meeting by phone as soon as a woman finished her working hours. Mira explained, "You could meet with three to five clients a night this way. Maybe you would only work from

[101] Interview with Tanya, November 23, 2011.

10:00 until 20:00 or from 20:00 until 23:00 [in the bar], but afterwards you might be working until five in the morning."[102] Often, bar owners ask for half of the earnings from sexual intercourse with clients. In other instances, bar owners are not involved in setting appointments for sexual intercourse, but benefit from the customers' bonds with the bar, which ensures that more drinks are sold. Sometimes bar owners try to access the additional income the women earn by asking the women to lend it to them or give it to them for safekeeping.

Through these working methods Tanya managed to pay off her debt, to which a weekly amount for rent and food had been added, within several weeks. Women from Serbia generally had lower debts, since they did not have to travel far.[103] Other women from Moldova mentioned amounts similar to what Tanya had to pay. Sofija said that her sister needed to give Edi around 500 euro for purchasing a plane ticket from Ukraine.[104] These amounts seem relatively high for plane tickets from Moldova or Ukraine to Kosovo and also for other journeys by land. A female bar owner confirmed that these were relatively high prices to charge, explaining, "I had two girls from Bulgaria working for me. Two sisters. I paid for the taxi that brought them to Kosovo. Someone asked, 'Do you want two girls from Bulgaria? Two sisters?' I looked at the pictures and they were pretty, so I said yes. He said, 'Then you have to pay for the taxi.' It was 150 euro for both. [...] It was a van full of girls. More than 10 girls from Bulgaria in the van. They worked for me to pay it back. They did not get salary until they paid it back. I earned like 100 euro per day from them."[105] Although the sisters earned 100 euro a day and the journey had cost them 75 euro each, it took them several weeks to pay back their debts.[106] The bar owner altered the amount of their debts and lowered their daily earnings. It was not uncommon for bar owners to inflate the costs of the journey, add extra costs for rent and food once in Kosovo, and calculate low earnings. Another bar owner testified the following in court about the salary of the women that worked for him: "It was 750 euro [per month] in the contract, but when accommodation, food and drinks, and clothes are calculated, I have given them 250 euro."[107]

The question that arises is: When is this deliberate miscalculation of debts and earnings "bad enough" to state that women are deceived, exploited and thus victims of human trafficking? In order to answer this question, the concept of human trafficking will be explored in the final section of this chapter alongside the experiences of foreign women, engaged in prostitution in Kosovo in the context of the peacekeeping mission, who have generally been labeled as victims of trafficking.

---

[102] Interview with Mira, December 8, 2011.

[103] Interview with EUL4, May 2, 2013.

[104] Interview with Elena, November 23, 2011; informal conversation with Sofija, January 6, 2014.

[105] Interview with Saranda, September 27, 2013.

[106] After these initial few weeks, the Bulgarian sisters started to earn an income. They worked for the bar owner for 6 months and then went back to Bulgaria for a holiday, after which they returned to the same bar and worked for an additional 6 months.

[107] Analysis of court files, February 13, 2013.

Fig. 5.6 Motel

5.7 One-Sided Representation of Victims of Trafficking Disputed

The Protocol to Prevent, Suppress and Punish Trafficking in Persons defines human trafficking on the basis of three constituent elements: the act, the means, and the purpose of exploitation. The act is defined by *what* is done: this can consist of recruitment, transportation, transfer, harboring, or the receipt of persons. The means subsequently relates to *how* this is done and can consist of threat or use of force, coercion, abduction, fraud, deception, abuse of power or vulnerability, or giving payments or benefits to a person in control of the victim. Finally, the purpose of exploitation concerns *why* this is done (UNODC, 2004).

This definition, however, fails to clarify the meaning of central terms such as "coercion" and "exploitation"—a lacuna that causes Anderson and O'Connell Davidson (2003, p. 7) to state that it is "virtually impossible to specify who has or has not been 'trafficked' into the commercial sex trade without becoming embroiled in the more general debate about the rights and wrongs of prostitution—a debate which is both highly polarized and hugely emotive." The two prominent discourses on the sex industry, which either describe prostitution as gender-based violence or emphasize the right to self-determination (Segrave, Milivojevic, & Pickering, 2009), indeed echo evaluations of whether a person should be seen as a victim of trafficking or not. The case of Sofija can illustrate this point.

Is Sofija deceived, coerced or forced into prostitution? Abolitionists would likely put forward that she is coerced, based on the assumption that women only enter the prostitution business as a consequence of economic, social or personal constraints. In Sofija's case, it could be argued that her low income and violent stepfather encompassed such constraints. On the other hand, pro-sex-work scholars would presumably emphasize the fact that Sofija opted to engage in prostitution and define her as a sex worker instead—a sex worker whose rights had been violated during her stay in Spain. Thus, more than clearly defined characteristics, these prominent discourses on the sex industry determine whether an individual is seen as a victim of trafficking or not.

Gould (2011) therefore suggests shifting the concern from human trafficking to a focus on labor exploitation and abuse in the sex industry—an approach that would immediately reject the false dichotomy between "innocent victims" and "voluntary prostitutes" whereby the latter cannot always count on support in case of labor exploitation or abuse. A similar appeal is made by Anderson and Andrijasevic (2008, p. 135), who state that:

> [T]he moral panic over trafficking is diverting attention from the structural causes of the abuse of migrant workers. Concern becomes focused on the evil wrongdoers rather than more systemic factors. In particular it ignores the state's approach to migration and employment, which effectively constructs groups of non-citizens who can be treated as unequal with impunity.

This chapter has aimed to show the lived experiences of foreign women engaged in prostitution in Kosovo and elucidate the structural factors (e.g., structural inequality and migration policies) that can make these women vulnerable. The stories of these women have underlined that an exclusive focus on foreign women engaged in prostitution (both in the context of the peacekeeping mission in Kosovo, and elsewhere) as completely disempowered victims does not do justice to the agency they attempt to assert in their lives within the means available to them. Moreover, it obscures the structural factors that actually increase their vulnerability.

Nonetheless, women engaged in prostitution, and especially foreign women engaged in prostitution in the context of a peacekeeping mission, rarely feature as independent subjects in their own right. Instead, these women are singularly represented as victims of trafficking. While this one-sided representation might not do justice to the lived experience of women, it can indeed be effective for some actors. Examples of such actors are aid agencies, which depend on the projects that are granted to them and therefore can be tempted to emphasize the helplessness of the women at whom their projects are aimed. As outlined by anthropologist Agustín (2007), aid agencies benefit from describing "ideal victims" (Christie, 1986)—who are innocent, deceived and exploited—versus "evil" pimps and other exploiters, since this generally makes them more successful in receiving projects and grants. Likewise, the media need straightforward stories that the public can grasp in a few headlines, and policymakers generally welcome brief representations of the situation with concrete policy recommendations (Autesserre, 2012, p. 207; see also Sect. 2.3).

However, the focus on completely helpless victims can also prevent well-intended projects and policy, developed in line with this representation, from achieving their goals. Highly symbolic and stereotypical images of victims of trafficking are at the core of posters and brochures warning about the dangers of trafficking worldwide (Andrijasevic, 2007, p. 42). This results in women not easily identifying with the helpless victims portrayed. In Kosovo, an organization that assists victims of trafficking published a brochure featuring a drawing of a girl with a rope around her neck to illustrate the slavery-like conditions in which victims of trafficking are kept. One day, flipping through some magazines with a woman involved in prostitution at the bar where we were sitting, I accidentally set this brochure on the table. Upon seeing the drawing, the woman said, "That poor girl. Terrible such things happen," although it could be argued that she was the intended target group of the brochure, given the fact that she could not leave her place of work whenever she wanted (although she agreed to being kept inside in order to earn money).[108] The overly dramatic depiction of victims of trafficking causes any links with the actual experiences of women to be lost.

References

Agustín, L. M. (2007). *Sex at the margins: Migration, labour markets and the rescue industry*. London, UK: Zed Books.

Amnesty International. (2004). So does it mean I have rights? In *Protecting the human rights of women and girls trafficked for forced prostitution in Kosovo*. London, UK: Author.

Anderson, B., & Andrijasevic, R. (2008). Sex, slaves and citizens: The politics of anti-trafficking. *Soundings, 40*, 135–145.

Anderson, B., & O'Connell Davidson, J. (2003). *Needs and desires: Is there a demand for "trafficked" persons*. Geneva, Switzerland: International Organization for Migration.

Andreani, A., & Raviv, T. (2004). *The changing patterns and trends of trafficking in persons in the Balkan region: Assessment carried out in Albania, Bosnia and Herzegovina, the province of Kosovo, the former Yugoslav Republic of Macedonia and the Republic of Moldova*. Geneva, Switzerland: International Organization for Migration.

Andrijasevic, R. (2007). Beautiful dead bodies: Gender, migration and representation in anti-trafficking campaigns. *Feminist Review, 86*(1), 24–44.

Andrijasevic, R. (2010). *Migration, agency and citizenship in sex trafficking*. New York, NY: Springer.

Appadurai, A. (1990). Disjuncture and difference in the global cultural economy. *Theory, Culture & Society, 7*(2), 295–310.

Aronowitz, A. A. (2001). Smuggling and trafficking in human beings: The phenomenon, the markets that drive it and the organisations that promote it. *European Journal on Criminal Policy and Research, 9*, 163–195.

Arsovska, J. (2015). *Decoding Albanian organized crime: Culture, politics, and globalization*. Oakland, CA: University of California Press.

[108] Informal conversation with Manda, November 2011.

Autesserre, S. (2012). Dangerous tales: Dominant narratives on the Congo and their unintended consequences. *African Affairs, 111*(443), 202–222.
Barber, B. R. (2007). *Consumed: How markets corrupt children, infantilize adults, and swallow citizens whole*. New York, NY: W. W. Norton.
Bauman, Z. (1998). *Globalization: The human consequences*. New York, NY: Columbia University Press.
Bickford, A. (2003). See the world, meet interesting people, have sex with them: Tourism, sex, and recruitment in the U.S. military. *American Sexuality Magazine*. Retrieved March 21, 2008, from http://nsrc.sfsu.edu/MagArticle.cfm?Article=113&PageID=8&SID=59FE2D7C4E0B33976D4CE7400DFFAD37&DSN=nsrcdsn
Bovenkerk, F., van San, M., Boone, M. M., Boekhout van Solinge, T., & Korf, D. J. (2006). *Loverboys of modern pooierschap*. Amsterdam, The Netherlands: Augustus.
Christie, N. (1986). The ideal victim. In E. A. Fattah (Ed.), *From crime policy to victim policy* (pp. 17–30). London, UK: Palgrave Macmillan.
Counter-Trafficking Regional Clearing Point. (2003). *First annual report: On victims of trafficking in South Eastern Europe*. Amsterdam, The Netherlands: La Strada International. Retrieved November 11, 2017, from http://lastradainternational.org/lsidocs/205%20First%20Annual%20Report%20(RCP%20IOM%202003).pdf
De Wildt, R. (2009). Tasten in het duister: Roemeense straatprostituees in Rome. In Y. van der Pijl, D. Raven, L. Brouwer, & B. Oude Breuil (Eds.), *Antropologische Vergezichten: Mondialisering, Migratie en Multiculturaliteit* (pp. 207–224). Amsterdam, The Netherlands: Aksant.
Doezema, J. (2000). Loose women or lost women? The re-emergence of the myth of white slavery in contemporary discourses of trafficking in women. *Gender Issues, 18*, 23–31.
Doezema, J. (2002). Who gets to choose? Coercion, consent and the UN trafficking protocol. *Gender and Development, 10*(1), 20–27.
Ehrenreich, B., & Hochschild, A. R. (2002). Introduction. In B. Ehrenreich & A. R. Hochschild (Eds.), *Global woman: Nannies, maids, and sex workers in the new economy* (pp. 1–13). New York, NY: Henry Holt and Company, LLC.
Espiritu, Y. L. (2003). *Home bound: Filipino American lives across cultures, communities, and countries*. Oakland, CA: University of California Press.
Ferrell, J., Hayward, K., & Young, J. (2008). *Cultural criminology: An invitation*. London, UK: Sage.
Friman, R., & Reich, S. (2007). *Human trafficking, human security, and the Balkans*. Pittsburgh, PA: University of Pittsburgh Press.
Godziak, E. M., & Bump, M. N. (2008). *Data and research on human trafficking: Bibliography of research-based literature*. Washington, DC: Institute for the Study of International Migration.
Goodey, J. (2008). Human trafficking: Sketchy data and policy responses. *Criminology and Criminal Justice, 8*(4), 421–442.
Gould, C. (2011). Trafficking? Exploring the relevance of the notion of human trafficking to describe the lived experience of sex workers in Cape Town, South Africa. *Crime, Law and Social Change, 56*(5), 529–546.
Hannerz, U. (2002). Where we are and who we want to be. In U. Hedetoft & M. Hjort (Eds.), *The postnational self: Belonging and identity* (pp. 217–232). Minneapolis, MN: University of Minnesota Press.
Haynes, D. F. (2009). Lessons from Bosnia's Arizona Market: Harm to women in a neoliberalized postconflict reconstruction process. U. Pa. L. Rev., 158, 1779.
Higate, P. (2003). Gender and peacekeeping. Case studies: The DRC and Sierra Leone. *Africa Portal*. Retrieved November 7, 2017, from https://www.africaportal.org/publications/gender-and-peacekeeping-case-studies-the-drc-and-sierra-leone/
Higate, P. (2007). Peacekeepers, masculinities, and sexual exploitation. *Men and Masculinities, 10*(1), 99–119.
Hughes, D. M. (2000). The 'Natasha' trade: The transnational shadow market of trafficking in women. *Journal of International Affairs, 53*(2), 625–651.

Jeffreys, S. (2009). *The industrial vagina: The political economy of the global sex trade*. London, UK: Routledge.
Jennings, K. M. (2015). Life in a 'Peace-kept' city: Encounters with the peacekeeping economy. *Journal of Intervention and Statebuilding, 9*(3), 296–315.
Jennings, K. M., & Bøås, M. (2015). Transactions and interactions: Everyday life in the peacekeeping economy. *Journal of Intervention and Statebuilding, 9*(3), 281–295.
Jennings, K., & Nikolić-Ristanović, V. (2009). *UN peacekeeping economies and local sex industries: Connections and implications* (Microcon Working Paper No. 17). Retrieved from http://www.peacewomen.org/assets/file/Resources/NGO/PK_SexIndustries_MICROCON_2009.pdf
Kempadoo, K. (2003). Globalizing sex workers' rights. *Canadian Woman Studies, 22*(3–4), 143–150.
Kursani, S., Haxholli, V., & Gjikolli, G. (2014). *Kosovo in regional context: Bilateral political relations*. Pristina, Kosovo: KIPRED.
Lazaroiu, S., & Alexandru, M. (2003). *Who is the next victim? Vulnerability of young Romanian women to trafficking in human beings*. Geneva, Switzerland: International Organization for Migration.
Leclerc-Madlala, S. (2003). Transactional sex and the pursuit of modernity. *Social Dynamics, 29*(2), 213–233.
Long, L. D. (2007). Trafficking exchanges and Economic responses: Reflections from Bosnia and Herzegovina and Serbia. In H. R. Friman & S. Reich (Eds.), *Human trafficking, human security, and the Balkans* (pp. 20–40). Pittsburgh, PA: University of Pittsburgh Press.
Martin, S. (2005). *Must boys be boys? Ending sexual exploitation & abuse in UN peacekeeping missions*. Washington, DC: Refugees International.
Matthews, R. (2008). *Prostitution, politics & policy*. London, UK: Routledge.
Mendelson, S. E. (2005). *Barracks and brothels: Peacekeepers and human trafficking in the Balkans*. Washington, DC: CSIS.
Mertus, J., & Bertone, A. (2007). Combating trafficking: International efforts and their ramifications. In R. Friman & S. Reich (Eds.), *Human trafficking, human security and the Balkans* (pp. 40–60). Pittsburgh, PA: University of Pittsburgh Press.
Muir, M. (1991). *The environmental context of AIDS*. New York, NY: Praeger.
Murray, J. (2002). Who will police the peace-builders? The failure to establish accountability for the participation of United Nations civilian police in the trafficking of women in post-conflict Bosnia and Herzegovina. *Columbia Human Rights Law Review, 34*(2), 475–528.
Nagy, V. (2018). Roma networks: Ethnic solidarity in an internet age. *Intersections. EEJSP, 4*(3), 158–179. (22 p.).
Nordstrom, C. (2004). *Shadows of war: Violence, power, and international profiteering in the twenty-first century*. Berkeley, CA: University of California Press.
O'Neill, M. (2001). *Prostitution and feminism: Towards a politics of feeling*. Cambridge, UK: Polity Press.
Oldenburg, S. (2015). The politics of love and intimacy in Goma, Eastern DR Congo: Perspectives on the market of intervention as contact zone. *Journal of Intervention and Statebuilding, 9*(3), 316–333.
Otto, D. (2007). Making sense of zero tolerance policies in peacekeeping sexual economies. In *Sexuality and the law* (pp. 259–282). Abingdon, UK: Routledge-Cavendish.
Oude Breuil, B. C. (2008). "Precious children in a heartless world"? The complexities of child trafficking in Marseille. *Children & Society, 22*(3), 223–234.
Oude Breuil, B. (2014). Fluid security? Home, care and belonging in prostitution migration. In M. Schuilenburg, R. Van Steden, & B. O. Breuil (Eds.), *Positive criminology. Reflections on care, belonging and security* (pp. 129–144). The Hague, The Netherlands: Eleven International Publishing.
Oude Breuil, B. C., Siegel, D., Van Reenen, P., Beijer, A., & Roos, L. (2011). Human trafficking revisited: Legal, enforcement and ethnographic narratives on sex trafficking to Western Europe. *Trends in Organized Crime, 14*(1), 30–46.
Petrunov, G. (2014). Human trafficking in Eastern Europe: The case of Bulgaria. *The Annals of the American Academy of Political and Social Science, 653*(1), 162–182.

Preston-Whyte, E., Varga, C., Oosthuizen, H., Roberts, R., & Blose, F. (2000). Survival sex and HIV/AIDS in an African city. In *Framing the sexual subject: The politics of gender, sexuality, and power* (pp. 165–191). Berkeley, CA: University of California Press.

Rathgeber, C. (2002). The victimization of women through human trafficking – An aftermath of war? *European Journal of Crime Criminal Law and Criminal Justice, 10*(2–3), 152–163.

Republic of Kosovo, Ministry of Internal Affairs, Koordinatori Nacional Kundër Trafikimit Me Qenie Njerëzore. (2010). *Rapport per Zbatimin e Strategjisë Nacionale dhe Plani i Veprimit Kunder Trafikimit të Qenieve Njerëzore. Vepro me Përgjegjësi. Të gjithë kundër Trafikimit me Qenie Njerëzore. Janar- Dhjetor*. Pristina, Kosovo: Author.

Republic of Kosovo, Ministry of Internal Affairs, Office of National Coordinator against Trafficking in Human Beings. (2009). *Progress report: Implementation of strategy and action plan against trafficking in human beings. Zero tolerance against organized crime*. Pristina, Kosovo: Author.

Sanghera, J. (2005). Unpacking the trafficking discourse. In K. Kempadoo (Ed.), *Trafficking and prostitution reconsidered: New perspectives on migration, sex work and human rights* (pp. 3–24). Boulder, CO: Paradigm Publishers.

Segrave, M., Milivojevic, S., & Pickering, S. (2009). *Sex trafficking: International context and response*. Devon, UK: Willan Publishing.

Shelley, L. (2010). *Human trafficking: A global perspective*. Cambridge, UK: Cambridge University Press.

Siegel, D. (2011). Mobility of sex workers in European cities. *European Journal on Criminal Policy and Research, 18*(3), 255–268.

Siegel, D. (2012). Meisjes, moeders en madams. In W. Koops, B. Levering, & M. de Winter (Eds.), *Boos! Over agressie, opvoeding en ontwikkeling* (pp. 117–127). Amsterdam, The Netherlands: Uitgeverij SWP.

Siegel, D. (2015). *Het Zandpad, closing brothels or closing eyes?: Utrechtse sekswerkers na de sluiting van het Zandpad*. Amsterdam, The Netherlands: Boom Lemma uitgevers.

Simic, O. (2012). *Regulation of sexual conduct in UN peacekeeping operations*. New York, NY: Springer.

Spencer, S. W. (2005). Making peace: Preventing and responding to sexual exploitation by United Nations peacekeepers. *Journal of Public and International Affairs, 16*(Spring), 167–181.

Surtees, R. (2005). *Second annual report on victims of trafficking in South-Eastern Europe*. Geneva, Switzerland: International Organization for Migration.

Surtees, R. (2008). Traffickers and trafficking in Southern and Eastern Europe: Considering the other side of human trafficking. *European Journal of Criminology, 5*(1), 39–68.

UNMIK. (2011). *Special measures for protection from sexual exploitation and abuse*. UNMIK. Retrieved from http://www.unmikonline.org/SiteCollectionDocuments/Conduct%20and%20Discipline%20FREQUENTLY%20ASKED%20QUESTIONS%20AND%20ANSWERS%20%2003%20JUNE%202011.pdf

UNODC. (2004). *United Nations convention against transnational organized crime and the protocols thereto*. New York, NY: United Nations. Retrieved from https://www.unodc.org/documents/treaties/UNTOC/Publications/TOC%20Convention/TOCebook-e.pdf

Verwijs, R., Mein, A. G., Goderie, M., Harreveld, C., & Jansma, A. (2011). Loverboys en hun slachtoffers. In *Inzicht in de aard en omvang problematiek en in het aanbod aan hulpverlening en opvang*. Utrecht, The Netherlands: Verwey-Jonker Instituut.

Weitzer, R. (2007). The social construction of sex trafficking: Ideology and institutionalization of a moral crusade. *Politics and Society, 35*(3), 447–475.

Weitzer, R. (2012). *Legalizing prostitution: From illicit vice to lawful business*. New York, NY: New York University Press.

Weitzer, R. (2014). New directions in research on human trafficking. *The Annals of the American Academy of Political and Social Science, 653*(1), 6–24.

Yea, S. (2005). Labour of love: Filipina entertainers' narratives of romance and relationships with GIs in US military camp towns in Korea. *Women's Studies International Forum, 28*(6), 456–472.
Zhang, S. X. (2009). Beyond the 'Natasha' story – A review and critique of current research on sex trafficking. *Global Crime, 10*(3), 178–195.
Zhang, S. X. (2011). Woman pullers: Pimping and sex trafficking in a Mexican Border City. *Crime, Law and Social Change, 56*(5), 509–528.

Fig. 6.1 Woman in a bar

Chapter 6
Kosovar Women Engaged in Prostitution: (The Consequences of) Being Defined as a Voluntary Prostitute

Some years after the war had ended, local women increasingly took the place of foreign women who no longer engaged in the prostitution business in Kosovo (Surtees, 2005).[1] The Kosovar Albanian women who became involved in prostitution in bars were seldom identified by Kosovar law enforcement as victims of trafficking. When speaking about Kosovar sex workers in bars, police officers often mentioned that "in the coffee bars we don't find or we find very few victims [of trafficking]."[2] In line with the central argument of Chap. 5, I welcome the initiative to consider women engaged in prostitution in terms other than one-dimensional victims of trafficking, as this rarely does justice to the lived experience of women depicted as such. However, this was not the reason that Kosovar law enforcement did not identify local women engaged in prostitution in bars as victims of trafficking—it had nothing to do with this depiction being considered inadequate. Local women simply were not expected to meet the criteria of victims of trafficking as

[1] Since 2005, figures from the National Authority against Trafficking in Human Beings show a rise in the numbers of domestic victims of trafficking for sexual purposes (Republic of Kosovo, 2009, 2010, 2015). These numbers are based on statistical data from the Kosovo police and primarily consist of cases of Kosovar women and girls who are identified as internal trafficking victims for the purpose of sexual exploitation. A small number of the cases refer to other forms of trafficking, such as exploitation of children for beggary and forced labor (Republic of Kosovo, 2015, p. 10). This statistical data does not necessarily reflect larger trends in the Kosovar prostitution business, as it excludes those who are engaged in prostitution but who are not defined as victims of trafficking. However, the increased tendency for Kosovar women to engage in the sex industry in their home country was confirmed during visits to premises that functioned as meeting grounds for sex workers and clients. There was only one Moldovan woman amongst the dozens of women I met in bars from 2013 onward; all the others were local and, to a lesser extent, from neighboring Albania. As outlined in the previous chapter, women from Albania were largely able to continue their work in the Kosovar sex industry when foreign women from other countries were sent back home. The experiences of foreign women—from Albania and elsewhere—who engaged in prostitution in the context of the peacekeeping mission in Kosovo have been analyzed in Chap. 5.

[2] Interview with KPO3, October 8, 2013.

R. de Wildt, *Post-War Prostitution*, Studies of Organized Crime 17,
https://doi.org/10.1007/978-3-030-19474-1_6

defined in the UN Optional Protocol to Suppress and Punish Trafficking in Persons, Especially Women and Children.[3]

In the contemporary discourse, women who are not considered to be victims of trafficking tend to be labeled as voluntary prostitutes. This also tended to be the case for the Kosovar women engaged in prostitution in bars in their home country. No international agreement exists on the definition of voluntary prostitution (Doezema, 2002, p. 41–42; Shelley, 2010, p. 10). It is a category that only exists as opposed to the category of victims of trafficking as defined in the UN Protocol. But what does it mean to act "voluntary"? Acting voluntary implies the presence of realistic alternatives. As argued in Chap. 2, abolitionist scholars put forward that such alternatives are non-existent because women only engage in prostitution as a consequence of economic, social and personal constraints (Aronowitz, 2001; Farley, 2003; Jeffreys, 2009; Matthews, 2008). In doing so, they set aside the whole notion of voluntary prostitution. This stance has been criticized by pro-sex-work scholars, who argue that abolitionists deny women any form of agency (Andrijasevic, 2007; Derks, 2000). In doing so, pro-sex-work scholars retain a distinction between forced victims of trafficking and voluntary sex workers. This can also be seen as problematic, however, as voluntary prostitution is thus not defined. Concepts like "victims of trafficking" (see Chap. 5) and "voluntary prostitutes" have been fiercely debated for decades (see, for instance, Doezema, 1998; Weitzer, 2010). This chapter aims to take this discussion a step further by examining the consequences of being identified as a voluntary prostitute.

The first section of this chapter will reflect on the notion of the voluntary prostitute by examining why local women, who are defined as such, engaged in prostitution in bars in Kosovo. Were there constraints that informed their decision to do so? And what do these possible constraints say about the notion of "voluntary prostitute"? In examining their motivations, I have differentiated between market forces, social factors and individual considerations. The second part of this chapter examines how local women involved in prostitution in bars experience their work. Specific attention is given to how their lives are impacted by being labeled voluntary prostitutes. By way of conclusion, I will postulate that the attention paid to alleged victims of trafficking during peacekeeping missions causes the often-precarious situation of women engaged in prostitution, but who are not defined as victims of trafficking, to remain unseen.

6.1 Market Forces

The increasing numbers of local women who engaged in prostitution in Kosovo can be explained, first of all, by looking at specific market forces in the early years of the millennium. These market forces encompass one pull factor and one push factor, both of which will be examined in more detail in this section.

[3] See Sect. 5.7 for a discussion of this UN Protocol, including the three constituent elements of human trafficking.

6.1.1 Demand to Replace Departing Foreign Women

As outlined in detail in Chap. 5, women from Moldova, Ukraine, Romania, Bulgaria, Albania and Serbia primarily engaged in prostitution in Kosovo when the sex industry started to grow in the wake of the war. Yet the ethnic makeup of the industry changed when Romanian and Bulgarian women, as well as Moldovan women holding Romanian passports, increasingly began to travel to affluent countries in Western Europe instead of Kosovo. They were exempted from visa requirements to the Schengen area in 2007, and they largely preferred to search for employment there (Surtees, 2005, p. 255). Foreign women who continued working in the Kosovar prostitution business largely departed in the years to follow. This was a consequence of stricter (enforcement of) rules to live and work in Kosovo.[4] Albanian women were an exception: they were the only foreign women who managed to continue their work in Kosovo as a consequence of the strong bilateral relations between Kosovo and Albania, which had resulted in a more lenient attitude toward Albanian citizens residing in Kosovo (see footnote 4).

At that point, the prostitution market had been solidly established and had a need for new women to replace the foreign women who had departed. Women from Kosovo—and, to a lesser extent, Albania—were an obvious group to fill this void.[5] They were "pulled" toward the prostitution business, since foreign women no longer offered commercial sex in Kosovo as they had previously done since the blossoming of the industry in the wake of the war.

Several push factors can also be identified that did indeed make some Kosovar women engage in prostitution in their home country. The first (market) factor relates to the dire economic situation of many Kosovar citizens and will be considered in the upcoming section.

6.1.2 Poverty-Based Need

Economic need is an unsurprising push factor that made Kosovar women consider prostitution. I say "unsurprising" since the desire to improve one's economic situation was a principal reason for foreign women to engage in prostitution in Kosovo; moreover, it is mentioned as a central motivation for women in studies on prostitution worldwide (Agustín, 2007; Siegel, 2011).

As outlined in Sect. 3.2.6, there was relative economic prosperity in Kosovo in the first few years after the war due to the peacekeeping economy. In 2015, how-

[4] See Sect. 5.1.

[5] Interview with KPO3, October 8, 2013. Also mentioned in interview with NGO2, October 2, 2013, and interview with KPO2, January 8, 2014.

ever, the World Bank (2015, p. 6) concluded that Kosovo was one of the poorest countries in Europe, with an average per capita income of about one-tenth the EU average. For years, there has been widespread pessimism amongst Kosovo's population regarding economic prospects and the rule of law (World Bank, 2015, p. 2). Economy-related pessimism within Kosovo only increased when its long-desired independence did not solve local problems. Furthermore, the availability of well-paying jobs at UNMIK and EULEX abated when these missions were downsized, widespread corruption and nepotism impeded vacancies from being filled by those most qualified, and unemployment remained extremely high.[6] A labor force survey by the Kosovo Agency of Statistics (2016, p. 21) estimated that 32.9% of people ages 15–64 were unemployed in 2015.[7] This number was even higher for young people in particular[8]: in 2015, 57.7% of young people were unemployed, and this percentage rose to 67.2% for young women (Kosovo Agency of Statistics, 2016, p. 22). However, it has to be noted that these percentages are based on an analysis of employment in the legal economy, and some of those listed as unemployed likely earn money in Kosovo's blossoming informal economy, for instance as taxi drivers or cigarette vendors. This means that unemployment rates are slightly lower than the official statistics show (Xhelili Krasniqi & Mustafa-Topxhiu, 2012, p. 13), but nevertheless remain substantial.

The economic situation in Kosovo deteriorated even further due to a decline in remittances (Elezaj, Bislimi, & Duri, 2012, p. 21). Its economy has strongly relied on remittance flows from the Kosovar diaspora since as early as the 1960s. Over the last decade, approximately one-quarter of the households in Kosovo received remittances (Kosovo Agency of Statistics, 2013). These households largely spent their remittances on basic needs such as food, housing, health and education. Yet in 2012, Kosovo received 14% fewer remittances than in 2010 (Elezaj et al., 2012). Some studies explain this decline as a consequence of the global economic crisis (Elezaj et al., 2012). Others point to the increasing integration of Kosovar migrants in their host countries. Increased integration allegedly leads to migrants spending their income on children's education and real estate instead of on remittances (UNDP, 2014, p. 35). While an in-depth examination of the reasons behind the decline in remittances is outside the scope of this research, it is notable here that, as observed by Elezaj et al. (2012, p. 19), a decline in remittances can "have detrimental impacts on vulnerable groups." The decline in remittances further deteriorated the economic disparity of households that depended on remittances as an essential livelihood strategy.

[6] Interviews with NGO2, October 2, 2013, and NGO1, November 8, 2013, as well as various informal conversations with citizens of Kosovo between 2011 and 2016.

[7] https://ask.rks-gov.net/media/1687/results-of-the-kosovo-2015-labour-force-survey.pdf, accessed January 23, 2017.

[8] In this study, young people are defined as those aged between 15 and 24.

These negative economic developments meant that part of Kosovo's population found themselves in an increasingly dire economic situation some years after the end of the war.[9] Police officers and representatives of NGOs working in the field of human trafficking and prostitution in Kosovo suggested to me that some women in economic need tried to improve their position through engagement in prostitution.[10]

Without exception, women from Kosovo who engaged in prostitution indeed told me that economic difficulties had informed their decision to do so. One could critically note that it is socially desirable to say that one only became involved in prostitution as a consequence of financial despair. As discussed in Sect. 5.3.1, women can be inclined to emphasize the lack of realistic alternatives to provide for themselves and their families outside the sex industry in order to receive more sympathy and less judgment from society. In their empirical studies on prostitution in Italy and South Africa, respectively, Andrijasevic (2010, p. 24) and Leclerc-Madlala (2003, p. 224) encountered similar presentations of women. However, as will be outlined in more detail in the upcoming sections, my female respondents who worked in bars often felt isolated. They were eager to share their everyday matters with a researcher with a non-judgmental attitude. These matters included discussing and observing their daily struggles with money—an unpleasant reality for all of them.

The ways in which Kosovar women struggled financially while working in bars can be illustrated by Saranda's experiences. Saranda was a waitress who supplemented her income by having sexual intercourse with regular clients:

> During a visit to the bar where she was working in mid-September 2013, Saranda said, "My daughter is very good and doing well in school. Only the books are very expensive, so I told the man who sold them that I could only pay a part. I pay the rest later."[11] She often touched her belly during our conversation; it belly was slightly swollen as a consequence of a liver condition that had caused Saranda pain for months. "I still did not have the operation for my liver," she explained (see footnote 11). She did not have the money for a medical intervention. A week later, Saranda asked me to pick her up in the city center in the afternoon and mentioned, "I was in the city just now to search for another job."[12] She planned to start working double shifts in two different bars because she was not managing to pay all her bills: "My daughter is starting to be quite expensive with schoolbooks and so on (see footnote 12)." Saranda succeeded in finding a second job in another bar; she started working during the day in one bar and during the evening in another. In the beginning of October, however, she shared with me that she had not managed to pay the rent.

[9] In the winter of 2014/2015, widespread discontent with economic prospects and the rule of law resulted in a mass exodus of an estimated 5% of the total population of Kosovo to the European Union. The majority of these migrants tried to enter the EU without the required visa and, as a consequence, were sent back to Kosovo or entered the EU illegally (World Bank, 2015, p. 2).

[10] Interviews with KPO3, October 8, 2013, and NGO2, October 2, 2013, as well as with NGO1, November 8, 2013.

[11] Informal conversation with Saranda, September 19, 2013.

[12] Informal conversation with Saranda, September 27, 2013.

> To her relief, her landlord allowed her to "pay it in parts" for the time being.[13] When I picked Saranda up from the bar where she finished her first shift and drove her to her evening shift one day in early November 2013, Saranda told me that she was not doing well. It was the first time that she had mentioned this explicitly, although she had gone through difficult periods over the years that we had been in contact. She was a strong, proud woman who was not quick to complain, but now really struggled with her health and the costs of both her apartment and her daughter's schoolbooks. Saranda showed me her belly: it had swollen further, and she could no longer sit for long periods of time. The doctor had advised her to come to the hospital for a MRI scan, but the MRI alone cost 200 euro. Saranda did not dare to think about the price of the operation. When I asked her if she thought if it would be possible to have the operation at all, she shrugged her shoulders: "I saved money, but then I had to buy [fire]wood for the winter. Every time I save money. But then something else is coming."[14] We arrived at the bar where Saranda would be working the evening shift, and I joined her inside. She walked to a table, closing her eyes every now and then to suppress the pain. "It's all about the money. If I did not need the money so bad, then I would go home right now (see footnote 14)." It would be eight more hours until her shift ended that day.

Studies on prostitution in the context of peacekeeping missions often suggest that local women engage in commercial sexual transactions out of economic need. According to Higate (2003) and Martin (2005), local women in Sierra Leone, the Democratic Republic of the Congo and Haiti only engaged in prostitution in their home countries in order to meet subsistence needs such as food, clothes and shelter. As outlined in Sect. 5.3.1, Jennings (2014) and Oldenburg (2015) expand upon this economic reasoning by outlining that commercial sexual transactions by local women in the context of peacekeeping missions are more diverse than "survival prostitution" alone. Jennings (2014, p. 319, 2015) found that local women in Liberia and the Democratic Republic of the Congo also engaged in prostitution in order to improve their standard of living, build up some savings, start a small business and invest in "maintaining their appearance." Likewise, and also based on an empirical study in the Democratic Republic of the Congo, Oldenburg (2015, p. 322) observed that women engaged in prostitution in order to consume and to increase their prestige in their communities through relative wealth.

I have argued in the previous chapter that foreign women engaged in prostitution in Kosovo for a range of economic reasons. These reasons varied from economic despair to a desire to consume luxury goods, such as holidays and houses with heated flooring. However, I have to debunk this insight when applied to the local women who engaged in prostitution in bars in Kosovo. In a comparable manner to Saranda, the motivations of the dozens of local women who engaged in prostitution in Kosovo whom I have gotten to know over the years tend more toward that of economic need on the abovementioned continuum. Kosovar women who engaged in prostitution constantly found themselves in economic distress. This was the case for Shqipe, who feared having to leave her apartment because she

[13] Informal conversation with Saranda, October 3, 2013.

[14] Informal conversation with Saranda, November 2, 2013.

had trouble paying the rent as a result of losing her job in the bar.[15] Likewise, Lorena, a woman from the north of Kosovo whom I briefly introduced in previous chapters, constantly worried about earning enough income to provide for food and rent; other women regularly mentioned having debts with various people in order to make ends meet.[16]

How can this difference between foreign and local women involved in Kosovo's sex industry be explained? I will argue that Kosovar women do not engage in prostitution in their home country to purchase a luxury lifestyle as a result of the stigmatization they encounter from society and authorities. This argument will be set out in more detail in Sect. 6.6 about the consequences of identifying as a "voluntary prostitute." First, however, let us examine why Kosovar women turn to prostitution in an economically dire situation. Concluding that Kosovar women tend to engage in prostitution in their home country out of economic necessity does not by itself explain why some Kosovar women engage in prostitution while others do not. Poverty is widespread in Kosovo, yet not all local women in a situation of economic despair engage in prostitution. Most notably, my data suggests that women involved in prostitution also came from disrupted families, often as a consequence of the war. This distinctive social feature is examined in the upcoming section.

6.2 Social Factors: Disruption of the Social Fabric

Family networks in Kosovo often protect individual family members from falling into poverty. This was illustrated by a respondent who told me that he and his five brothers, all married men with families of their own, would put their income together in a pot. Subsequently, the money would be divided amongst all brothers according to their needs. This meant that my respondent donated more money than he took from the family pot during his employment by the government, but he took more money from the pot then he had contributed during a subsequent period of unemployment.[17] Likewise, a Kosovar woman described arrangements in which her unemployed husband received a monthly allowance from his family in order to pay for rent and food until he found a job and would be expected to help out the others.[18] These setups between parents and siblings allowed my respondents to meet their basic needs, even in difficult economic times. Core family ties thus functioned as a safety net in a national context of widespread unemployment and no social welfare system to speak of. Similar coping strategies are described in other low-income countries where informal

[15] Informal conversation with Shqipe, October 1, 2013.

[16] Informal conversation with Lorena, June 2, 2013.

[17] Informal conversations with HTE5 between 2011 and 2015.

[18] Informal conversations with KLA2 in 2013.

arrangements are established to deal with harsh economic blows (Alderman & Paxson, 1994; Haddad & Zeller, 1996; Morduch, 1995, 1999).

However, none of the Kosovar women who engaged in prostitution in bars in their home country had a husband. Women had either been divorced, widowed or had never been married at all. The majority of the women had neither parents nor siblings to rely on: their parents had either passed away, or relationships with parents and siblings (if any) had been disrupted. Consequently, these women had to fend for themselves. These observations indicate that erosion of the social fabric (e.g., marital bonds and family ties) severely affected the economic resilience of Kosovar women, eventually pushing some of them into sex work.

Travis Hirschi's theory of bonding and social control (Gottfredson & Hirschi, 1990; Hirschi, 1969; Lanier, Henry, & Desire, 2015) comes to mind here. Hirschi argues that people are inclined to break the law as a consequence of inadequate bonding with law-abiding people and institutions, especially parents. He puts forward that connections with parents and conventional society at large teach us to foresee the long-term consequences of our behavior. Some examples of long-term consequences of deviant behavior include punishment—such as imprisonment and fines—or disappointed family members. Individuals generally want to avoid such consequences; therefore they will be inclined to avoid deviant behavior. Thus, according to Hirschi, bonds with parents or other significant (conventional) others instill self-control. However, he also suggests that people do not develop self-control if they do not have many (or any) such bonds. Hirschi maintains that individuals without adequate bonds with parents and other law-abiding people are more inclined to exhibit impulsive, possibly deviant, behavior (idem). Chaukar (1998, p. 121) and Walkowitz (1980, p. 20) can be seen to adopt such a perspective in debating the involvement of women in sex work. Chaukar (1998, p. 121) puts forward that Indian women became engaged in prostitution following a lack of "parental supervision." Likewise, Walkowitz (1980, p. 20) points out that women who were not emotionally attached to a parent in the context of England's Victorian era might have found it easier "to act against conventional norms." However, following my empirical findings, I believe we need an alternative interpretation of Hirschi's work—or we even need to disregard altogether his interpretation of the link between weak relationships with parents and deviant behavior. In the upcoming sections, I will introduce five Kosovar women. Their stories illustrate how disrupted family ties meant that women in situations that were already economically dire were left to rely on their own resources, which eventually pushed them toward the sex industry. Let's take a closer look at these findings and then consider Hirschi once more.

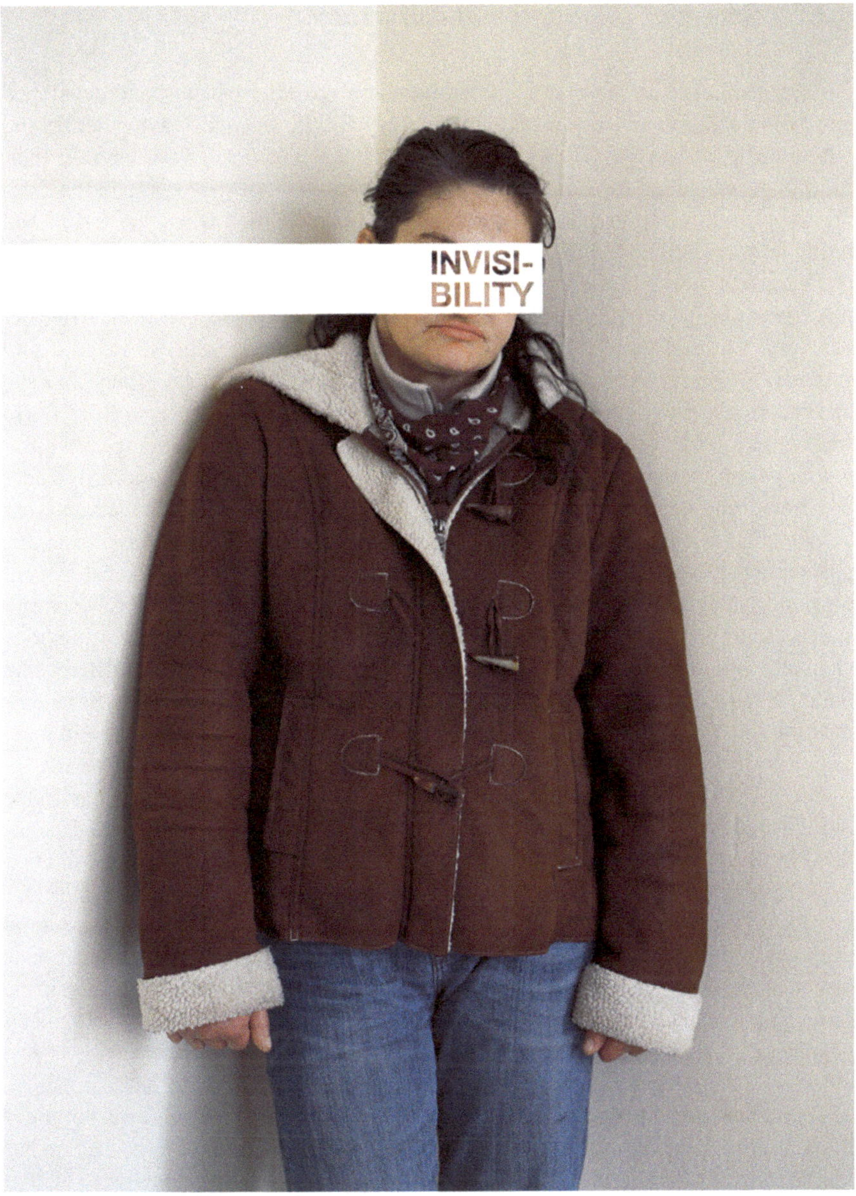

Fig. 6.2 Woman in a bar

6.2.1 Saranda: Dissolution of a Marriage

Saranda explained to me that her marriage dissolved after her husband developed psychological problems and went to live in a psychiatric hospital, leaving her behind with their little daughter. Saranda's younger sister also depended on her after their parents passed away. Saranda provided for the three of them by working in the laundromat at Camp Bondsteel.[19] However, she lost this position when she fell ill and needed an operation. Camp Bondsteel allowed employees like Saranda to be off work for two weeks in a row at most; Saranda was fired before the operation took place because the doctor had told her she needed four weeks to recover. After her recovery, Saranda decided to try to earn money by opening a bar close to Camp Bondsteel. She served drinks and food to the international peacekeepers that she had met at her previous job. At times, she also had commercial sexual intercourse with them in order to supplement her income.[20] Saranda thus first engaged in commercial sexual transactions incidentally. After several years, she temporarily had a boyfriend, and the two opened a business where foreign and local women were employed as waitresses who also provided commercial sex. After some prosperous years as a bar owner with her boyfriend, both the business and the relationship went downhill, and her relatively wealthy years came to an end. She applied for jobs and started working in the bar owned by Bujar, who has been introduced in previous chapters. Bujar said that he was initially surprised when "a successful lady like Saranda" asked him for work.[21] However, some years and bar jobs later, Saranda's position did not differ from the other women who engaged in prostitution in bars. Like my other respondents, she was struggling to make ends meet every month.

Saranda's experiences do vary from most other local women who work in bars in the sense that she was temporarily involved in the facilitation of prostitution. As also outlined by Siegel and De Blank (2010), women can play leading roles in prostitution networks (see also Siegel, 2007). Yet when speaking about Kosovo, local female bar owners are exceptional. As also outlined by Arsovska (2015, p. 203), Kosovo is a relatively male-dominated society. A 2014 analysis of gender differences in Kosovo reveals that no other country in Europe has such a limited number of women participating in the formal labor market and that less than 10% of Kosovar businesses are led or owned by women (Färnsveden, Qosaj-Mustafa, & Farnsworth, 2014). This gender divide is also reflected in the sex industry, where female bar owners like Saranda are an exception.

As mentioned, the relative wealth that Saranda's business brought was not long-lived; however, the dissolution of her marriage had a more long-term impact on her life. Her divorce meant that Saranda turned from housewife to breadwinner, with a daughter and younger sister both depending on her. The fact that she had to provide for an income in a socio-economic context dominated by men made her situation increasingly difficult. Options for women were limited, but engaging in prostitution was one of them. Like Saranda, two other Kosovar respondents mentioned that they became involved in prostitution after getting divorced. Divorce made it so that women with no further family to rely on had to fend for themselves.

---

[19] Interview with Saranda, November 4, 2013.

[20] Informal conversation with Saranda, September 25, 2013.

[21] Informal conversation with Bujar, November 2, 2013.

6.2.2 *Lorena: Ethnic Tensions After Being Widowed*

Lorena also had to provide for herself after her marriage came to an end. She did not experience a divorce, but rather found herself widowed. Lorena wrote a letter to human rights organizations about the death of her husband and the effect it had on her life. The letter is shared here with her permission, since it clearly describes the experiences of Lorena in her own words:

> My name is Lorena. I grew up in North Mitrovica with my Bosnian family. After my marriage to my husband Ylli, who was ethnic Albanian, I moved in with my family- in- law in a village close to South Mitrovica. My husband and I had five children together.
>
> On a morning in early 2000, fighting broke out around the bridge in Mitrovica. During this shooting, French KFOR soldiers shot my husband. He was brought to the French hospital where they refused to treat him. Upon arrival in the [nearby] Moroccan hospital, my husband died of his injuries.
>
> Initially KFOR said that my husband was a sniper. They said he had been shooting at French KFOR and probably wounded a French KFOR soldier. They explained that this was the reason why they shot him. This explanation is false. Evidence shows that my husband wasn't carrying a weapon when he was shot. KFOR later also acknowledged this. Further evidence shows that a bullet from French KFOR has killed my husband.
>
> After the death of my husband, I was in a very difficult situation. I was left behind with five children, had no source of income and my house was burned in the war. I went to Camp Film City [the KFOR headquarters in Pristina] to speak with a commander of KFOR. He initially refused to see me. A lady from Amnesty International visited me one time and I told her that I was refused to have a meeting with a commander at KFOR. She then arranged a meeting for me.
>
> During the meeting, the commander of KFOR asked me what I wanted. He promised me a new house if we could visit my village and see my burned house. We went to my burned house and the commander made some measurements. He also promised me 10.000 mark.[22] I went back to Film City regularly to remind them of their promises but have never been given a new house or any financial compensation for their killing of my husband. The last thing they said was that I had to go to France and talk to the Ministry of Foreign Affairs there. Without money, visa and five children to care for, this was of course no option.
>
> My children and I continued to live with my family-in-law. I suffered from domestic abuse [by the family-in-law] and eventually saw no other alternative than to flee from them. I had to leave my children behind, whom I haven't seen in seven years.[23] I now work in a bar in Peja to ensure income. The work is hard and I would really like to stop working there. The financial compensation that was initially promised to me by KFOR would allow me to stop my work in the bar and try to move on.

The domestic abuse Lorena mentioned was rooted in the ethnic differences between herself, on the one hand, and her late husband and family-in-law, on the other. Lorena is Bosnian, while her family-in-law is Albanian. Lorena's family-in-law started to lock her in the house, used her as a servant, called her Serbian names and turned her children against her. She eventually couldn't handle this situation

[22] The German mark was unofficially but widely used in Kosovo before the war. In September 1999, UNMIK legalized its use in Kosovo and the population adopted the German mark as its common currency. The euro was adopted as the legal currency on January 1, 2002 (Maloku & Badivuku Pantina, 2011).

[23] In Kosovo, it is not completely exceptional for children to stay with the family of the father after a divorce. In my conversations with other divorced women, they often mentioned their struggles to keep their children with them.

anymore and decided to return to her parents in North Mitrovica. After the death of her father, Lorena, who has no siblings, needed to take care of herself and her mother. She did so by engaging in prostitution.[24]

Fig. 6.3 Women in a bar

[24] Informal conversations with Lorena, April 27 and 29, 2013; May 3, 2013; and October 9, 2013.

Fig. 6.3 (continued)

6.2.3 *Kaltrina: Wartime Sexual Violence*

Like Lorena, Kaltrina traced the problems within her family back to wartime events. Kaltrina's family rejected her after she had been raped during the war. Wartime rape is a sensitive subject in Kosovo. No accurate estimates on the incidence of sexual violence exist, but Human Rights Watch (2001, p. 130) collected 96 accounts of sexual assault by Serbian and Yugoslav forces during the NATO bombing campaign. Furthermore, local NGOs documented over 100 cases of wartime rape and sexual assault (Rames, 2013, p. 32). The vast majority of these cases describe Kosovar Albanian women who had been assaulted by Serbian paramilitary, police or military forces. A small number refers to Kosovo Albanian men who sexually abused Kosovo Albanian, Kosovo Serb or Roma women. Both Human Rights Watch and local NGOs, however, believe that the total number of incidents of wartime sexual assault is much higher, as many cases have gone unreported (Human Rights Watch, 2001; Rames, 2013).

An international special prosecutor working on war crimes in Kosovo linked this underreporting to cultural dynamics in Kosovo, explaining, "If the woman is not married, then this will not happen if she speaks about what happened to her. If she is married, maybe she will get divorced."[25] Likewise, Linda Gusia, a Kosovo Albanian sociologist who conducted research on wartime rape, mentioned that fear of repercussions keeps victims from coming forward. Women do not want to shame themselves and their families by acknowledging that they are victims of wartime rape. Gusia also identified another reason for women to remain silent: "Rape doesn't fit the dominant story of the war. The war is being remembered as heroic. The UCK was fighting. Brave men and women were fighting. But the majority of the victims were women and children, among which women that have been raped. This story of raped women doesn't fit in the dominant discourse. Because where was the UCK to protect them?" Aside from reasons of fear and shame, Gusia estimated that it is hard for women to speak up because of the way in which the war is (heroically) remembered.[26]

Kaltrina was my only respondent who shared her story of sexual violence during the war with me. I simply do not know if any of my other respondents experienced wartime rape. The abovementioned fears that women might have, and which cause them to remain silent, became a reality for Kaltrina. She mentioned that she had been distanced from her family due to the fact that she had been raped. Kaltrina suddenly had to take care of herself, and she considered that this could only be feasible through engagement in prostitution.[27]

---

[25] Interview with EUL6, March 26, 2013.

[26] Interview with ACA3, March 21, 2013.

[27] Interview with Kaltrina, April 20, 2013.

6.2.4 Elira: Unexcused Behavior

Several other women mentioned how the war had changed the social fabric within families. Examples of such changes in the social fabric include families that are dispersed across different countries, families that moved from a village to a city (where different forms of interaction rule), and individual family members' altered roles and responsibilities together with new "freedoms" to move around. Some of my respondents described how these changes, in retrospect, laid the foundation for their later involvement in prostitution. Elira's account is illustrative of this: she grew up in a small town close to the Macedonian border, and her stories of childhood overlap with Arsovska's (2015, p. 202–203) descriptions of traditional Kosovar Albanian families, in which girls are strongly protected and controlled by their families.

> As a girl, Elira explained, "I never went out. Just with my mother and father and sometimes with someone else from the family."[28] But her life abruptly changed at age 16 when the war broke out.
>
> Elira's family decided to flee to Macedonia. They left on foot toward the main border crossing in the village of Blace. The family walked for days in a row with hundreds of other refugees.[29] Elira got lost during this journey: "I paused for a moment in the forest. I was so tired. We had walked so long and did not have any food. I fell asleep in that forest. We walked in enormous groups, and my family was in the first group. When I woke up I did not recognize anyone. Then I went back to the village of my uncle. He was the nearest person that I knew. The Serbs separated us—me and my family. They were in Blace and I lost them (see footnote 28)." Elira stayed with her uncle when the violence increased and NATO conducted an 11-week bombing campaign. Elira's family didn't know if she survived and feared for her wellbeing.
>
> When Elira was reunited with her parents, brothers and sister, she explained that they were ecstatic with joy: "When I survived during the war, my family carried me in their hands. They spoiled me too much because I survived the war in Kosovo (see footnote 28)." One of Elira's brothers gave her money to buy new clothes. She decided to buy sneakers for herself and her best friend. For the first time in Elira's life, she went to the city with a friend: "We bought Nikes. I remember the store. I was so happy (see footnote 28)." In the city, Elira and her friend met a boy who invited them to a birthday party. The girls agreed and ended up partying for three days. "I did not come to the city with the idea to not go back. But after three days I was afraid to go back home. Everybody said, 'Your brother will kill you (see footnote 28).'" Elira and her friend decided to stay in the city out of fear of repercussions from their families. Elira initially earned money by cleaning, but after a year, she started working in prostitution in one of the many bars that were opening.
>
> Elira did not have contact with her family for 13 years. Contact was re-established in 2012. Since then, she regularly tries to visit her mother. These are tense undertakings: her oldest brother still does not accept her. One afternoon, her brother came to search for Elira in the bar where she was working at the time. She ran away when she saw him coming, but she could hear him shout, "You are no longer family. You embarrass us (see footnote 28)." Elira's oldest brother is the only family member who knows that she is working in a bar, "but he does not speak. The rest of the family thinks that I am working in a restaurant on the way to Pristina. That I am doing the dishes in the kitchen there (see footnote 28)."

---

[28] Interview with Elira, March 16, 2013.

[29] See also Rohde (1999) for a description of the stream of Kosovar Albanian refugees who tried to enter Macedonia in April 1999.

Elira was quite suddenly left to care for herself when she did not dare to return home out of shame for her behavior and fear of repercussions. Without a family safety net and in need of income, one way to make ends meet was to engage in prostitution.

Fig. 6.4 Inside a bar

6.2.5 *Genta: Ill Family Members*

Genta's story is a final example of local women's entrance into prostitution that seems related to troubled family relations. Genta was living with her uncle, aunt and nephew at the time we met. Her aunt and uncle were suffering from mental disorders and other illnesses. It was a 2-h walk from Genta's house to the bar where she normally hung out and picked up clients; she did not have money for the bus ride. Genta told me that she had started to come to the bar in order to escape from the tension at home. Sometimes she could scrape money together for medicine for her family members. Genta did not want to come home without any earnings in order to avoid violence. Engaging in prostitution became a way to secure some income as well as physical wellbeing.[30]

[30] Interview with Genta, October 20, 2013.

6.2.6 *What to Do About Travis Hirschi?*

Kosovar families often function as a safety net in a national context of widespread unemployment, with limited to no social security systems to rely on. In these cases, informal arrangements between parents and siblings prevent individual family members from falling into poverty. Nevertheless, the accounts of Saranda, Lorena, Kaltrina, Elira and Genta illustrate that family ties can be disrupted for a plethora of reasons. Sometimes this occurred as a direct consequence of wartime experiences. This has also been observed in studies on Second World War and Vietnam veterans and their families (e.g., Catherall, 1992; Figley & McCubbin, 1983; Hill, 1949). In other instances, women such as Saranda and Genta simply did not know whether events would have transpired as they did if not for the war.

This erosion of the social fabric increased the vulnerability of the women concerned and influenced their decision to engage in prostitution. This is not to say that women engaged in prostitution because of a lack of "parental supervision," as argued by Chaukar (1998, p. 20) and Walkowitz (1980). Rather, it is to say that weak family bonds increased the financial despair of these Kosovar women, which eventually "pushed" them toward the sex industry. This further develops the frequently heard suggestion that poverty drives women toward prostitution (this is argued in the context of peacekeeping missions by Higate (2003) and Martin (2005)). A dire economic situation alone does not explain why some women engage in prostitution while others do not. People have fewer options to make ends meet when family ties are disrupted in a context of widespread poverty with no social security system to speak of. My empirical findings in Kosovo suggest that this combination of factors increasingly make women consider prostitution.

This finding calls for an alternative interpretation of the link between weak family relations and deviant behavior as elaborated upon by Hirschi in his theory of bonding and social control. Hirschi argues that the "failure to bond [...] produce[s] low self-control and allow[s] deviance to go unchecked" (Lanier et al., 2015, p. 175). In other words, Hirschi suggests that weak family bonds increase impulsive behavior in the form of risk-taking. Yet my data suggests that engagement in prostitution is no matter of poor self-control. It is a way to sustain oneself, not a matter of risk-taking; it is a way to achieve relative security in an already risky situation.[31] The lack of family bonds did not mean that women like Saranda, Lorena, Kaltrina, Elira and Genta did not foresee the long-term consequences of their behavior. Rather, this lack of bonds meant that their need to provide for themselves simply overruled the extent to which long-term consequences could be taken into account.[32]

[31] Security, as presented here, follows a more positive notion of security as elaborated upon by Oude Breuil (2014). Such a notion not only considers security in the negative light of crime, disorder, and fear, but is concerned, for instance, with the ways in which individuals try to care for themselves and their loved ones.

[32] Hirschi's theory of bonding and social control has, of course, been subject to other critiques. Blanc, Ouimet, and Tremblay (1988) question the scope of the theory by suggesting it is only applicable to specific crimes such as violence. Likewise, Thio (1978) puts forward that the theory applies only to unsophisticated crimes. Furthermore, it has been suggested that the theory of bonding and social control fails to explain why a lack of social bonds will cause one person to turn to theft while another turns to drug use (Walklate, 2007, p. 26).

6.3 Individual Considerations: Drug Use

Fig. 6.5 Needles and syringes

Aside from the market forces and social factors outlined so far, some local women also mentioned that a drug habit pushed them toward the sex industry. These respondents primarily used heroin, which they purchased by engaging in commercial sexual transactions. Drug use is presented as an individual factor here, since it can be seen as an individual practice with individual causes and consequences. Nevertheless, the behavior and decisions of female drug users in post-war Kosovo have been influenced by the social context in which these women found themselves. Durkheim (1897) made this point with regard to suicide. Suicide is a seemingly individual act, but one which, according to Durkheim, can be explained by various characteristics of capitalist society such as the increasing uncertainty and difficulty of life. Durkheim therefore posed that suicide can be seen as a social phenomenon. Likewise, the presentation of drug use as an individual factor does not imply that it can be understood apart from the social context of post-war Kosovo, in which drugs were widely available and drug dealers sometimes deliberately tried to get young women to use them. Let us briefly consider these characteristics of post-war Kosovo in more detail before turning to the link between drug use and prostitution.

After the war, drugs—heroin in particular—were widely available in Kosovo (see also Agani, Landau, & Agani, 2010, p. 146). This can be explained by Kosovo's position as a transit country for the smuggling of heroin on the route from Afghanistan to countries within the European Union (EMCDDA, 2010, p. 14).[33] In 2010, the European Monitoring Centre for Drugs and Drug Addiction (2010, p. 14) noted that since the beginning of the millennium, increasing amounts of heroin en route to the European Union were remaining in Kosovo for local consumption. The staff of a Kosovar NGO that provided psychomedical treatment to those using drugs attested to this observation, noting a substantial increase in drug use since the end of the war (Muqaj, 2012). Heroin in particular was the popular drug of consumption in the first 10 years after the conflict.[34] One man, who had been injecting heroin for years, said about these initial years after the war, "You won't believe what I've seen after the war. It took 10 min to get all the drugs you wanted."[35] The widespread availability of drugs like heroin allegedly meant that more people came into contact with it and started using.

At the time, drug dealers sometimes deliberately tried to stimulate drug use amongst girls. Lindita, a Kosovo Albanian woman who injected heroin during this period, explained, "Sometimes a dealer gives a girl drugs for a little bit of money. He wants her to get addicted and come back. And then, when she gets addicted and she gets into a crisis for drugs, he will tell her, "OK, I will give you drugs, but if I do something for you, you do something for me." He wants her to have sex with him

---

[33] The main transit routes for heroin through Kosovo that are identified by the European Monitoring Centre for Drugs and Drug Addiction (2010, p. 14) are: Afghanistan–Iran–Turkey–Bulgaria–former Yugoslav Republic of Macedonia or Albania–Kosovo–Serbia–EU member states, and Afghanistan–Iran–Turkey–Greece–Albania–Kosovo–Montenegro–EU member states.

[34] http://www.kosovapress.com/en/news/-blakaj-a-growing-number-of-drug-users-in-kosovo-26809/, accessed January 27, 2017.

[35] Transcript of interview by Guido van Eijck (historian involved in Willem Poelstra's photo project), February 5, 2016.

or with his friends and other men to make some money. Dealers detect girls that are already using small amounts and try to keep them with them."[36] In this way, drug dealers thus may "help" create their own market by trying to get women or girls addicted to drugs, subsequently making sure that they have money to buy drugs by arranging commercial sexual encounters for them.

The local female heroin users that I met in Kosovo sometimes started using drugs after contact with a drug dealer, as described by Lindita, but women also developed a drug habit in other ways (e.g., after exploring drugs with friends or partners). Without exception, these women subsequently sustained their drug habits by offering sexual services for drugs or money.[37] This interdependence between sex work and drugs has been observed in studies worldwide (e.g., Hope Ditmore, 2013; Kensy, Stengel, Nougier, & Birgin, 2012; Stengel & Fleetwood, 2014). The story of Zamira, a Kosovo Albanian woman, is illustrative in this regard. Zamira fled to Switzerland with her husband in the 1990s. They often partied in discotheques and started using drugs. When Zamira returned to Kosovo after the war, she told me, she would be "thinking about drugs all day" and found heroin to be widely available: "I used to buy drugs from a dealer but sometimes I didn't have money. When you are without heroin, you accept any price to take a shot. You pay with money, or if you don't have money, something else." Zamira started to exchange sex for drugs or money that would allow her to buy heroin. "Sometimes clients wanted me to do things I didn't want to do. But I had to do it, because when you are in a drug crisis you do anything."[38] As outlined in a study amongst clients in the Netherlands (Zaitch & Staring, 2009, p. 94) and experienced by Zamira, women who are addicted to drugs can be attractive to clients, who get a kick out of getting sexual services as cheaply as possible from women in need of drugs and therefore money.

In other instances, women started using drugs after they became involved in the prostitution business. Women emphasized that heroin made them able to deal with life in the bars, which they experienced as tough. One young woman, who had been addicted to several kinds of drugs, explained why she and her colleagues preferred to use heroin: "I used cocaine, but my body needed heroin more. I wanted to forget about my life. Heroin made me sleep. Cocaine made me happy and more confident. I didn't want that. I preferred heroin. I just wanted to forget."[39] By no means did all women engaged in prostitution use drugs,[40] yet the Kosovar women who used drugs often noted that heroin was their preferred drug.

[36] Interview with Lindita, December 5, 2011.

[37] For instance, I met these women in drop-in centers for people affected by drugs.

[38] Interview with Zamira, November 25, 2011.

[39] Interview with Dua, March 20, 2013.

[40] Most women did use alcohol. Amongst other reasons, they did so to deal with their experiences in the bar—see Sect. 6.6.1.

6.4 Intersecting Constraints

Various factors have been identified that could influence Kosovar women's decisions to engage in prostitution in their home country. These factors have been divided into market forces, social factors and individual considerations and consist of one pull factor as well as various push factors. This is not to say that the presence of these factors in women's lives inevitably led them to the sex industry; not every divorced Kosovar woman with weak family ties in an economically dire situation engages in prostitution. Yet the intersection of various constraints (such as poverty, being widowed, ethnic tensions and having no parents or siblings to rely on) increases the vulnerability of women in Kosovo and therewith the likelihood that they turn to prostitution in order to make ends meet.

Intersection, as it is used here, refers to the term "intersectionality" coined by Kimberlé Crenshaw (1989, 1991) to deal with the fact that social justice problems such as racism and sexism are often overlapping. She initially took the example of African American women to illustrate her point: a company might not employ African American women, but this is seldom recognized as racism, since a company might hire African American men as technicians, or as sexism, since a company might hire white women for administrative tasks. The problem then lies in the combination of a race and gender claim. Crenshaw observed that there was no name to point to such a discriminatory combination. In search of an alternative frame to allow people to grapple with the simultaneous impact of racism and sexism, as well as other oppressive social categorizations such as homophobia, xenophobia and classism, Crenshaw coined the term intersectionality. Intersectionality thus refers to the fact that social justice problems often come together and do not act independently of each other (idem).

When the idea of intersectionality is applied to the situation of Kosovar women who eventually engaged in prostitution in their home country, it becomes apparent that the socio-economic disadvantages of these women cannot be encapsulated by looking at disadvantages separately. Their struggles with poverty, erosion of the social fabric, or drugs were interrelated and often created unique challenges. Yet for all of these women, engaging in the prostitution business—which at the time was asking for the involvement of local women—offered a way to deal with these challenges.

Drawing attention to the constraints that influence local women's decisions to engage in prostitution can be tied to the abolitionist rhetoric. Abolitionists argue that women only enter the prostitution business after economic, social and personal constraints "coerce" them to do so (Aronowitz, 2001; Farley, 2003; Hughes, 2000; Matthews, 2008; Miriam, 2005; see also Sect. 2.1). Because of these constraints (as well as the sexual exploitation that abolitionists believe to be inherent to prostitution), abolitionists describe the experiences of women involved in the sex industry as "abusive, degrading, and harmful to their health and well-being" (Hughes, 2000, p. 653). As outlined in Sect. 2.1.3, academics who published work in line with this rhetoric (Barry, 1979; Dworkin, 1997; Farley, 2004; Jeffreys, 2009; Raymond, 1998) have been critiqued for presenting one-dimensional and ideologically tainted findings (Agustín, 2007; Vanwesenbeeck, De Graaf, Van Zessen, Straver, & Visser, 1993; Weitzer, 2005,

2009, 2010; Zhang, 2009). This critique is underlined by the observations in this study. The abolitionist perspective does not do justice to the narratives of Lorena and the other women as described above. It can also be posited that prostitution offered them an opportunity to provide for themselves and achieve relative security.

Yet the moment critical attention is drawn to the fact that a woman does not behave as completely passive and coerced victim but simply negotiates her situation, she is suddenly deemed into a voluntary prostitute. As outlined in the introduction of this chapter, in the contemporary discourse a woman is generally labeled as such when the classification of "victim of trafficking," as defined in the UN Protocol to Prevent, Suppress and Punish Trafficking in Persons Especially Women and Children, does not apply.[41] I have underlined the importance of considering women engaged in prostitution beyond the simple notion of their being victims of trafficking, which essentializes suffering. But in this regard, the notion of the voluntary prostitute is problematic as well. In line with the critique on pro-sex-work scholars, who tend to draw attention to prostitution as a form of work that has the potential to be empowering (Agustín, 2007; Chapkis, 1997), the label of "voluntary prostitute" has the tendency to ignore the negative experiences of those defined as such. As shown, and as will be elaborated upon in more detail in the upcoming sections, local women generally experience their engagement in prostitution as being difficult. Moreover, far from considering prostitution a job like any other, local women often engaged in prostitution as one of the final possibilities for earning a livelihood in a challenging situation—one that they would very much like to exchange for another profession. I do not draw attention to this to enforce the "constraints-as-force" rationale, which (morally) stigmatizes those who are not driven by economic or other burdens, but instead engage in prostitution in order to purchase a luxury lifestyle.[42] I would simply like to reiterate that the label "voluntary prostitute" does not do justice to the lived experiences of the Kosovar women discussed above.

Imaginations of being a voluntary prostitute do, however, influence the experiences of people involved in the sex industry. In other words, as touched upon in Chap. 2, "if men define situations as real, they are real in their consequences" (Thomas & Thomas, 1928, p. 572). In the upcoming sections, I will therefore examine the consequences of being identified as a voluntary prostitute. The leading questions here include: How do Kosovar women experience their engagement in prostitution, and how does the label of "voluntary prostitute" impact their lives?

6.5 At Work in the Bars

Let us first consider the ways that women can work in bars that facilitate commercial sex in Kosovo.

[41] The definition of the Protocol to Prevent, Suppress and Punish Trafficking in Persons, Especially Women and Children, supplementing the UN Convention against Transnational Organized Crime, is given in Annex One. See also UNODC (2004).

[42] See Sect. 5.3.1.

6.5.1 Commercial Sexual Encounters

The ways in which women can make money in bars, which function as meeting grounds for clients in search of—and women who offer—commercial sex, were described in Sect. 5.6.4. During their work, women earn money by accompanying guests at the bar, making clients buy them (expensive) drinks or giving performances of (pole) dancing or singing. Further money is earned though sexual intercourse with clients, which generally takes place in a motel after working hours.

Commercial sexual transactions have not always been organized this way. Right after the war, sex workers in Kosovo could mainly be found working in coffee bars and nightclubs. Women also provided their clients with sexual services within these premises. This is not unique to Kosovo: "[…] being a waitress in Albania is just like being a 'waitress' in Italy or Greece […] serve in the front room, fuck in the back room […]" (Davies, 2009, p. 154). This citation, which is a combination of statements by an informant who is presented in Davies' (2009) ethnography on Albanian women in the sex industry of Lyon, France, shows that there is a well-known pattern anywhere in Europe for sexual acts to take place in coffee bars, nightclubs and comparable establishments.

Sex workers in Kosovo, however, have changed their working habits over the past few years. At the time of my research, commercial sexual transactions increasingly took place in hotels instead of a room in the bar itself. In these hotels, rooms could be rented per hour, and clients usually paid for the costs of the hotel. Furthermore, women no longer tended to have intercourse during working hours; they met with clients after their work in the bar was finished. The bar thus turned into a meeting ground. Saranda explained this way of working as follows: "If you have a guest, then you drink. After your shift you can meet a client. Not during your shift."[43] Lorena clarified how such appointments with clients were made: "Men ask you when you sit with them at their table and when you serve them. Than they say, 'Let's go somewhere.'"[44] The time and place to meet are generally agreed upon by phone.

Lorena tended to work in the bar from four until twelve o'clock in the evening and then met with clients until three o'clock at night.[45] Elira worked double shifts: in a bar during the day and in a nightclub in the evening. After her work in the nightclub finished at three o'clock, Elira had sexual intercourse with clients (one or more) until approximately five o'clock in the morning.[46] Due to these long working hours, women often remarked having limited time to sleep, which made them feel tired and sick.

The change in working methods can be attributed to the strengthening of police control (see also Surtees, 2008, p. 55). As indicated in Chap. 3, the months in the wake of the war were characterized by a virtual absence of law enforcement (Yannis, 2001), which allowed the sex industry to flourish in public despite its illegality. Law enforcement remained weak in the years that followed, but as a legal system was slowly established (see also Perritt, 2010, p. 66; Picarelli, 2002, p. 17; Serwer & Thomson, 2008, p. 367–370), bar owners increasingly found themselves accused of facilitating prostitution. In order to avoid prosecution, bar owners tried to make it

[43] Interview with Saranda, September 27, 2013.

[44] Informal conversation with Lorena, May 14, 2013.

[45] Informal conversation with Lorena, April 29, 2013.

[46] Informal conversation with Elira, March 16, 2013.

difficult for themselves to be linked to prostitution. As one former bar owner recalled, it became a popular strategy to organize commercial sexual transactions outside their bars: "My girls were not allowed [to have sexual intercourse] during working hours. I did not want to be a victim of the police because of my children."[47] By removing the commercial sexual act from bars, bar owners shifted responsibility to the women, which made it tricky to accuse bar owners of facilitating prostitution. A police officer from the anti-trafficking unit in Pristina explained that this tactic indeed hindered them from making a case against bar owners:

> They have found a new method without breaking the law and also benefiting a lot, gaining a lot. We have a lot of bars where you find like 10 women employed. The bar owner uses this ten 10 women for dancing purposes, expensive drinks. So he uses these women to attract clients to spend on drinking. But the bar owner does not allow clients to use this women for sexual services. [...] They meet privately. Now we [the police] know there is something, but there is no way to argument it. Because every court will bring down this argument (see footnote 2).

The abovementioned features of the sex industry, as it takes place around bars in Kosovo, are general trends. Exceptions exist, since naturally every bar has its own dynamics: Zamira, for instance, worked in several bars where the bar owner would allow and even push her to go with clients during working hours. At times, the bar owner would tell her to go with a client and set the price. It was difficult for her to refuse: "One time a boss hit me when I didn't want to go with a really old client. I didn't go to the police, but I did quit that job (see footnote 38)." If Zamira left the bar to go with a client during working hours, then she would split the money she had earned with the bar owner.

Similar exceptions exist with regard to the place a woman and a client meet. Although the sexual act generally takes place in a motel or private house, some working places allowed women to meet their clients in a private room in the same building. This was illustrated by the working experiences of Sofija from Ukraine in the previous chapter.[48]

6.5.2 Circulation Between Sex Work Premises

While women could sometimes be found working in a single bar or club for many years in a row, many women tended to circulate between bars in the same city or (to a lesser extent) in different cities in Kosovo. Women often decided to change their working place after problems with a specific bar owner. Zamira explained: "I often changed my working place. Sometimes the boss wanted me to go with a client, and if I didn't want it then I was fired, or I quit and changed my job. It is almost self-employment. Usually I would only work in a place for a few weeks. I would leave when the boss started to force me to do things or when he wanted to take all my money (see footnote 38)." She never encountered problems with finding new employment: "When you do this kind of job you have many contacts. People know you. There are many coffees [coffee bars], and if you cannot find one in Mitrovica then you will in Vushtrri. It never

[47] Interview with Saranda, March 13, 2013.

[48] The owners of the premises where Sofija was working took other measures to protect themselves from law enforcement (see Sect. 5.4.2).

took long—maybe one or two days (see footnote 38)." In other instances, women decided to change their working places after receiving a tempting offer from another establishment. Saranda and Elira, for instance, opted to work in a nightclub that was popular amongst "schatzis" during the summer months, since they expected that they would be able to earn more money there. When they did not like the people and working hours in the nightclub, they decided to return to their previous place of work.[49]

A limited number of women also circulate between bars in Kosovo and abroad. Some women worked in beach towns in Montenegro or Albania for several weeks during the summer.[50] Two of the women I spoke with also managed to work in Western Europe every now and then. One woman explained that she had been going back and forth between Switzerland and Kosovo for two years. She always worked in Switzerland for three months, returned to a bar in Kosovo for three months and then went back to Switzerland again. In Switzerland she managed to earn much more money than in Kosovo. Her passport, however, did not allow her to stay in Switzerland for more than 90 days in a row, which is why she needed to alternate between Switzerland and Kosovo. Another woman had similar arrangements. Both Kosovar Albanian women had an exceptional position because they also had an Albanian passport,[51] which allows individuals to be in Switzerland for half the time every 180 days, whereas a Kosovar passport does not.[52]

6.5.3 Independent Sex Workers

While the previous sections describe the situation of women who engage in prostitution while being employed in a bar or nightclub, local women who hang out in bars that function as a meeting ground for clients and women engaged in prostitution are not all actually employed there. Some women instead work as "independent" prostitutes. This is illustrated by the experiences of Lindita, a Kosovar Albanian woman who created a network of local and international clients with whom she met in order to have paid sex: "I had a number of regular clients from Kosovo, but internationals as well. I lived in Germany for a while [during the war], so I could speak German or English with the internationals (see footnote 36)." Lindita met her clients by approaching them in coffee bars and occasionally on the street. "I would go into a bar and try to join a man at a table, get close to him and then make a deal. I was my own boss and could decide when I worked or not. At the beginning it was difficult, but then I created a network of people and it became easier (see footnote 36)." Lindita mentioned that she usually made appointments with clients by phone once she managed to create a network of clients of her own: "Local clients would introduce me to other guys. They would give them my number and they would call me to set a meeting. I had a special mobile number for that: one number for my family and one number for clients (see footnote 36)." The use of mobile phones

[49] Interview with Elira, September 25, 2013.

[50] Informal conversation with Shqipe and Mimoza, October 1, 2013.

[51] In one case, the young woman also had an Albanian passport because her father was from Albania.

[52] https://www.sem.admin.ch/dam/data/sem/rechtsgrundlagen/weisungen/visa/bfm/bfm-anh01-liste1-e.pdf, accessed November 28, 2017.

is widely practiced in arranging commercial sex. On silent days, women who are employed in the bars also call regular clients in order to tempt them to come to the bar.[53]

During my observations in bars and nightclubs, I regularly met women who were not employed there but tried to join clients. Genta, introduced earlier, was one such woman who worked this way. Women who were employed in bars were not necessarily hostile to outsiders who offered extra competition for clients; usually all women were (vaguely) familiar with one another and just let each other be, as they knew they were trying to deal with a difficult situation. Moreover, bar owners would not allow women to make a fuss, since they would benefit from the extra drinks that were sold to the independently working women and the clients that joined them.

6.6 Experience of Being a "Voluntary Prostitute"

How, then, do local women experience their work? The narratives in the previous chapter showed that foreign women often considered their involvement in prostitution in Kosovo to be physically and emotionally challenging. The fact that they frequently had plans or goals that they wanted to achieve through their sex work, however, meant that most foreign women thought it was worthwhile to deal with the downside of engagement in prostitution. Kosovar women, on the other hand, only tended to express the downside of their involvement in prostitution. The hardships that these women faced were central to almost all of the meetings I had in bars. The following field notes are illustrative of this:

> Saranda and I went to the bar where Shqipe and Mimoza were working. It was a bit of a cold evening, so we seated ourselves around the woodburning stove that was placed in the middle of the bar during the winter months. The television on the bar was showing a program about Islam. A mufti stated that you would pay the price if you behaved improperly in this life (or something along those lines). We were only half-paying attention until Mimoza mumbled, "Maybe you go to hell if you do wrong in this life."
>
> Shqipe shook her head. "How can you know if another life exists when you have never been there, and no one else has ever been there and come back to tell that such a life exists." She turned to me and asked, "Do you believe in heaven and hell, Roos?" I shrugged my shoulders and said that I personally did not think that there was something as an afterlife. Shqipe agreed. She smiled and gave me a high five. Mimoza said, "Maybe you don't believe in heaven because you haven't lived in hell."[54]

[53] Observations in bars and informal conversation with Saranda on September 25, 2013, who stated, "It wasn't a busy day in the bar so far. I called some friends to ask if they wanted to come to the bar for food or drinks, but they were all busy." However, some women, like Lorena, did not like their mobile numbers to circulate freely. Lorena's boyfriend, a married man, would get jealous if she received phone calls from other men; therefore, she did not share her number with people whom she did not know very well. After we exchanged numbers, Lorena said, "Please don't give my number to Saranda. Nobody has it and I don't know Saranda very well. I don't know what she would do with it, to whom she would give it. The other day a client told my colleague that he wanted to have the number of 'that one'—and then he pointed at me. He said, 'I give you 50 euro for her number.' But my colleague did not have my number. I don't want people to share it for money, so I don't give it to anyone" (informal conversation with Lorena, May 21, 2013).

[54] Discussion with Shqipe and Mimoza, April 16, 2013.

Mimoza continued the conversation by saying that her life had been close to a living hell so far. When I asked her what had made her life so hard, she first referred to the war and the flashbacks to wartime experiences she had during police raids of the bar. She then referred to her engagement in prostitution, specifically the emotional and physical strain of the contact with clients. Most local women highlighted these negative aspects of engagement in prostitution, as well as the challenges related to stigmatization, limited access to healthcare and being denied legal protection. These aspects will be discussed in the upcoming paragraphs with a discussion about how this relates to being identified as a voluntary prostitute.

6.6.1 Emotional Challenges

When women mentioned that they considered their engagement in prostitution to be emotionally challenging, they often referred to the contact they had with men while serving and accompanying them. Aferdita wore a disapproving expression when explaining, "Men come and sit with you and just say, 'I want to fuck you.'"[55] Along similar lines, Lorena exclaimed, "I can't stand this work anymore. I just need peace. In my job, you have to sit with clients and all of them ask for your telephone number. Always the same. I am tired of it. This job... it makes me so angry, so bored."[56] Elira noted, "I don't like to sit with men. I get too bored. I would like to give money to them just to leave".[57] Yet a few minutes later, she stood up from our table in the bar and served drinks to two men sitting in another corner. One of them was around 60 years old. Elira softly touched his arm and gave him a flirtatious smile before he put his arm around her and pulled her in to sit with him at the table. Money needed to be earned. However, in line with Ukranian Sofija's experience, this has an emotional backlash on women, who must constantly force themselves to engage in conversations and sexual intercourse with men while simultaneously being repulsed by it.

Women often mentioned that alcohol consumption helped them to get through emotionally challenging situations. When we went for lunch in a restaurant before the start of her working day, Saranda explained this:

> Drinks?" asked the waiter. I asked what the others felt like; Saranda ordered vodka with Schweppes. When the waiter left, she said, "I always drink at least three strong drinks before I go to work. Otherwise I cannot deal with the shit that the clients are speaking about. What they say. You can't sit with them for one or two hours without them saying, 'How much does it cost to fuck you?' You see them put the *raki* on the table and they'll start

[55] Informal conversation with Aferdita, September 19, 2013.

[56] Informal conversation with Lorena, October 18, 2013.

[57] Informal conversation with Elira, September 25, 2013.

speaking like that.[58] I can't deal with it without drinking." The alcohol made her calmer, she said: "I always drink at least eight per day (see footnote 12)."[59]

Farley (Farley, 2003; Farley & Barkan, 1998; Farley et al., 2004) has extensively published work on how women are emotionally affected by engagement in commercial sexual transactions and acknowledges the stress it can cause. Farley is a known advocate of the abolitionist rhetoric. As shown by the following citation from her in an edited volume entitled *Prostitution, Trafficking and Traumatic Stress*, Farley's analyses are tainted by ideological reasoning on the sex industry at large:

> In 1995 I spoke with Sara, a woman prostituting in what was called a high-class brothel in Johannesburg, South Africa. She asked me why I was there. I told her the truth: I thought that prostitution caused tremendous harm to women, but since there were few studies that asked about the experience of prostitution across different cultures, I wanted to know about her (and others') experiences of rape, physical assault, psychological effects, and childhood trauma (Farley, 2003, p. xii).

Farley generalizes the emotional effects of prostitution on women and assumes that all those engaged experience rape and trauma. However, my respondents varied in the ways in which their involvement in the prostitution business caused stress. Sofija and the Kosovar women quoted above found sex work emotionally challenging, but others did not share with me that it had an emotional backlash on them.

There is limited attention paid to the (emotional) hardships these women encounter during their work when considering them as voluntary prostitutes. As previously mentioned, the contemporary discourse on prostitution distinguishes between voluntary and forced prostitution (i.e., human trafficking). This discourse suggests that the latter should be abolished, while the former symbolizes women's right to self-determination. In her groundbreaking article "Forced to Choose: Beyond the Voluntary v. Forced Prostitution Dichotomy," Doezema (1998) warns that this distinction promotes a whore–Madonna division between those engaged in prostitution:

> The Madonna is the "forced prostitute"—the child, the victim of trafficking; she who, by virtue of her victim status, is exonerated from sexual wrong-doing. The "whore" is the voluntary prostitute: because of her transgression, she deserves whatever she gets (idem: 47).

Since the status of the Kosovar women engaged in prostitution in bars is considered to be voluntary, they are considered responsible for what befalls them, including the emotional backlash that contact with clients can cause.

---

[58] *Raki* is a popular drink in Kosovo. It is a collective term for all sorts of fruit brandies.

[59] As outlined in Sect. 5.2.1 as well, women are further inclined to drink since it provides them with income: they can earn money if clients buy them drinks. Women generally received half the price of each drink that a client bought for them. A young woman explained that she thus preferred to drink vodka Red Bull: "Vodka Red Bull is expensive. It costs like five euro. Just Red Bull is cheaper. It's not that I always prefer to drink alcohol. Sometimes I prefer to be conscious. If my client drinks and I drink, then I might lose control" (interview, March 16, 2013). Yet in the end, she mostly opted for vodka Red Bull in order to have more earnings. Alcohol use is therefore a central element of the work in bars, both as a way to make a living and as a coping mechanism.

6.6.2 Dealing with Stigma

Women in Kosovo face stigmatization when it is known that they engage in behavior that is considered sexually promiscuous (see also Arsovska, 2015, p. 204), such as voluntary prostitution. Lorena referred to this stigmatization when she expressed her dissatisfaction with working in a bar: "I hate it. I really hate it. It is horrible. Also when you are not working, people look at you exactly as a whore. They don't see anything else."[60] On several occasions, people on the street called Lorena names because they knew of her engagement in prostitution; it stopped her from going outside. Lorena preferred to stay at home and spent her free days, every other Sunday, sleeping, watching television and browsing the internet. Out of fear of similar reactions, Kosovo Albanian Elira tried to hide her work in the bar from her family and neighbors. She was well aware that it is unusual for women to work in a bar as a waitress in Kosovo; female waitresses like her are often involved in prostitution.[61] Elira explained, "People think bad of you if they know you are serving in a bar."[62] She therefore constantly declined neighbors' invitations to come over for a coffee, anxious that the nature of her work would be revealed, while at the same time longing for social interaction outside the sex industry. Elira dreamed of having just one friend, other than her colleagues, who wouldn't judge her, "someone with whom you can speak about everything and doesn't tell it (see footnote 62)," but fear of the stigma attached to prostitution kept her and other Kosovar women from having social contacts outside the sex industry.[63]

Throughout the world, those involved in commercial sexual transactions encounter some form of social stigma, but perceptions and attitudes vary between cultures (Scambler, 2007; Tomura, 2009; Weitzer, 2012, 2017). When focusing on empirical research on prostitution alongside peacekeeping missions, Oldenburg (2015), for instance, points out that local women engaged in prostitution in the Democratic Republic of the Congo can be looked down upon. These women are especially judged by young men, who are unable to provide bridewealth and feel marginalized by women's power to accumulate money and goods through commercial sexual encounters. At the same time, however, Oldenburg notes that these commercial sexual encounters also provide women with money and consequently with social status. This is different in the case of women in Kosovo: Local women who are known to engage in prostitution are often shunned by their family and community and are no longer considered suitable marriage candidates. While Kosovar women involved in the sex industry often had long-lasting relationships with married men, these relationships never developed beyond extra-marital affairs.

[60] Interview with Lorena, April 17, 2013.

[61] Some trendy restaurants, nightclubs, and bars in Pristina are notable exceptions to this unwritten rule.

[62] Informal conversation with Elira, November 2, 2013.

[63] For the most part, the only social contacts women had outside the sex industry consisted of a family member who would not have broken off contact completely and/or a boyfriend (who was always already married). As mentioned in Sect. 4.3.3, however, women had usually met the latter through sex work as well.

The stigma encountered by Kosovar women engaged in prostitution in their home country brings me back to the question posed in Sect. 6.1.2: Why don't local women engage in prostitution in bars in Kosovo in order to enjoy a more luxurious lifestyle, as was observed for the foreign women involved in prostitution in Kosovo and for local women during peacekeeping missions in other parts of the world (e.g., in the Democratic Republic of the Congo; see Jennings, 2014, 2015; Oldenburg, 2015)? The answer to this question, I argue, lies in the social exclusion that women identified as voluntary prostitutes experience as a consequence of the stigmatization of those involved in sex work. With social repercussions, such as those described by Lorena and Elira, in mind, raising one's socio-economic status to middle- or higher-class levels through sex work is simply not an option for Kosovar women.

This is especially true because local women engaged in prostitution in Kosovo can barely hide the nature of their work from their social environment; Kosovo is a small and close-knit society. A human rights activist explained, "Here we are in a very small country. Everybody knows everybody. It is like a spiderweb."[64] As a consequence, it tends to be known within communities if a woman works in a bar and engages in commercial sexual transactions—this leaves them irreversibly tainted. This is even the case when a woman opts to engage in prostitution in a city on the other side of the country, since "the other side of the country" is still no more than two hours away.

With regard to managing stigma, foreign women who engaged in prostitution in Kosovo had a great advantage over local women. Working abroad allows foreign women to save face toward their local communities, as they can try to keep their involvement in the sex industry a secret (Scambler, 2007). This advantage of prostitution migration has also been observed by Oude Breuil (2014, p. 135), who studied Bulgarian women involved in sex work in France. The Kosovar women who eventually engaged in prostitution in bars in Kosovo also often dreamed about migration and marriage or work abroad (in the sex industry or other sectors) in order to escape stigma. Remarks that reflected this were often heard in the bars: "Maybe it is better abroad. If I could, I would leave today. I would do anything. Go with old people. [...] If the day will come for visa liberalization, then I will leave as soon as possible."[65]

Like the foreign women who migrated to Kosovo in order to work in its booming sex industry, the possibilities of Kosovar women to cross borders were hindered by visa restrictions. While foreign women illegally crossed borders with the help of smugglers or traffickers in order to arrive in Kosovo, and large numbers of Kosovo's citizens used similar means in order to travel illegally to Western Europe over the past few years, the Kosovar women who worked in the bars did not try to do this. These women did not opt to be smuggled or trafficked to Western Europe, first of all because they often did not have money to pay a smuggler or trafficker. Similar to

64 Interview with NGO2, October 2, 2013.

65 Informal conversation with WP5, April 14, 2013.

observations on the current refugee crisis, those who illegally cross borders—either as a refugee or in this case as a (prostitution) migrant—are not necessarily the poorest of the poor.[66] Often some money is necessary in order to make a deal with a smuggler or trafficker. Second, the women in the bars were familiar with the arduous routes taken by irregular migrants from Kosovo and some of their foreign former colleagues, whose stories discouraged them from being smuggled or trafficked themselves. Saranda, for example, explained, "I would go if someone would take me from here and arranged an apartment and work for me. Not if I have to cross all kind of borders."[67] Third, and most importantly, if these women had children, they mentioned not wanting to leave them behind. As a consequence, these Kosovar women were stuck in their home country to experience what Bauman (1998, p. 2) calls "the discomforts of [a] localized existence." In line with the stigmatization faced by Kosovar women, defined as voluntary prostitutes, who are engaged in prostitution in bars in their home country, he describes the condition of being localized as "neither pleasurable nor endurable" (Bauman, 1998, p. 2).[68]

However, being defined as a voluntary prostitute not only leads to social and emotional hardships, but also to the tangible disqualification of one's human rights, such as the right to healthcare provision and legal protection (see also Goodyear & Cusick, 2007; Peate, 2006). Women thus not only encounter stigmatization by society, but also by authorities that criminalize prostitution in some cases. Criminalization of prostitution has been the dominant trend worldwide (Weitzer, 2012, p. 48).[69] It aims to abolish the prostitution business at large by not only fighting human trafficking, but any form of commercial sexual transaction—including what is considered voluntary prostitution. The ways in which criminalization can impede those identified as voluntary prostitutes in accessing basic human rights can be seen in Kosovo. Let us first consider the barrier it creates to accessing healthcare.

[66] See, for instance, Bregman (September 9, 2015).

[67] Informal conversation with Saranda, April 14, 2013.

[68] As Goffman (1963) has put forward, stigma is a social construction. It is the outcome of a relationship between various actors and not inherent in an act itself (e.g., engagement in sex work). Consequently, Weitzer (2017) argues that efforts can and should be made to reduce or eliminate stigma from sex work. Possibilities to do so in the specific context of Kosovo have been outlined in an unpublished report drafted for Global Fund, "Programmatic Mapping and Size Estimation of Female Sex Workers in Kosovo" (De Wildt, 2015). Suggestions include raising public awareness about the lived experiences of women engaged in prostitution. This has been done, for instance, through a photo exhibition in Pristina (October 7–17, 2016) and the publication of a book (Poelstra, 2017) in which pictures of women are featured alongside stories that give an insight into their lived experiences.

[69] Decriminalization of prostitution in New Zealand (Abel et al., 2009; Rottier, 2018) and legalization of prostitution in Belgium, Germany, and the Netherlands are notable exceptions (Weitzer, 2012).

6.6.3 Hindered Access to Health Services

The only organization in Kosovo that has implemented projects aimed at providing health services to women involved in prostitution (e.g., regular medical checkups and treatment of sexually transmitted infections) has faced severe difficulties with law enforcement. According to the law on peace and public order in Kosovo, facilitation of prostitution and trafficking in human beings is a crime, while engaging in prostitution is a minor offense.[70] People are expected to inform the police if one is aware of any such acts. As a consequence, NGO representatives and doctors who aim to deliver health services to women engaged in prostitution are in an extremely vulnerable position. They cannot provide anonymous services while simultaneously passing on information to law enforcement regarding individuals' engagement in prostitution. This tension led to the (temporary) cancelation of all services specifically targeting women involved in the sex industry in Kosovo when law enforcement explicitly communicated that incriminating information should be shared. These events underline the Doezema's statement (Doezema, 2002, p. 45) that the voluntary prostitute is ignored; health services with a non-judgmental attitude toward women engaged in prostitution are closed down, and the alleged voluntary prostitute has to fend for herself.

Hampered access to healthcare is especially harrowing since those engaged in prostitution are generally considered to be a key population at risk for HIV infection and other sexually transmitted infections (UNAIDS, 2016; WHO, 2015); Kosovo is no exception. As shown by a study on health risks for commercial sex workers in Kosovo, most of those engaged in prostitution know that condom use can protect them from diseases, yet only 25% use a condom on a regular basis (KOPF, 2010). Reasons for not using a condom are manifold: clients pay more if the sexual act can be performed without one; a middleman (e.g., bar owner or drug dealer) might push women to have unprotected sex; or a woman might not want to spend money on condoms, which makes her dependent on the whims of the client. The limited use of condoms causes health risks for women engaged in prostitution, as well as their clients, spouses and clients' other sexual partners outside the sex industry.

6.6.4 Denied Legal Protection

Finally, being identified as a voluntary prostitute, especially in a national context where prostitution is criminalized, impedes access to legal protection. Kosovar women regularly mentioned that they needed such protection, as they had encountered violence. Let us first examine the incidence of violence.

[70] Engaging in prostitution is an offense according to Article 7: Law on public peace and order, Law No. 03/L-142. In case of force, the act could also fall under Article 171: Trafficking in persons; Article 241: Facilitating or compelling prostitution; and Article 169: Slavery of the criminal code of the Republic of Kosovo, Code No. 04/L-082.

Narratives of aggressive traffickers quickly come to mind when considering violence in the prostitution business.[71] In her study on traffickers and trafficking in Southern and Eastern Europe, Surtees (2008, p. 58–61) refers to the violence traffickers use in order to resolve conflicts and discipline women. However, she also observes that the use of violence by middlemen in order to make women obey is seemingly declining and is being replaced by other "manipulating tactics such as the payment of minimal wages" (see also De Wildt, 2009). Surtees thus suggests that in the Balkans, and in Kosovo in particular, bar owners and other facilitators of prostitution do not need to turn to the use of violence in order to make women work. Women are motivated to do so if they can earn a bit of money. Surtees' suggestion is confirmed in my own study: my respondents rarely mentioned the use of violence by facilitators of prostitution. Rumors and observations, however, indicated that violence from these actors did sometimes take place. On one occasion, I noticed that one of my informants was bruised when I visited her in the bar where she was working:

> When we came into the bar, Aferdita was sitting at a table with a client. She stood up and came to greet us with a hug. When my face was close to hers, I noticed something like a little open wound on her right cheek. I later looked at Aferdita from a distance and saw that her face was bruised all along her cheeks up to her forehead. Aferdita was sitting with a client; she smiled at us every now and then. She did not look good: she was wearing the same clothes as the last time we saw her and is uncomfortably moving back and forward on her chair. She stayed with her client during our whole visit to the bar. As we were leaving, Aferdita stood up to wave goodbye to us. In German, I asked her if she was all right; Aferdita had been a refugee in Germany, and she sometimes communicated in German if she did not want other people to understand her. She smiled and said, "Oh yes, no, I'm good. I just took some hairs from my face."[72]

Saranda, who was working in the same bar as Aferdita at the time, later suggested that the bruises had to do with a fight with the bar owner. Aferdita changed her place of work a few weeks later. Incidental use of violence by bar owners or other middlemen thus takes place, yet my respondents identified clients as the primary source of aggression.

Women shared that clients became aggressive when they wanted to have more sex, a different kind of sex, sex without a condom or if they wanted a woman to have sex with another person as well. This experience of one female respondent is illustrative in this regard:

> One time I told a client to take me home after we were finished. We were in his car. He didn't stop at my house, but just continued to drive. I didn't know where we were going. I was afraid, so I hit him and took over the steering wheel. Then we crashed. The guy started to beat me up very badly after we crashed. He was mad because the car was damaged. I was seriously injured and couldn't work for two months. I didn't dare to go to the police after

[71] Hughes (2000), Hughes and Denisova (2001) and Malarek (2004), for instance, describe instances in which physical violence and rape by traffickers—intended to break a woman's will—prevail. Weitzer (2005, 2007) and Zhang (2009) have criticized such accounts for their lack of empirical evidence.

[72] Notes, September 25, 2013.

> the accident. It would only cause problems. But I did go to the hospital and told them I fell from the stairs.[73]

Lindita, introduced earlier, decided to quit prostitution after a client used excessive violence toward her:

> One evening I agreed to go to a motel with a client. He called a friend and told him where we were going. When we finished, he brought in his friend. I didn't want to do it with his friend. I never agreed to have sex with him as well. They started to hit me when I refused. Then they took all the money I had on me and left. I really wanted to go to the police, but didn't because I was afraid that they would arrest me. Instead I decided to quit this way of living. I went back to working as a housekeeper. I work eight hours a day and barely earn enough to feed my daughter (see footnote 36).

As illustrated by the stories above, women rarely go to the police after they have encountered violence; instead, they stay away from the police because they are afraid to get arrested for being a voluntary prostitute. Lindita explained, "The police will also arrest you, and then you are without work and without money (see footnote 36)."

Like women's impeded access to health services, fear of the police is directly related to the criminalization of prostitution in Kosovo. Criminalization means that women's engagement in prostitution is considered a crime for which one can be arrested. The policy of criminalization is rooted in the widespread belief that prostitution is degrading and dishonorable (Weitzer, 2012, p. 3); it is an attempt to make prostitution disappear. This moral argument, however, only increases the vulnerability of women who are already in a vulnerable situation, as outlined by the factors that explained why Kosovar women tended to engage in prostitution in their home country. As the narratives of the Kosovar women illustrate, such abolitionist measures turn social issues—such as poverty, disrupted families, drug use and tactics to make ends meet—into criminal ones.

Since women feel that they cannot rely on the police, they try to reinforce their safety through other means, one example being that women primarily go to motels with regular clients. Women feel they run the biggest risk of encountering violence if they have not met with a client before: "If you meet someone for the first time, then you don't know anything about him. You don't know how he will be, and you don't have any information about him."[74] Sociologist Teela Sanders (2005, p. 53) has deemed the mutual assessment of sex worker and client in order to decrease risks as the "prostitution trust game." According to Sanders, sex workers often try to protect themselves from violence by gathering some information about a potential client. This thesis was confirmed by my study: women often tried to meet a client several times in the bar before heading to a motel in order to have commercial sex.

[73] Interview with Jehona, November 23, 2011.

[74] Interview with Katarina, November 30, 2011.

6.7 Simple Narratives Make Dangerous Tales[75]

The experiences of the foreign and local women engaged in prostitution in Kosovo debunk the suggestion that the demand for prostitution in the context of peacekeeping missions is met through human trafficking. Moreover, the narratives show that definitions of women as victims of trafficking or voluntary prostitutes do not meet lived experiences; both concepts simplify complex life trajectories. This not only creates a false dichotomy between innocent victims and voluntary prostitutes, but also often leaves women labeled as the latter without any form of support. The needs and rights of those defined as voluntary prostitutes are not considered in Kosovo; they remain unseen as all attention is focused on those considered to be victims of trafficking. Consequently, local women engaged in prostitution in bars, who are generally defined as voluntary prostitutes, are largely denied access to both healthcare services and legal protection and find themselves stigmatized and criminalized.[76] Simple narratives about prostitution in the context of peacekeeping missions, however productive they might be for some actors (see Sect. 2.3), thus make "dangerous tales" (Autesserre 2012).

References

Abel, G. M., Fitzgerald, L. J., & Brunton, C. (2009). The impact of decriminalisation on the number of sex workers in New Zealand. *Journal of Social Policy, 38*(3), 515–531.

Agani, F., Landau, J., & Agani, N. (2010). Community-building before, during, and after times of trauma: The application of the LINC model of community resilience in Kosovo. *The American Journal of Orthopsychiatry, 8*(1), 143–149. https://doi.org/10.1111/j.1939-0025.2010.01017.x

Agustín, L. M. (2007). *Sex at the margins: Migration, labour markets and the rescue industry*. London, UK: Zed Books.

Alderman, H., & Paxson, C. H. (1994). Do the poor insure? A synthesis of the literature on risk and consumption in developing countries. In *Economics in a changing world* (pp. 48–78). London, UK: Palgrave Macmillan.

Andrijasevic, R. (2007). Beautiful dead bodies: Gender, migration and representation in anti-trafficking campaigns. *Feminist Review, 86*(1), 24–44.

Andrijasevic, R. (2010). *Migration, agency and citizenship in sex trafficking*. New York, NY: Springer.

---

[75]This title refers to Autesserre's (2012) study of narratives about Congo. Autesserre argues that three prominent "simple narratives" actually cause an increase in human rights violations and therefore can be seen as "dangerous tales."

[76]This reality is rooted in the moral argument that those who engaged in prostitution voluntarily (the meaning of which has been disputed) are responsible for their own path (i.e., they deserve whatever they get). These women are not considered ideal victims (Christie, 1986), and consequently their often-precarious situation is ignored. However, morality, with discriminatory laws and practices in its slipstream, only worsens the situations of women who already find themselves in precarious circumstances.

Aronowitz, A. A. (2001). Smuggling and trafficking in human beings: The phenomenon, the markets that drive it and the organisations that promote it. *European Journal on Criminal Policy and Research, 9*, 163–195.
Arsovska, J. (2015). *Decoding Albanian organized crime: Culture, politics, and globalization*. Oakland, CA: University of California Press.
Autesserre, S. (2012). Dangerous tales: Dominant narratives on the Congo and their unintended consequences. *African Affairs, 111*(443), 202–222.
Barry, K. (1979). *Female sexual slavery*. New York, NY: New York University Press.
Bauman, Z. (1998). *Globalization: The human consequences*. New York, NY: Columbia University Press.
Catherall, D. R. (1992). *Back from the brink: A family guide to overcoming traumatic stress*. New York, NY: Bantam.
Chapkis, W. (1997). *Live sex acts: Women performing erotic labor*. New York, NY: Routledge.
Chaukar, S. (1998). *Problems of Mumbai's bar girls*. Mumbai, India: Rāmabhāū Mhālagī Prabodhinī.
Christie, N. (1986). *The ideal victim. In From crime policy to victim policy* (pp. 17–30). Palgrave Macmillan, London.
Crenshaw, K. (1989). Demarginalizing the intersection of race and sex: A black feminist critique of antidiscrimination doctrine, feminist theory and antiracist politics. *The University of Chicago Legal Forum, 140*, 139–167.
Crenshaw, K. (1991). Mapping the margins: Intersectionality, identity politics, and violence against women of color. *Stanford Law Review, 43*(6), 1241–1299.
Derks, A. (2000). *Combating trafficking in South East Asia: A review of policy and programme responses*. Geneva, Switzerland: International Organization for Migration.
Davies, J. (2009). *"My name is not Natasha": How Albanian Women in France Use Trafficking to Overcome Social Exclusion (1998-2001)*. Amsterdam, The Netherland: Amsterdam University Press.
De Wildt, R. (2009). Tasten in het duister: Roemeense straatprostituees in Rome. In Y. van der Pijl, D. Raven, L. Brouwer, & B. Oude Breuil (Eds.), *Antropologische vergezichten: Mondialisering, migratie en multiculturaliteit* (pp. 207–224). Amsterdam, The Netherlands: Aksant.
De Wildt, R. (2015). In the wake of war: A cultural criminological perspective on the growth of the sex industry in Kosovo. In F. de Jong, J. A. E. Vervaele, M. M. Boone, C. Kelk, F. A. M. M. Koenraadt, F. G. H. Kristen, D. Rozenblit, & E. Sikkema (Eds.), *Overarching views of crime and deviancy – Rethinking the legacy of the Utrecht School* (pp. 507–526). The Hague, The Netherlands: Eleven International Publishing.
Doezema, J. (1998). Forced to choose: Beyond the voluntary v. forced prostitution dichotomy. In K. Kempadoo & J. Doezema (Eds.), *Global sex workers: Rights, resistance, and redefinition* (pp. 34–50). New York, NY: Routledge.
Doezema, J. (2002). Who gets to choose? Coercion, Consent and the UN trafficking protocol. *Gender and Development, 10*(1), 20–27.
Durkheim, E. (1897). *Suicide: A study in sociology*. New York, NY: The Free Press.
Dworkin, A. (1997). *Life and death*. New York, NY: The Free Press.
Elezaj, E., Bislimi, F., & Duri, U. (2012). *Kosovo remittance study 2012*. New York, NY: UNDP.
European Monitoring Centre for Drugs and Drug Addiction. (2010). *Kosovo (under UNSCR 1244/99). Country Overview 2010*. Lisbon, Portugal: European Monitoring Centre for Drugs and Drug Addiction.
Erving, G. (1963). *Stigma: Notes on the management of spoiled identity*. New York, NY: A Touchstone Book Published by Simon & Schuster Inc.
Färnsveden, U., Qosaj-Mustafa, A., & Farnsworth, N. (2014). *Country gender profile: An analysis of gender differences at all levels in Kosovo*. Stockholm, Sweden: Orgut. Retrieved from http://www.swedenabroad.com/ImageVaultFiles/id_20757/cf_2/Orgut_Kosovo_Gender_Profile_FINAL_2014-05-08.PDF
Farley, M. (Ed.). (2003). *Prostitution, trafficking and traumatic stress*. New York, NY: Routledge.

Farley, M. (2004). 'Bad for the body, bad for the heart': Prostitution harms women even if legalized or decriminalized. *Violence Against Women, 10*(10), 1087–1125.

Farley, M., & Barkan, H. (1998). Prostitution, violence, and posttraumatic stress disorder. *Women & Health, 27*(3), 37–49.

Farley, M., Cotton, A., Lynne, J., Zumbeck, S., Spiwak, F., Reyes, M. E., ... Sezgin, U. (2004). Prostitution and trafficking in nine countries: An update on violence and posttraumatic stress disorder. *Journal of Trauma Practice, 2*(3-4), 33–74. https://doi.org/10.1300/J189v02n03_03

Figley, C. R., & McCubbin, H. I. (1983). *Stress and the family: Coping with catastrophe*. New York, NY: Routledge.

Goffman, E. (1963). *Stigma: Notes on the Management of Spoiled Identity*. Penguin Books Ltd.

Goodyear, M. D., & Cusick, L. (2007). *Protection of sex workers*. London, UK: BMJ Publishing Group Ltd. Retrieved from https://www.ncbi.nlm.nih.gov/pmc/articles/PMC1767242/

Gottfredson, M. R., & Hirschi, T. (1990). *A general theory of crime*. Stanford, CA: Stanford University Press.

Haddad, L. J., & Zeller, M. (1996). How can safety nets do more with less? General issues with some evidence from southern Africa (No. 583-2016-39645).

Higate, P. (2003). "Gender and peacekeeping. Case studies: The DRC and Sierra Leone." *Africa Portal*. Retrieved November 7, 2017, from https://www.africaportal.org/publications/gender-and-peacekeeping-case-studies-the-drc-and-sierra-leone/

Hill, R. (1949). *Families under stress: Adjustment to the crises of war separation and reunion*. New York, NY: Harper & Brothers.

Hirschi, T. (1969). *Causes of delinquency*. New York, NY: University of California Press.

Hope Ditmore, M. (2013). *When sex work and drug use overlap: Considerations for advocacy and practice*. London, UK: Harm Reduction International.

Hughes, D. M. (2000). The 'Natasha' trade: The transnational shadow market of trafficking in women. *Journal of International Affairs, 53*(2), 625–651.

Hughes, D. M., & Denisova, T. A. (2001). The transnational political criminal nexus of trafficking in women from Ukraine. *Trends in Organized Crime, 6*(3–4), 43–67.

Human Rights Watch (2001). *Under Orders: War Crimes in Kosovo* (report). New York: Human Rights Watch.

Jeffreys, S. (2009). *The industrial vagina: The political economy of the global sex trade*. London, UK: Routledge.

Jennings, K. M. (2014). Service, sex, and security: Gendered peacekeeping economies in Liberia and the Democratic Republic of the Congo. *Security Dialogue, 45*(4), 313–330.

Jennings, K. M. (2015). Life in a 'Peace-kept' city: Encounters with the peacekeeping economy. *Journal of Intervention and Statebuilding, 9*(3), 296–315.

Kensy, J., Stengel, C., Nougier, M., & Birgin, R. (2012). *Drug policy and women: Addressing the negative consequences of harmful drug control*. IDPC briefing paper. London: International Drug Policy Consortium.

Kosovo Agency of Statistics. (2013). *Study on remittance in Kosovo*. Pristina, Kosovo: UNDP.

Kosovo Agency of Statistics. (2016). *Results of the Kosovo 2015: Labour force survey*. Washington, DC: World Bank Group.

Kosova Population Foundation. (2010). Research Study: HIV Risks among Commercial Sex Workers. KOPF.

Lanier, M. M., Henry, S., & Desire, J. M. A. (2015). *Essential criminology*. Boulder, CO: Westview Press.

Blanc, M. L., Ouimet, M., & Tremblay, R. E. (1988). An integrative control theory of delinquent behavior: A validation 1976–1985. *Psychiatry, 51*(2), 164–176.

Leclerc-Madlala, S. (2003). Transactional sex and the pursuit of modernity. *Social Dynamics, 29*(2), 213–233.

Malarek, V. (2004). *The Natashas: Inside the new global sex trade*. New York, NY: Arcade.

Maloku, E., & Badivuku Pantina, M. (2011). How acceptable are the costs compared to benefits brought by Euroisation of Kosovar economy? *Journal of Knowledge Management, Economics and Information Technology, 5*, 1–20.

Martin, S. (2005). *Must boys be boys? Ending sexual exploitation & abuse in UN peacekeeping missions*. Washington, DC: Refugees International.

Matthews, R. (2008). *Prostitution, politics & policy*. London, UK: Routledge.

Miriam, K. (2005). Stopping the traffic in women: Power, agency and abolition in feminist debates over sex trafficking. *Journal of Social Philosophy, 36*(1), 1–17.

Morduch, J. (1995). Income smoothing and consumption smoothing. *The Journal of Economic Perspectives, 9*(3), 103–114.

Morduch, J. (1999). Between the state and the market: Can informal insurance patch the safety net? *The World Bank Research Observer, 14*(2), 187–207.

Muqaj, D. (2012). "The impact of a postconflict situation on drug use: A study from Kosovo." Bethesda, MD: National Institute on Drug Abuse. Retrieved from https://www.drugabuse.gov/international/abstracts/impact-postconflict-situation-drug-use-study-kosovo

Oldenburg, S. (2015). The politics of love and intimacy in Goma, Eastern DR Congo: Perspectives on the market of intervention as contact zone. *Journal of Intervention and Statebuilding, 9*(3), 316–333.

Oude Breuil, B. (2014). Fluid security? Home, care and belonging in prostitution migration. In M. Schuilenburg, R. Van Steden, & B. Oude Breuil (Eds.), *Positive criminology. Reflections on care, belonging and security* (pp. 129–144). The Hague, The Netherland: Eleven.

Peate, I. (2006). Paying the price: Health care and prostitution. *British Journal of Nursing, 15*(5), 245–247.

Perritt, H. (2010). *The road to independence for Kosovo: A chronicle of the Ahtisaari plan*. Cambridge, UK: Cambridge University Press.

Picarelli, J. T. (2002). *Trafficking, slavery and peacekeeping: The need for a comprehensive training program* (conference paper). UN Interregional Crime and Justice Research Institute & Transnational Crime and Corruption Center. Retrieved from http://traccc.gmu.edu/pdfs/publications/human_trafficking_publications/TIP&PKO_EWG_Report_Final.pdf

Poelstra, W. (2017). *For Hanna, future stories from the past....* Amsterdam, The Netherlands: Stichting For Hanna Foundation.

Rames, V. (2013). *Healing the spirit: Reparations for survivors of sexual violence related to the armed conflict in Kosovo*. Pristina, Kosovo: OHCHR Stand-Alone Office in Kosovo.

Raymond, J. (1998). Prostitution as violence against women. *Women's Studies International Forum, 21*(1), 1–9.

Republic of Kosovo, Ministry of Internal Affairs, Office of National Coordinator against Trafficking in Human Beings. (2009). *Progress report: Implementation of strategy and action plan against trafficking in human beings. Zero tolerance against organized crime*. Pristina, Kosovo: Ministry of Internal Affairs, Office of National Coordinator against Trafficking in Human Beings.

Republic of Kosovo, Ministry of Internal Affairs, Koordinatori Nacional Kundër Trafikimit Me Qenie Njerëzore. (2010). *Rapport per Zbatimin e Strategjisë Nacionale dhe Plani i Veprimit Kunder Trafikimit të Qenieve Njerëzore. Vepro me Përgjegjësi. Të gjithë kundër Trafikimit me Qenie Njerëzore. Janar- Dhjetor*. Pristina, Kosovo: Ministry of Internal Affairs, Koordinatori Nacional Kundër Trafikimit Me Qenie Njerëzore.

Republic of Kosovo, Ministry of Internal Affairs, National Authority against Trafficking in Human Beings. (2015). *National strategy against trafficking in human beings in Kosovo 2015–2019*. Retrieved from http://www.kryeministri-ks.net/repository/docs/NATIONAL_STRATEGY_AGAINST_TRAFFICKING_IN_HUMAN_BEINGS_IN_KOSOVO.pdf

Rohde, D. (1999). Crisis in the balkans: The expulsions. Kosovo Albanians trickle across Macedonia line. *The New York Times*. Retrieved from https://www.nytimes.com/1999/04/10/world/crisis-balkans-expulsions-kosovo-albanians-trickle-across-macedonia-line.html

Rottier, J. I. M. (2018). *Decriminalization of sex work: The New Zealand model: An analysis of the integrative sex industry policy in New Zealand (Aotearoa)* (Doctoral dissertation, Eleven international publishing).

Sanders, T. (2005). *Sex work: A risky business*. Devon, UK: Willan Publishing.

Scambler, G. (2007). Sex work stigma: Opportunist migrants in London. *Sociology, 41*(6), 1079–1096. https://doi.org/10.1177/0038038507082316

Serwer, D., & Thomson, P. (2008). A framework for success: International intervention in societies emerging from conflict. In C. A. Crocker, F. O. Hampson, & P. Aall (Eds.), *Leashing the dogs of war: Conflict management in a divided world* (p. 369387). Washington, DC: United States Institute of Peace.

Shelley, L. (2010). *Human trafficking: A global perspective*. Cambridge, UK: Cambridge University Press.

Siegel, D. (2007). Nigeriaanse madams in de mensenhandel in Nederland. *Justitiële Verkenningen, 33*(7), 39–49.

Siegel, D. (2011). Mobility of sex workers in European cities. *European Journal on Criminal Policy and Research, 18*(3), 255–268.

Siegel, D., & De Blank, S. (2010). Women who traffic women: The role of women in human trafficking networks–Dutch cases. *Global Crime, 11*(4), 436–447.

Stengel, C., & Fleetwood, J. (2014). *Developing drug policy: Gender matters*. Swansea, UK: Global Drug Policy Observatory.

Surtees, R. (2005). *Second annual report on victims of trafficking in South-Eastern Europe*. Geneva, Switzerland: International Organization for Migration.

Surtees, R. (2008). Traffickers and trafficking in Southern and Eastern Europe: Considering the other side of human trafficking. *European Journal of Criminology, 5*(1), 39–68.

Thio, A. (1978). *Deviant behavior*. Boston, MA: Houghton Mifflin Company.

Thomas, W. I., & Thomas, D. S. (1928). *The child in America*. Oxford, UK: Knopf.

Tomura, M. (2009). A prostitute's lived experiences of stigma. *Journal of Phenomenological Psychology, 40*(1), 51–84.

UNAIDS. (2016). *Global AIDS Update 2016*. Geneva, Switzerland: UNAIDS.

UNDP. (2014). *Kosovo Human Development Report 2014: Migration as a force for development*. Geneva, Switzerland: UN.

UNODC. (2004). *United Nations convention against transnational organized crime and the protocols thereto*. New York, NY: United Nations. Retrieved from https://www.unodc.org/documents/treaties/UNTOC/Publications/TOC%20Convention/TOCebook-e.pdf

Vanwesenbeeck, I., De Graaf, R., Van Zessen, G., Straver, C. J., & Visser, J. H. (1993). Protection styles of prostitutes' clients: Intentions, behavior, and considerations in relation to AIDS. *Journal of Sex Education and Therapy, 19*(2), 79–92.

Walklate, S. (2007). *Understanding criminology: Current theoretical debates*. Maidenhead, UK: Open University Press.

Walkowitz, J. R. (1980). The politics of prostitution. *Journal of Women in Culture and Society, 6*(1), 123–135.

Weitzer, R. (2005). The growing moral panic over prostitution and sex trafficking. *The Criminologist, 30*(5), 1–4.

Weitzer, R. (2007). The Social construction of sex trafficking: Ideology and institutionalization of a moral crusade. *Politics & Society, 35*(3), 447–475.

Weitzer, R. (2009). Sociology of sex work. *Annual Review of Sociology, 35*, 213–234.

Weitzer, R. (2010). The mythology of prostitution: Advocacy research and public policy. *Sexuality Research and Social Policy, 7*(1), 15–29.

Weitzer, R. (2012). *Legalizing prostitution: From illicit vice to lawful business*. New York, NY: New York University Press.

Weitzer, R. (2017). Resistance to sex work stigma. *Sexualities, 21*, 1–13. https://doi.org/10.1177/1363460716684509

WHO. (2015). *A technical brief: HIV and young people who sell sex*. Geneva, Switzerland: WHO.

World Bank. (2015). *The World Bank Group in Kosovo. Country Snapshot, April 2015*. Pristina, Kosovo: World Bank Group.

Xhelili Krasniqi, F., & Mustafa-Topxhiu, R. (2012). The informal economy in Kosovo: Characteristics, current trends and challenges. *Journal of Knowledge Management, Economics and Information Technology, 11*(2), 1–25.

Yannis, A. (2001). Kosovo under international administration. *Survival, 43*(2), 31–48.

Zaitch, D., & Staring, R. (2009). The flesh is weak, the spirit even weaker: Clients and trafficked women in the Netherlands. In A. Di Nicola, A. Cauduro, M. Lombardi, & P. Ruspini (Eds.), *Prostitution and human trafficking: Focus on clients* (pp. 67–121). New York, NY: Springer.

Zhang, S. X. (2009). Beyond the 'Natasha' story – A review and critique of current research on sex trafficking. *Global Crime, 10*(3), 178–195.

Fig. 7.1 Motel

Chapter 7
Conclusion

The hegemonic discourse claims that women engaged in prostitution in the context of peacekeeping missions are singular victims of trafficking who meet the demand of peacekeepers. The suggestion that UN peacekeepers engage in (forced) prostitution in war-torn and other vulnerable regions where they are expected to "do good" has provoked concerned reactions in academic and popular publications alike. However, claims that, first, international peacekeepers create the demand for prostitution and, second, that this demand tends to be met through the trafficking of women for sexual purposes are poorly substantiated by empirical data that takes insider perspectives into account. This ethnographic study has aimed to fill this knowledge gap.

In doing so, this study offered alternative ways to understand the growth of the sex industry in the wake of the war, as well as the situation of the women involved. Moreover, it deciphered the negative impact of the hegemonic discourse on the lives of the foreign women depicted as victims of trafficking, as well as the lives of the local women who do not fit this label.

I have brought ethnographic specificity to my analysis by situating the agency of the women at the heart of this study within the ethnographic context. This takes into account demand and supply of sex work but, in addition, considers the specific (geo-) political and socio-economic context, which is invaded by power structures that are dynamic and ever-changing. Insights from the structure-and-agency debate within the social sciences, which contests whether individuals control their own actions and destinies (i.e., agency; see Weber, 1978; Barth, 1967) or simply obey powerful social forces (i.e., structures; see Durkheim, 1938; Radcliffe-Brown, 1940) have therefore echoed throughout this study.

The purpose of this final chapter is threefold. First, it summarizes the main findings of this study. Next, it explores why simple narratives on prostitution in the context of peacekeeping missions tend to take the foreground in academic and popular discussions. Finally, it considers the main additions of this study to the contemporary debate on prostitution in the context of peacekeeping missions.

R. de Wildt, *Post-War Prostitution*, Studies of Organized Crime 17,
https://doi.org/10.1007/978-3-030-19474-1_7

7.1 Main Findings

The two stances that dominate the academic debate on prostitution have been examined in Chap. 2. On the one hand, abolitionists view prostitution as gender-based violence since, in this view, women never engage in prostitution out of free choice. Following the structure-and-agency debate this is a slightly naïve approach as individuals never hold complete free choice but always act under given social structures which they recreate at the very same time. On the other hand, pro-sex-work scholars emphasize women's right to self-determination and to earn money in the sex industry. It has been argued that both perspectives are not two competing views of reality, but rather two instrumental discourses. Both perspectives have significant goals that differ. Individuals and groups inspired by the abolitionist rhetoric, who take the lead in presenting prostitution in the context of peacekeeping missions as a form of sexual exploitation, hold similarities with what Howard Becker defined as "moral entrepreneurs." These moral entrepreneurs undoubtedly have good intentions, but in lieu of empirical data on the situation of women actually engaged in prostitution during peacekeeping missions, it remains to be seen if women identify themselves as victims and indeed want to be saved.

Chapter 3 set the stage for the study by providing a contextual analysis of the Kosovo War and its aftermath. Therewith, the chapter focuses on the social structures and power hierarchies wherein the prostitution business in Kosovo flourished. Yet it also shows how these structures exist in a discursive loop together with the agency of people in Kosovo, who constantly recreate these very same structures. I argued that solely focusing on peacekeepers as clients obscures other contextual factors that enabled the growth of the post-war prostitution business in Kosovo, which include weak law enforcement, corruption, socio-cultural attitudes adopted during the (prelude to) war that do not simply disappear when hostilities come to an end, the existence of regional smuggling and trafficking rings, Northern Kosovo as a nexus point for smuggling and trafficking and, finally, the establishment of a peacekeeping economy. Weak law enforcement was the result of the disappearance of original law and order institutions that had been in Serbian hands and subsequent institutional problems within UNMIK and EULEX. The prostitution business could flourish in plain sight despite its illegality as a consequence of this weak law enforcement. Corruption further affected the prostitution business in Kosovo: corrupt border police allowed foreign women to enter the country illegally, and officials in charge of stay and work permits provided foreign women with the papers necessary to live and work in Kosovo. Corrupt police warned bar owners about upcoming raids and obstructed the prosecution of people in the higher echelons of society. The Kosovar Albanian population's tendency of indifference toward official institutions in Kosovo further strengthened the idea that the law could be disregarded. This attitude developed as a reaction to experiences in former Yugoslavia, when Kosovar Albanians became accustomed to arranging their lives through unofficial channels, and it did not simply disappear when the war came to an end. It meant that in the aftermath of the war, some people opportunistically took any chance possible to earn money while paying little attention to the legality of their actions. It simply did not seem to occupy the minds of bar owners that their actions were illegal when they started to facilitate prostitution.

These same facilitators of prostitution benefited from cooperation with existing regional smuggling and trafficking rings, irrespective of the ethnicities of those involved. Northern Kosovo became a particularly popular route for the smuggling and trafficking of Eastern European women toward prostitution businesses in various cities throughout Kosovo. This disputed area tends to be described as a hotspot for crime. Finally, the arrival of peacekeepers and other internationals that broker peace, together with the influx of large sums of money aimed at the reconstruction of Kosovo, contributed to the establishment of a peacekeeping economy. This economy enabled relative economic prosperity; as a result, more people could afford to pay for commercial sex. This latter argument of increased demand, which triggers supply, has been pivotal in the flourishing of the post-war prostitution business in Kosovo, but it needs to be seen in tandem with the other factors mentioned, such as the relative inaccessibility of other prosperous markets in Western Europe.

In Chap. 4, I discussed in more detail my observation that clients of prostitution were more diverse than international peacekeepers alone. International peacekeepers have been clients of the nascent sex industry, despite special measures that forbid UN staff to visit premises where prostitution is allegedly taking place. Aside from peacekeepers, the international clientele has been comprised of civilian and police staff, diplomats, and relief workers dispatched in Kosovo. Nevertheless, the majority of the clients were local men. Furthermore, the diaspora, jokingly described as "schatzis" by inhabitants of Kosovo, return to their motherland in large numbers during the summer and winter holidays. This causes peak seasons in the sex industry. The suggestion that sex industries in the context of peacekeeping missions are prone to becoming destinations for sex tourists—as women are considered accustomed to catering to international clients—has also been discussed. This suggestion has not been confirmed by the empirical data from Kosovo, as it overlooks part of the current structure in which the atmosphere in bars does not exude an international air at all.

Chapter 5 turned to address the insider perspectives of women engaged in prostitution in Kosovo. Those who offered commercial sexual services in Kosovo in the wake of the war were predominantly Moldovan, Ukrainian, Romanian, Bulgarian, Serbian and Albanian. Exclusively focusing on the victimhood of these women does not do justice to their lived experiences. Unambiguous accounts essentialize suffering while less stereotypical and more complex aspects of the lives of these women are ignored. The lived experiences of these women have shown that there was no "typical" reason for Eastern European women to engage in prostitution in post-war Kosovo. An array of intentions has been grouped into three principal reasons: economic need and desires; the will to leave abusive relationships or otherwise difficult home situations; and the accessibility of Kosovo's relatively lucrative sex market in the wake of war. In the early days of the Kosovar sex industry, women went to Kosovo after bar owners advertised international job opportunities or traveled abroad to meet interested women. Furthermore, some international entrepreneurs experienced in the facilitation of prostitution took their businesses and the women working for them to Kosovo. However, the majority of the women that came to Kosovo in the years that followed were "recruited" by women from their native countries who had already been engaged in prostitution in Kosovo. Women did not always foresee that they would be involved in prostitution, nor were they always aware that Kosovo was their final destination. Nevertheless, in later years women tended to make a well-considered decision to migrate in order to engage in prostitution in Kosovo. They traveled via illegal border crossings over land, through the use of holiday packages or by plane with falsely arranged papers. Most women tended to reimburse the costs of their journey by working in prostitution upon arrival. For many of the foreign women who were involved in this study, prostitution in the context of the peacekeeping mission in Kosovo proved to be a way to resist structural inequalities and negotiate their situations as well as the power hierarchies that impacted their agency. Border controls and visa restrictions rendered them vulnerable, as they prompted women to travel with the help of middlemen. Heightened border security in order to prevent alleged human trafficking only increased this vulnerability. Such barriers do not necessarily prevent women from migrating; they only cause women to take more arduous routes and further increases their dependence on middlemen. All of these factors result in higher costs or agreements on debt bondage, but they largely go unchecked as a result of the overwhelming focus on the victimhood of these women.

Chapter 6 examined the situation of the Kosovar women who engaged in prostitution in bars in their home country after the foreign women had largely departed. Most of these women did not fit the label "victim of trafficking." In the contemporary discourse, those engaged in prostitution who are not considered to be victims of trafficking tend to be labeled "voluntary prostitutes." This label further does not do justice to the situation of the Kosovar women if market forces, as well as social and individual factors, are taken into account. Economic need is one of the market forces that made Kosovar women consider prostitution. While foreign women engaged in prostitution in Kosovo for a range of economic reasons, including the desire to purchase luxury goods, local women only did so out of economic distress. I have argued that this is a direct consequence of the stigmatization that Kosovar women engaged in prostitution encounter from society and authorities. However, economic disparity by itself does not explain why local women engage in prostitution; the women who did so also came from disrupted families, often as a consequence of war. In Kosovo, family relations often protect family members from falling into poverty, and consequently, erosion of the social fabric severely affects women's economic resilience. Some Kosovar women also mentioned that a drug habit pushed them toward the sex industry, as drugs were widely available in Kosovo after the war. Prostitution offered these women an opportunity to provide for themselves and achieve relative security, but they tend to be identified as voluntary prostitutes and their (often precarious) situation is ignored as a consequence. These women have to deal with stigma and are denied healthcare attuned to their needs, as well as legal protection. The stigma results in the social exclusion of Kosovar women who engage in prostitution; they tend to be shunned by their family and the community at large. Their hindered access to health services, amongst other forms of assistance, results in limited condom use and a lack of treatment of sexually transmitted infections, which in turn affects the health of clients and their families. The denial of legal protection means that women rarely go to the police after they have been raped, robbed or encounter violence by clients or bar owners. The attention paid to alleged victims of trafficking means that women who are not labelled as such are ignored, as they are considered voluntary prostitutes. But simple narratives about voluntary prostitutes obscure their negative experiences, thus making for "dangerous tales."

7.2 Underlying Motives for Simple Narratives

The above findings illustrate that assumptions about foreign victims of trafficking and local "voluntary prostitutes" do not correlate with actual experiences, at least not as one-dimensionally as the simple narratives suggest. Why are these claims brought to the fore, then? I have argued that various actors benefit from the dissemination of simple narratives about post-war prostitution.

Simple narratives that describe prostitution in the context of peacekeeping missions as forced prostitution justify regulation that prohibits peacekeepers from exchanging money for sexual intercourse. The Bulletin on Special Measures for Protection from Sexual Exploitation and Sexual Abuse promulgated by the UN is an example of such regulation, which aims to limit the demand for prostitution entirely. These measures subscribe to the abolitionist agenda that tends to conflate prostitution with human trafficking and strives to make sure that fewer (or, ideally, no) women engage in prostitution. First of all, therefore, abolitionists can benefit from simple narratives.

A one-sided representation can furthermore prove effective for non-governmental organizations that aim to fight human trafficking. These organizations usually depend on projects that are granted to them. They can be tempted to emphasize the helplessness of the women who are the beneficiaries of their projects, as donors eagerly spend money on "helpless victims" of trafficking. This is most definitely the case in donor darling Kosovo, where embassies and other donors have financed multiple large-scale initiatives aimed at countering human trafficking and rehabilitating victims exploited in post-war prostitution businesses.

Likewise, popular media need straightforward stories that the public can grasp in a few headlines. Such popular publications are often accompanied by narrow visual representations of women engaged in prostitution as completely powerless victims.

More generally, simple narratives of exploitation and victimization move attention away from contemporary mechanisms of exclusion and unequal mobility. The experience of a Ukrainian woman who graduated in information technology is illustrative here (see Chap. 5). She preferred to work in her field of expertise in Western Europe or the United States in order to earn a decent income. Visa restrictions, however, proved to be one of her main obstacles to realizing this dream. Refusing to let go of her ambition to leave Ukraine and make a good living, she eventually settled for the post-war prostitution business in Kosovo. Portraying this woman as a one-dimensional victim of trafficking exploited by peacekeepers does not do justice to her experience. However, doing so means that rescue organizations can set out to offer her assistance without considering the measures that cause structural inequalities, which in turn create instances of prostitution on the entire continuum from voluntary to forced. Simple narratives can hence be comforting for the general public, as they mean that the impact of exclusion mechanisms—such as border controls and visa restrictions—on the sex industry need not be considered.

7.3 What Is New?

In sum, these conclusions provide three main additions to the contemporary debate on prostitution in the context of peacekeeping missions. First, this study contributes to filling the gap of empirical knowledge that takes into account the insider perspectives of those actually engaged in post-war prostitution. Why is it important to provide such narratives? Precisely because these lived experiences provide the empirical data on which macro theories (i.e., on structure and agency) are built. On a more practical level, the lived experiences of foreign and local women engaged in the Kosovar sex industry illustrate that the attention paid to alleged victims of trafficking during peacekeeping missions negatively impacts those defined as such, as well as those who are not considered to be victims of trafficking and consequently ignored. This again points out that research amongst women engaged in prostitution is crucial in order to reach an understanding of their situation that is driven by actual experiences instead of ideology.

Second, the specific ethnographic details of my analysis illustrate the importance of situating the agency of women engaged in prostitution within their ethnographic context. Insights from the structure-and-agency debate within the social sciences—as well as those from critical criminology on the ways in which power hierarchies impact crime and criminalization—allow for an analysis whereby narratives are tied with their contemporary (geo-) political and socio-economic context. This context is impacted by power structures (i.e., structural inequality, immigration policies) that tend to be obscured if victimization is the sole focus within research on post-war prostitution. These debates thus provide important tools for future studies on prostitution.

Third, this study shows that prostitution is inherent to peacekeeping missions. This understanding changes the focus of regulations and actions concerning prostitution in this context. Measures that concentrate on punishing delinquent individuals, who allegedly give rise to the industry and can be dismissed, are not expected to have an impact. Other actions could be more effective in combatting cases of exploitation and protecting the rights of women who opt to engage in commercial sex. Examples of such actions include ensuring free health services with a non-judgmental attitude toward women engaged in prostitution, as well as providing legal services that can come to their aid in cases of rape or exploitation. However, these measures can only succeed in an environment where prostitution is decriminalized.

References

Barth, F. (1967). On the study of social change. *American Anthropologist, 69*(6), 661–669.

Durkheim, E. (1938). *The rules of sociological method*. New York, NY: The Free Press.

Radcliffe-Brown, A. R. (1940). On social structure. *The Journal of the Royal Anthropological Institute of Great Britain and Ireland, 70*(1), 1–12.

Weber, M. (1978). *Economy and society*. Berkeley, CA: University of California Press.

Annex One: Protocol to Prevent, Suppress and Punish Trafficking in Persons, Especially Women and Children, Supplementing the United Nations Convention Against Transnational Organized Crime

For the purposes of this Protocol:

(a) "Trafficking in persons" shall mean the recruitment, transportation, transfer, harbouring or receipt of persons, by means of the threat or use of force or other forms of coercion, of abduction, of fraud, of deception, of the abuse of power or of a position of vulnerability or of the giving or receiving of payments or benefits to achieve the consent of a person having control over another person, for the purpose of exploitation. Exploitation shall include, at a minimum, the exploitation of the prostitution of others or other forms of sexual exploitation, forced labour or services, slavery or practices similar to slavery, servitude or the removal of organs;
(b) The consent of a victim of trafficking in persons to the intended exploitation set forth in subparagraph (a) of this article shall be irrelevant where any of the means set forth in subparagraph (a) have been used;
(c) The recruitment, transportation, transfer, harbouring or receipt of a child for the purpose of exploitation shall be considered "trafficking in persons" even if this does not involve any of the means set forth in subparagraph (a) of this article;
(d) "Child" shall mean any person under 18 years of age (UNODC, 2004).

R. de Wildt, *Post-War Prostitution*, Studies of Organized Crime 17,
https://doi.org/10.1007/978-3-030-19474-1

Annex Two: Overview of Informants

This overview distinguishes between four categories of informants:

- Women engaged in prostitution;
- Others engaged in the facilitation of the prostitution business;
- Experts in the field of human trafficking and prostitution in Kosovo; and
- Others

Each category of informants is described in a separate table.

Long-term relationships have been established with some informants. In these cases, the start of the relationship is mentioned (i.e., "since…") together with the dates of the main interviews and informal conversations.

Women engaged in prostitution

Pseudonym/ code	Position	Country of origin	Approx. age (at first meeting)	Place of interview(s)	Date(s)
Aferdita	Sex worker	Kosovo	25	Ferizaj	Since Sept. 2013, e.g., on Sept. 19 and 25, 2013 Oct. 3, 2013 Nov. 2, 2013
Aleksandra	Sex worker	Bulgaria	35	Prizren	Dec. 2, 2011
Constanta	Sex worker	Moldova	40	Ferizaj	Since May 2013, e.g., on May 13, 2013 Sept. 25, 2013 Nov. 3 and 12, 2014
Dea	Sex worker	Albania	30	Prizren	Dec. 2, 2011
Elira	Sex worker	Kosovo	30	Ferizaj	Since July 2011, e.g., on March 16, 2013 April 1, 2013 Sept. 25, 2013 Nov. 2, 2013 Nov. 3 and 12, 2014

R. de Wildt, *Post-War Prostitution*, Studies of Organized Crime 17,
https://doi.org/10.1007/978-3-030-19474-1

Pseudonym/ code	Position	Country of origin	Approx. age (at first meeting)	Place of interview(s)	Date(s)
Elena	Sex worker	Moldova	25	Ferizaj	Nov. 23, 2011
Genta	Sex worker	Kosovo	35	Ferizaj	Since April 2013, e.g., on Oct. 20, 2013
Jehona	Sex worker	Kosovo	40	Ferizaj	Nov. 23, 2011
Julia	Sex worker	Moldova	25	Ferizaj	Nov. 30, 2011
Katarina	Sex worker	Moldova	25	Prizren	Nov. 30, 2011
Katya	Sex worker	Ukraine	25	Ferizaj	Nov. 16, 2011
Kaltrina	Sex worker	Kosovo	30	Ferizaj	April 20, 2013
Lindita	Sex worker	Kosovo	35	Pristina	Dec. 5, 2011
Lorena	Sex worker	Kosovo (northern part)	40	Ferizaj and Pristina	Since April 2013, e.g., on April 27 and 29, 2013 May 3, 9, 14 and 21, 2013 June 2, 2013 Aug. 28, 2013 (Skype) Sep. 19 and 24, 2013 Oct. 9 and 18, 2013 Nov. 15, 2013
Manda	Sex worker	Kosovo	25	Ferizaj	Since Nov. 2011
Mimoza	Sex worker	Kosovo	35	Ferizaj	Since April 2013, e.g., on April 16 and 23, 2013 May 13, 2013 Oct. 1, 2013
Mira	Former sex worker	Serbia	25	Gjilan	Dec. 8, 2011
Rea	Sex worker	Albania	18	Prizren and Pristina	Dec. 2, 5 and 8, 2011
Rita	Sex worker	Moldova	30	Sojevo and Skype	Since May 2013, e.g., on May 15, 21 and 28, 2013 Aug. 16, 2013 Feb. 17 and 19, 2014 March 21, 2014 April 1, 2014
Saranda	Sex worker/ former bar owner	Kosovo	35	Ferizaj	Since July 2011, e.g., on July 3, 2011 March 3, 13 and 16, 2013 April 1, 14 and 16, 2013 Sept. 19, 25 and 27, 2013 Oct. 3, 2013 Nov. 2 and 4, 2013 December 8, 2014

(continued)

Pseudonym/ code	Position	Country of origin	Approx. age (at first meeting)	Place of interview(s)	Date(s)
Shqipe	Sex worker	Kosovo	40	Ferizaj	Since April 2013, e.g., on 16, 23 April 2013 9, 13 May 2013 1 Oct. 2013
Sofija	(Former) sex worker	Ukraine	25	Ferizaj and Pristina	Since 2011 e.g., on: Nov. 16, 2011 Jan. 3, 4, 6, 8, 9 and 16, 2014
Tanya	Sex worker	Moldova	25	Ferizaj	Since July 2011, e.g., on July 3, 2011 Nov. 23, 2011
Valbona	Sex worker	Kosovo	25	Ferizaj	Sept. 25, 2013
Vera	Sex worker	Albania	20	Prizren	Dec. 2, 2011
Vesna	Former sex worker	Serbia	20	Pristina	March 20, 2013
Vlora	Sex worker	Albania	20	Ferizaj	Nov. 17, 2011
WP1	Sex worker	Albania	25	Ferizaj	April 14, 2013
WP2	Sex worker	Moldova	28	Prizren	Nov. 30, 2011
WP3	Sex worker	Kosovo	30	Ferizaj	Nov. 23, 2011
WP4	Sex worker	Kosovo	25	Ferizaj	Nov. 23, 2011
WP5	Sex worker	Kosovo	40	Ferizaj	April 14, 2013
WP6	Sex worker	Ukraine	20	Ferizaj	Nov. 16, 2011
WP7	Sex worker	Ukraine	30	Ferizaj	Nov. 16, 2011 Jan. 3, 2014
WP8	Sex worker	Kosovo	30	Gjilan	Dec. 8, 2011
WP9	Sex worker	Kosovo	25	Gjilan	Dec. 8, 2011
WP10	Sex worker	Kosovo	25	Ferizaj	March 13, 2013 Nov. 3, 2014
WP11	Sex worker	Albania	45	Ferizaj	March 13, 2013 Sept. 25, 2013 Nov. 2, 2013
WP12	Sex worker	Albania	25	Ferizaj	March 16, 2013
WP13	Sex worker	Albania	35	Ferizaj	Since April 2013, e.g., on April 27 and 29, 2013 Sept. 24, 2013 Oct. 9 and 18, 2013 Nov. 2, 2013
WP14	Sex worker	Albania	25	Ferizaj	Nov. 2, 2013
Yana	Sex worker	Bulgaria	25	Ferizaj	Nov. 23, 2011
Zamira	Sex worker	Kosovo	35	Pristina	Nov. 25, 2011

Others engaged in the facilitation of the prostitution business

Pseudonym/ code	Position	Country of origin	Approx. age (at first meeting)	Place of interview(s)	Date(s)
BAR1	Bartender/son of bar owner	Kosovo	25	Ferizaj	May 3, 2013
BAR2	Male bartender	Kosovo	30	Sojevo	May 21, 2013
BAR3	Female bar owner	Albania	50	Ferizaj	Sept. 19 and 25, 2013 Oct. 3, 2013
Bujar	Male bar owner	Kosovo	50	Ferizaj	Since June 2011, e.g., on March 3, 13 and 16, 2013 April 14, 2013 Sept. 25, 2013 Oct. 17, 2013 Nov. 2 and 12, 2013 April 14, 2014 Nov. 2 and 3, 2014

Experts in the field of human trafficking and prostitution in Kosovo

Code	Position	Country of origin	Place of interview(s)	Date(s)
ACA1	Professor of criminology	Serbia	North Mitrovica	April 26, 2013
ACA2	PhD student in field of human trafficking	Ukraine	Utrecht (NL)	July 31, 2016
ACA3	Sociologist	Kosovo	Pristina	March 21, 2013
DOC1	Gynecologist	Kosovo	Prizren	Since July 2011, e.g., on December 8, 2011 December 6, 2015
DOC2	Gynecologist	Kosovo	Ferizaj	Since July 2011, e.g., on December 8, 2015
DOC3	Gynecologist	Kosovo	Ferizaj	Since July 2011 e.g., on December 8, 2015
EUL1	(Former) senior analyst, EULEX	The Netherlands	Pristina, Utrecht (NL)	Since June 2011 e.g., on August 17, 2017
EUL2	EULEX prosecutor	Finland	Pristina, Ferizaj	Since October 2013 e.g., on Oct. 29, 2013 Jan. 3, 2014

(continued)

Code	Position	Country of origin	Place of interview(s)	Date(s)
EUL3	EULEX prosecutor	The Netherlands	Pristina	Since October 2013 e.g., on Oct. 23 and 25, 2013
EUL4	EULEX prosecutor	Australia	Pristina	Since May 2013 e.g., on May 2 and 15, 2013 Oct. 16 and 29, 2013
EUL5	EULEX legal advisor	Kosovo	Pristina and Ferizaj	Since May 2013 e.g., on May 15, 2013 Sept. 16 and 17, 2013 Jan. 3, 2014 June 26, 2014
EUL6	EULEX prosecutor	Italy	Pristina	March 26, 2013
EUL7	Assistant to EULEX prosecutor	Italy	Pristina	March 26, 2013
EUL8	EULEX legal advisor	Nigeria	Skype	April 29, 2014
EUL9	EULEX prosecutor	Norway	Pristina	Sept. 16, 2013
EUL10	EULEX interpreter	Kosovo	Pristina	Nov. 12, 2013
EUL11	EULEX advisor to directorate for trafficking in human beings	Ireland	Pristina	Since March 2013, e.g., on March 22, 2013 May 27, 2013
HTE1	Human trafficking program officer	Kosovo	Pristina	Since 2008, e.g., on Feb. 6, 2011 Sept. 20, 2013 Oct. 8, 2013
HTE2	Legal advisor	USA	Pristina	Oct. 24, 2013
HTE3	Former researcher on sex industry	Kosovo	Pristina	Since June 2011
HTE4	Director shelter for VoT	Kosovo	Pristina	Since June 2011, e.g., on Feb. 14, 2013
HTE5	(Former) member of the inter-ministerial working group on anti-trafficking	Kosovo	Pristina	Since June 2011
HTE6	Legal advisor on human trafficking at Ministry of Health; brother of bar owner	Kosovo	Pristina and Ferizaj	Nov. 12, 2013 Nov. 3, 2014
HTE7	Deputy Minister of Internal Affairs and National Anti-Trafficking Coordinator of Kosovo	Kosovo	Pristina	Since March 2012, e.g., on March 22, 2012 June 5, 2012
KFO1	Translator, KFOR	USA/Bosnia Herzegovina	Pristina	April 17, 2013

(continued)

Code	Position	Country of origin	Place of interview(s)	Date(s)
KFO2	Translator, KFOR	USA/Croatia	Pristina	April 17, 2013
KPO1	Police officer	Kosovo	Peja	Oct. 30, 2013
KPO2	Police officer, anti-trafficking unit	Kosovo	Pristina	Since June 2011, e.g., on Jan. 8, 2014
KPO3	Police officer, anti-trafficking unit	Kosovo	Pristina	Since June 2011, e.g., on Oct. 8, 2013
KPO4	Police officer, anti-trafficking unit	Kosovo	Pristina	Since June 2011, e.g., on April 13, 2012 Feb. 14, 2013 March 22, 2013
NGO1	Human rights activist	Kosovo	Pristina	March 13, 2013 Nov. 8, 2013
NGO2	NGO representative	Albania	Pristina	Since 2008, e.g., on October 2, 2013
NGO3	NGO representative	USA	North Mitrovica	May 8, 2013
NGO4	NGO representative	Kosovo	Pristina	Feb. 12, 2013
NGO5	NGO representative	Kosovo	Pristina	Feb. 12, 2013
NGO6	NGO representative	Kosovo	Pristina	Since June 2011, e.g., on Feb. 6, 2013
NGO7	NGO representative	Kosovo	Pristina	Since June 2011, e.g., on Feb. 6, 2013
NGO8	NGO representative	Kosovo	Pristina	Since June 2011, e.g., on Feb. 6, 2013
NGO9	NGO representative	Kosovo	Ferizaj and Pristina	Since June 2011
NGO10	NGO representative	The Netherlands	Pristina	Since Feb. 2013, e.g., on Feb. 15, 2013
NGO11	NGO representative	Kosovo	Pristina	Since June 2011
NGO12	NGO representative/legal expert	Serbia	North Mitrovica	April 26, 2013
SP1	Special prosecutor	Kosovo	Pristina, Peja and Gjakova	Since June 2011, e.g., on Feb. 5, 7, 13 and 26, 2013 March 25, 2013 Sept. 23, 2013

(continued)

Code	Position	Country of origin	Place of interview(s)	Date(s)
UNM1	(Former) UNMIK police officer, specialized in anti-trafficking	USA	Pristina	Since Feb. 2013, e.g., on May 2, 2013 Oct. 7, 2013
UNM2	UNMIK police officer	USA	South Mitrovica	March 18, 2013

Others

Code	Position	Country of origin	Place of interview(s)	Date(s)
FST1	Former student	Kosovo	Pristina	Since June 2011, e.g., on March 16, 2016
JOU1	Journalist previously based in Kosovo	The Netherlands	Skype	Nov. 14, 2013
KLA1	Former KLA combatant	Kosovo	Pristina	Since June 2011, e.g., on Feb. 2, 2013
KLA2	Former KLA combatant	Kosovo	Pristina	Since July 2012
KLA3	Mother of KLA combatant killed in war	Kosovo	Ferizaj	September 26, 2013
KLA4	Former KLA combatant/ KLA spokesman	Kosovo	Pristina	July 3, 2014
KLA5	Former KLA combatant	Kosovo	Pristina	Since Feb. 2013
SUNM1	Spouse of UNMIK employee	Kosovo	Pristina	Since Sept. 2013
WAI1	Waiter	Kosovo	Pristina	July 1, 2011
RA1	Psychologist/research assistant	Kosovo	Peja, Deçan, Pristina, Ferizaj and Prizren	Since June 2011, e.g., on Sept. 25, 2013

Reference

UNODC. (2004). *United Nations convention against transnational organized crime and the protocols thereto*. New York, NY: United Nations. Retrieved from https://www.unodc.org/documents/treaties/UNTOC/Publications/TOC%20Convention/TOCebook-e.pdf

Index

R. de Wildt, *Post-War Prostitution*, Studies of Organized Crime 17,
https://doi.org/10.1007/978-3-030-19474-1

Kolibri 360 GmbH
Ferdinand-Jühlke-Straße 7
99095 Erfurt, Deutschland
produktsicherheit@kolibri360.de